JN016043

ストーリーを
楽しむだけで
いい！

ビジネス英語奮闘記

31日目→60日目

著

晴山陽一
クリストファー・ベルトン

SANSHUSHA

はじめに

This book represents the second half of a story outlining the events that occur in a business environment throughout the course of one year. Together with the first book, 『ストーリーを楽しむだけでいい! ビジネス英語 奮闘記 1 日目〜30 日目』, this book shines a light on the working lives of two people working for an IT company: Osamu Yonezawa, the director of the Global Logistics Department, and Shinnosuke Nitobe, an office clerk headhunted into Yonezawa's department.

Although the plotline showcasing Shinnosuke Nitobe as he struggles to learn English fluently within one year continues through both books, each can be read to great effect independently, so don't worry if you have not yet read the first book. The main objective is, after all, to learn all four aspects of English reading, writing, speaking and listening, and the story is a secondary element.

The first book commenced at the beginning of April and ran through to September, and this book starts from the beginning of October and runs through to March the following year. Nitobe is currently assigned to the Customer Support Section, and Yonezawa is on assignment to the London office to stand in for the president, who is undergoing hospital treatment.

The book is packed full of material to aid in your quest to learn English, and I hope you will find it useful. Good luck!

Christopher Belton

お待たせしました。物語の続きをお届けします。

　この2巻目では、新渡戸と岬の1年間の英語修行の結果が明らかになります。帰国子女ではないというハンディを負った新渡戸の成長の行方が気になります。2人は無事に海外事業部の一員になれるのでしょうか。

　新渡戸は意中の人である柴田彩と一緒に仕事できるようになるでしょうか。

　また、社内コンペの行方はいかに？

　著者である僕とベルトンさんは、この物語を追体験することで、読者のあなたの英語力が、バランスよく、リアリティーを伴いながら大きな成長を遂げることを祈っています。

　この本は、いわば「書物留学」。いながらにして、グローバルなビジネスの臨場感を味わい、さまざまな外国人とのコミュニケーションを疑似体験できます。

　あとのことは、あなたにお任せします。思い切り感情移入し、物語を楽しんでください。

　遠慮はいりません。どうか本書を通じて、英語を好きになってください。

晴山陽一

本書の使い方

　１日目〜30日目では、どこにでもいる普通の新入社員・新渡戸慎之助（主人公）に突然降ってきた海外事業部への異動辞令。それを機に与えられた「１年で英語をペラペラにする」ための英語猛特訓研修。そんなに好きでもない英語と奮闘しながらも、１年後には英語を読んで、書いて、聞いて、話すことが不自由なくできて仕事をしなければならない新渡戸は、様々な葛藤を乗り越えてみるみるうちに成長していく…。

　そんな新渡戸を厳しくも温かく見守るのは海外事業部・部長の米澤修。新渡戸を中心とする部下たちの活躍と失敗を見届けながら、周りからの人望と期待を背負っていく米澤部長もまた人生の新たな転機と出くわすことになる。31日目〜60日目では、成長した新渡戸と米澤部長の大きな人生の絶頂を見ながらストーリーを楽しみましょう。

　本書は、主人公の新渡戸慎之助とその上司の米澤修の「英語の日誌」を時系列に交互に紹介することでストーリーを楽しみながら、仕事で必要な４技能「読む・書く・聞く・話す」を一気に習得できる１冊です。

▶ **入社数年目、突然仕事で英語が必要になった!**

▶ **入社して数年で海外研修・海外赴任がある企業に勤めることになった!**
　　→新渡戸慎之助の視点から「日誌」を楽しんでください

▶ **勤務年数20〜30年で突然英語が必要になった!**

▶ **英語があまり得意でない部下のために英語研修が必要になった!**
　　→米澤修の視点から「日誌」を楽しんでください

READING: JOURNAL

　１年間で英語を使いこなすため、書くことになった新渡戸と海外事業部に配属されてから習慣として書き続けている米澤部長の英語の日誌とその訳。時系列にそれぞれの視点からどんな心境でどんなことが起きているのかストーリーを楽しみつつ、英語が必要な仕事の現場の臨場感を味わってください。

WRITING: MATERIAL 1

「日誌」で出てくるビジネス書類・文書や説

4

明文などで書き方を知っておくと便利なものを紹介しています。内容をキチンと理解できているかのクイックQ&Aや書き方や書類・文書・説明文のポイントも掲載。（クイックQ&Aの答えはページ下にあります）

READING: MATERIAL 2

「日誌」で出てくるビジネス書類・文書や説明文などで読み方を知っておくと便利なものを紹介しています。内容をキチンと理解できているかのクイックQ&Aや読み方や書類・文書・説明文のポイントも掲載。（クイックQ&Aの答えはページ下にあります）

LISTENING & SPEAKING: CONVERSATION

「日誌」で触れているある会話の具体的な中身を掲載。自分に一番等身大の主人公になりきって会話を聞いて、真似して話して会話力をつけましょう。

LISTENING & SPEAKING: KEY WORDS & PHRASES

「日誌」で出てきたビジネスで必要なキーワードやキーフレーズが身につきます。すべてのワードとフレーズには２つの例文がついていますので、より実践的で定着しやすくなっています。最後の「マナーのヒント」（海外文化におけるビジネスマナーのヒント）などのコラムは、グローバルなビジネス現場で活躍す

る人に必要なビジネススキルやコミュニケーションの基礎となる知識です。英語力だけでなく知識も習得することでより円滑にビジネスコミュニケーションが可能となるでしょう。

　　主人公と一緒にめきめき英語力を身につけて、ビジネスの第一線で活躍できる人材に！！

新渡戸慎之助　　米澤修　　岬一郎　　富沢秀幸　　ポール・ウィンストン

新渡戸慎之助（にとべ・しんのすけ）

　主人公。２６歳。PCゲームが好きでIT会社に入社。一見どこにでもいそうな若手新入社員。IT企業に入社すればみんなソフト開発できると思って入社するも、最初に総務部配属になりがっかり。さらにその後、突然海外事業部に異動の辞令が下りる。そんなに英語が好きなほうでもない新渡戸が、１年で流暢な英語を４技能まんべんなく身につけなければならなくなる。渋々書き始めた「英語の日誌」をはじめ、毎日多くの英語の課題と研修レッスンをこなす中でだんだんと英語が好きになり、自分でも気づかなかった英語の才能が少しずつ開花し始める…。

　失敗と挫折、思わぬ才能の開花と成功を繰り返し、厳しくも温かい上司・米澤修に見守られながら成長していく。躊躇しつつも社内で恋する姿に新近感がわく。

米澤修（よねざわ・おさむ）

　主人公。海外事業部・部長。55歳。取締役の１人。仕事ができて、誰からも尊敬される鑑のような人物。誠実で紳士的な見た目からわかるように部下には温かくも、間違ったことは間違っていると厳しく愛を持って指導する。その人柄から社内でも社長をはじめ、多くの人からの人望も厚い。家族仲もよく、最近孫ができた。

岬一郎（みさき・いちろう）

　新渡戸の同僚。新渡戸と同じく研修中。26歳。帰国子女（中学生のときにニュージーランドに3年間滞在）。帰国子女なので英語がペラペラで、自信がある。英語を話すと、より自信に満ちた話し方としぐさをするので帰国子女だろうなと想像できる。新渡戸と同じく上司から好感が持たれるようなさわやかな見た目。

富沢秀幸（とみざわ・ひでゆき）

　（株）富沢インテグレーティッド・ソリューションズ代表取締役社長。70歳。1986年10月に会社を立ち上げる。自身が72歳になるのを目前に、自分がこれ以上主導権を握っているのは会社の害になると考え、若い人材に役目を引き継がせようとするような客観的で有能な社長。モットーは「誰にでもなにかしらの特技（才能）がある」で、その人が能力を発揮できる仕事を割り当てるのが会社の義務だと考え、多くの社員を大切に育ててきた。

ポール・ウィンストン

　新渡戸と岬の英語研修を1年間担当する英語講師。アメリカ人。1984年生まれ34歳。交友関係が広く明るくフレンドリーで授業も楽しい。本書の途中で婚約者と結婚する。新渡戸と岬に「文法よりも使える英語を」と楽しくも実践的な英語を日々教え、2人の英語力をぐんぐん伸ばす有能な英語講師。

サブ登場人物

小林誠司　取締役部長で共同設立者。63歳。取締役の1人。
武田宏　一見冷たく見えるが実はいい人。創業メンバーの1人だがいまだに課長。自分の限界を知っていてあまり責任を負いたくないので昇進をいつも断っている謙虚さも。
柴田彩　新渡戸とほぼ同じ年。人懐っこくて素直でかわいい。インターナショナルスクールから上智大。新渡戸と…!?
ケネス・ルイス　ロンドン支社長。楽天的。60歳くらい。
スティーブン・ジョーンズ　静かで誠実な人柄。仕事も非常に優秀。自分の仕事の限界を理解しているが、みんなから信頼を得ている。ロンドン支社取締役。50代後半。

　他にもたくさんの人物が登場するので、ストーリーと臨場感を楽しみましょう！

CONTENTS

UNIT

4 人生に無駄はない！

UNIT

5 ロンドン武者修行

UNIT

6 未来へのステップ

UNIT

人生に
無駄は
ない！

OCTOBER 6TH (SUNDAY)

It is now past nine o'clock on Sunday night, and I have just returned home from work. Work on a Sunday! This is the first time I have ever had to work on a weekend, but it was an emergency.

On Thursday last week, we received an urgent call from one of our clients, a travel agency in Melbourne, Australia, to say that the system we had developed was malfunctioning. The System Engineering Section asked the Customer Support Section to provide an interpreter, and Ms. Haraguchi assigned me to the job. I therefore spent most of Thursday afternoon in the SE Section. First of all, I spoke to the local system administrator on the phone and asked him to send us an **e-mail outlining the problem (p.16)**. I then translated the e-mail for the system engineers, and they worked on the problem for about an hour. I was then given a briefing on what to tell Melbourne, after which I **called the system administrator (p.20)** and explained the situation. And finally, I **followed this up with an e-mail (p.18)**.

The computer we have in the System Engineering Section is able to connect directly into the Melbourne mainframe, so the engineers were able to patch up the problem temporarily. However, they also needed to add a permanent patch, which wouldn't be ready until Sunday (today). Once the permanent patch was created, they had to upload it to the Melbourne computer and then compile it. That meant that the system administrator needed to be in the office, so I was asked to work today in order to communicate with him.

Although I had heard the word "compile" many times in the past (unavoidable when you work for a software developer), it was not until today that I found out what it means. Apparently, computers are unable to directly understand the programing language that has been used for software, so it has to be converted into the machine code language that they can understand. This process is known as "compiling."

Anyway, everything went smoothly, and the Melbourne system is once again up and running normally. To be honest, I really enjoyed myself. It was the first time in a long time that I felt as if I was being useful.

Nitobe

キーワード＆キーフレーズ→p.22

１０月６日（日曜日）

　今は日曜の夜9時過ぎで、僕はちょうど仕事から帰ってきたところだ。日曜日に働くなんて！　週末に働かなければならなかったのはこれが初めてだけど、緊急事態だったのだ。

　先週の木曜日、我が社の顧客の1社、オーストラリアのメルボルンにある旅行代理店から、我が社が開発したシステムが誤作動を起こしているという緊急の電話があった。システムエンジニアリング課が顧客サポート課に通訳者の提供を頼んで、原口課長が僕にその仕事を振ったのだ。というわけで、僕は木曜日の午後のほとんどをSE課で過ごした。まず、現地のシステム管理者に電話して、そのトラブルの概要を説明するメールを送ってくれるように頼んだ。次に、そのメールをシステムエンジニアのために翻訳して、SEたちは1時間ほどかけてそのトラブルの解決に当たった。そのあと僕はメルボルンへ報告する内容の簡単な指示を受け、システム管理者に電話して状況を説明し、最後にメールでフォローアップした。

　システムエンジニアリング課にあるコンピュータがメルボルンのメインフレームに直接接続できるので、エンジニアたちは応急的にそのトラブルを修正することができた。でも彼らは恒久的な処置も追加しなければならなくて、こっちは日曜日（今日）まで完成しない。恒久的な修正が完成したら、今度はそれをメルボルンのコンピュータにアップロードしてコンパイルしなければならなかった。これはシステム管理者がオフィスにいなければならないということで、僕は彼と連絡を取るために今日働くよう頼まれたのだ。

　「コンパイル」という単語は今まで何回も聞いたことがあるけど（ソフトウェア開発会社で働いていればいやでも聞くからね）、今日初めてその意味がわかった。どうやら、コンピュータというものはソフトウェアに使われているプログラミング言語を直接理解することはできなくて、理解のできる機械語に変換する必要があるらしい。その過程を「コンパイルする」と呼ぶそうだ。

　何はともあれ、すべて順調に進んで、メルボルンのシステムは再び正常に稼働している。正直に言うと、僕はとても楽しかった。自分が役に立っていると感じるのは久しぶりだったのだ。

新渡戸

e-mail outlining the problem ►

問題の概要を伝えるEメールを書いてみよう！

From: Mark Harrison <mharrison@outbackfuntours.com.au>
Sent: Thursday, October 03, 3:16 PM
To: Shinnosuke Nitobe <snitobe@tomizawais.co.jp>
Subject: Trouble in the system (Outback Fun Tours)

Mr. Nitobe,

This is Mark Harrison at Outback Fun Tours. As I mentioned on the phone, we had a power cut about an hour ago, and when the power came back on, the people who had been logged onto the system were refused access.

From what I can gather, it looks like the access authority file was left open and still thinks these people are logged on. It therefore refuses additional log-ons. People who weren't logged on at the time of the power cut can log on without any trouble. I've tried fiddling with it, but nothing works.

I'll be waiting for your call.

Regards, Mark

POINT

特に、初めての人にメールを書く際は、冒頭ではっきりと自分の氏名や所属を明らかにしましょう。そして、まず問題がずばり何なのかを簡潔に説明し、次に、想定される原因や自分なりに対処したことなどを具体的に述べます。

差出人: マーク・ハリソン<mharrison@outbackfuntours.com.au>
送信: 10月3日(木曜日)午後3:16
宛先: 新渡戸慎之助<snitobe@tomizawais.co.jp>
件名: システムトラブル(アウトバック・ファン・ツアーズ)

新渡戸様

アウトバック・ファン・ツアーズのマーク・ハリソンです。お電話でお話ししたように、1時間ほど前に停電があり、電気が戻った際、システムにログオンしていた人がアクセスできなくなってしまいました。

私が集めた情報では、アクセス権限のあるファイルが開いたままだったようで、このファイルの持ち主がまだログオンしていると想定しているようです。そのため追加のログオンが拒否されています。停電の時点でログオンしていなかった人は、何も問題なくログオンできています。あちこち触ってみたのですが、効果はありません。

お電話をお待ちしております。

よろしくお願いいたします。
マーク

31

クイックQ&A

Q The computer problem started when the electricity unexpectedly failed. True or false?
(コンピュータのトラブルは突然停電が起きたとき始まりました。正しいですか、誤りですか)

POINT

メールの送り主のマーク・ハリソンはオーストラリア人なので、アメリカ人の場合おそらく使わない表現を用いています。第2段落にあるfiddle with「〜をいじくり回す」は一般的にイギリス英語・オーストラリア英語の表現で、アメリカ英語でも問題なく通じますがあまり使われません。fiddle以外でイギリス英語・オーストラリア英語で同じ意味を表す動詞は他にtinker(I've tried tinkering with it)やtoy(I've tried toying with it)などがあります。また、同じ意味を表すのにアメリカ人ならおそらく以下のような言い回しをするでしょう。
・I've tried messing with it　・I've tried fooling with it　・I've tried playing with it

A True(正しい)

followed this up with an e-mail ►
フォローアップ・メールを読んでみよう！

From: Shinnosuke Nitobe <snitobe@tomizawais.co.jp>
Sent: Thursday, October 03, 4:37 PM
To: Mark Harrison <mharrison@outbackfuntours.com.au>
Subject: Re: Trouble in the system (Outback Fun Tours)

Dear Mr. Harrison,

This is just to confirm the details of our conversation of a few minutes ago.

- The problem was caused by the access authority file remaining open after the system shut down abnormally due to a power cut.
- The cause of the problem was a bug that was overlooked at the time of development.
- A temporary patch will be installed from the Tokyo office within today (this afternoon).
- A permanent patch will be prepared for installation on Sunday, October 06, at 2 p.m.
- The modified files will need to be compiled, which may take a few hours.
- You are respectfully requested to be available in the Melbourne office at 2 p.m on Sunday (Oct. 06).

And that's about it. Sorry again for all the trouble. I look forward to speaking to you again on Sunday.

Best Regards, Shinnosuke Nitobe

POINT

箇条書きにするとわかりやすいです。

差出人: 新渡戸慎之助<snitobe@tomizawais.co.jp>
送信: 10月3日（木曜日）午後4:37
宛先: マーク・ハリソン<mharrison@outbackfuntours.com.au>
件名: Re: システムトラブル（アウトバック・ファン・ツアーズ）

ハリソン様

数分前の私たちの会話の詳細を確認させてください。

- 停電のためにシステムが異常シャットダウンした後にアクセス権限のあるファイルが開いたままだったことによって、問題が起きた。
- 問題の原因は、開発時点で見逃されていたバグだった。
- 一時的な修正は本日中（今日の午後）に東京本社からインストールされる。
- 恒久的な修正は10月6日（日曜日）午後2時にインストール準備がされる。
- 修正ファイルはコンパイルする必要があり、それには数時間かかるかもしれない。
- 日曜日（10月6日）の午後2時にメルボルンのオフィスにいらしていただけますようお願い申し上げます。

以上になります。改めてすべてのトラブルについてお詫び申し上げます。日曜日にまたお話しできることを楽しみにしています。

よろしくお願いいたします。
新渡戸慎之助

クイックQ&A

Q What caused the system to shut down?
（システムのシャットダウンの原因は何でしたか）

POINT

本文冒頭のThis is just to confirm...というフレーズは、話し合いの内容や特定の行動についての詳細が文字として残るようにメールを送るときによく使われます。これは以下のように様々な状況で使えます。
・This is just to confirm the details of next week's meeting. （来週の会議に関する詳細の確認です）
・This is just to confirm that I received your e-mail of yesterday and will reply within this week. （昨日のメールを確かに受信いたしました。今週中にはご返信いたします）
・This is just to confirm that we have received your inquiry and will reply as soon as possible. （確認:御社のお問い合わせを拝受しました。迅速にご返答させていただきます）

A A power cut (停電)

実際の会話を聞いて話してみよう!

SETTING:

Nitobe calls Mark Harrison, the system administrator for Outback Fun Tours, on the telephone to explain the situation regarding the computer problem.

Nitobe: Mr. Harrison? This is Shinnosuke Nitobe at Tomizawa, Tokyo.

Harrison: Hi! Thanks for getting back to me. Good news, I hope.

Nitobe: Well, we've isolated the problem and our system engineers are working on a patch right now. It should be ready in about an hour.

Harrison: That's great! Thank you. What was the problem?

Nitobe: You were right about the access authority file. It was still open when the system was powered up, and was refusing access to people who tried to log-on a second time. We are still not sure how the bug was overlooked during development, but we'll fix it for you now.

Harrison: Okay, that's great. Is there anything you need me to do?

Nitobe: Not at the moment. Our engineers will patch it up from this side, but it will only be a temporary measure. They'll start work on a permanent patch immediately, which should be ready by Sunday. We'll need you to be available on Sunday, though. Is that a problem?

Harrison: No, that's okay. I have nothing special planned.

Nitobe: It may take some time. After the system files have been transferred to your computer, they need to be compiled. That means you'll have to stay in the office for several hours.

Harrison: Okay. I'll make sure I bring a book with me. What time on Sunday?

Nitobe: Shall we say two o'clock in the afternoon?

Harrison: Yes, that's fine. I'll be here.

Nitobe: Thank you very much. We're also very sorry for the problem. We'll be sending you a full report within a week or two. In the meantime, I'll follow this conversation up with an e-mail confirming the details.

Harrison: Okay, I'll look forward to that. Thanks for your help.

Nitobe: Our pleasure. Sorry again for the trouble.

called the system administrator

場面：

> 新渡戸がアウトバック・ファン・ツアーズのシステム管理者マーク・ハリソンに電話をして、コンピュータのトラブルに関する状況を説明する。

N：ハリソンさんですか。東京の富沢の新渡戸慎之助です。

H：やあ！　お電話ありがとう。よい知らせだといいのだけど。

N：はい、問題を特定しまして、現在弊社のシステムエンジニアが修正しているところです。1時間ほどで終わるはずです。

31

H：それはよかった！　ありがとうございます。問題は何だったのです？

N：アクセス権限のファイルについて、そちらがおっしゃった通りでした。システムの電源が入ったときにファイルが開いたままで、再びログオンしようとした人のアクセスを拒否していました。なぜ開発中にこのバグが見落とされていたのかはわかっていませんが、問題はすぐに解決します。

H：わかりました、助かります。私がしなければならないことは何かありますか。

N：今のところはありません。弊社のエンジニアがこちら側から修正しますが、これは応急的な措置にすぎません。彼らは早急に恒久的な修正に取りかかり、それは日曜日には完成する予定です。ただ、日曜日にハリソンさんにオフィスにいていただく必要があります。それで問題ないですか。

H：ああ、それで大丈夫です。特に予定はありませんから。

N：その日は少々時間がかかると思われます。システムファイルがそちらのコンピュータに転送された後、それをコンパイルしなければならないので、ハリソンさんには数時間オフィスにいてもらわなければならないでしょう。

H：了解です。本でも持ってくることにしますよ。日曜日の何時です？

N：午後2時はいかがですか。

H：うん、それでいい。その時間にここに来ますよ。

N：どうもありがとうございます。この問題につきましては誠に申し訳ございません。1、2週間以内に詳細な報告書をお送りいたします。その間に、私からこの会話の詳細をメールでフォローアップしておきます。

H：わかりました、楽しみにしています。対応ありがとう。

N：お役に立てて幸いです。今回の件については重ねてお詫び申し上げます。

キーワードやフレーズをチェック!

☐ urgent call　緊急の電話（連絡）

We received an **urgent call** to say that our client's flight had been cancelled.
私たちは顧客のフライトがキャンセルになったという緊急の電話を受けた。

The manager put an **urgent call** in to the president to inform him of the problem.
部長は社長にその問題を報告するため緊急で電話をかけた。

☐ outline the problem　問題の概要を述べる

She **outlined the problem** during the meeting.
彼女は会議でその問題の要点を述べた。

He was not looking forward to **outlining the problem** to the angry stockholders.
彼は怒っている株主たちにその問題の概要を説明するのは気が進まなかった。

☐ give a briefing　簡単な報告をする

The police were **given a briefing** over the factory accident.
警察はその工場での事故について簡潔な状況説明を受けた。

He solved the problem himself, and then **gave a briefing** to his department head.
彼は自分でその問題を解決し、そのあと部長に簡潔な報告をした。

☐ communicate with ～　～と連絡を取る

It is essential that all staff **communicate with** each other at all times.
すべての社員が常にお互いにコミュニケーションを取ることは必須だ。

He was told to **communicate with** the sales office to prevent the same problem from arising in the future.
彼は将来同じような問題が起こることを防ぐため、営業所と連絡を取るように指示された。

☐ unavoidable when 〜   〜であるときは回避できない

Raising prices is **unavoidable when** the cost of imports continues to increase.

輸入コストが上がり続けていれば、値上げはやむを得ない。

Delays in production are **unavoidable when** facilities are badly maintained.

施設の管理が悪ければ、生産の遅れは避けられない。

31

☐ up and running   稼働して

The new system is scheduled to be **up and running** before the end of the year.

新しいシステムは年末までには稼働している予定だ。

The production line was **up and running** three days after the flooding.

生産ラインは冠水の3日後には問題なく稼働していた。

マナーのヒント

英語では「お世話になっております」などのようなフレーズがEメールなどのビジネス文書の冒頭に用いられることはありません。ですが、ビジネス文書には2つのタイプがあり、それによって本題への入り方が異なります。この2つのタイプとは「求められていない文書」と「求められた文書」です。つまり、連絡が来ることを予期していない相手に手紙やメールを送る場合、それは「求められていない文書」で、そのようなメッセージは以下のような簡単な挨拶で始めるのが一般的です。

　・くだけた挨拶：I hope everything is fine with you. （お変わりなくお過ごしでしょうか）

　・正式な挨拶：I hope this letter finds you enjoying good health and prosperity. （時下ますますご清栄のこと存じます）

しかし、送る手紙やメールが相手に求められたもの、もしくは一連の手紙・メールの1つである場合、文章の始めに挨拶を入れる必要はなく、直接本題に入るべきです。この31日目での新渡戸とマーク・ハリソンの間の2通のメールはこちらのタイプです。

DAY

OCTOBER 6TH (SUNDAY)

It appears as if Aya Shibata is not Shinnosuke Nitobe's bulbul after all. Hiroshi Takeda sent me an e-mail the other day saying that they had broken up. He mentioned that they have remained friends and seem to have no problem working together. Although, of course, I am sad for them, I must admit to feeling a sense of relief. Hopefully, Nitobe will now begin to search for his bulbul outside of the company.

And while I am on the subject of Shinnosuke Nitobe, Masami Fujiwara, head of the General Affairs Department in Tokyo, **e-mailed me a copy (p.26)** of his Kaizen Competition proposal on Tuesday. Reading through it, I nearly fell off my chair. It's absolutely amazing! He has only been working in the department for a few months, yet he casually came up with a proposal for establishing a nursery within the company for the children of employees. And, he came up with a plan for funding this by cutting down on the amount of outsourced translation by using special software and freelance translators. According to his plan, this will save the company more than sixty million yen per year, which he assumes will be enough to run the nursery. Sixty million yen! I've never seen anything like it. The usual Kaizen proposals consist of improving productivity in some small way to save a few yen here and there. Nitobe's proposal, on the other hand, approaches the way in which daily operations are handled by the Documentation Section. There are quite a few holes in his proposal and he has been a little too generous with his figures, but the sheer magnitude of what he is suggesting is mind-boggling!

I **forwarded it onto the president (p.28)** yesterday and then **called him to discuss the matter (p.30)** later in the day. He was as amazed as I was. I asked him to talk to Nitobe, just to give him a little encouragement, and also asked him to record the meeting and get Nitobe to transcribe it and translate it into English as an extra homework assignment. Paul Winston sends me regular updates on his progress, but I get the feeling that the homework assignments are a little too easy. Something a little more challenging may be useful.

Yonezawa

キーワード＆キーフレーズ→p.32

１０月６日（日曜日）

　結局のところ、どうやら柴田彩は新渡戸慎之助のヒヨドリではないようだ。先日、武田宏さんから2人が別れたというメールが送られてきた。彼によると2人はその後も友達でいるらしく、問題なく一緒に仕事をしているようだ。もちろん彼らのことは残念に思うが、少しほっとしていることも確かだ。新渡戸が今度は会社の外で彼のヒヨドリを探し始めてくれるといいのだが。

　新渡戸慎之助といえば、東京本社の藤原正美総務部長が火曜日に、新渡戸の改善コンペの提案書のコピーをメールで送ってきたのだが、それを読んで私は椅子からずり落ちそうなくらいに驚いた。全く素晴らしい！　彼はまだほんの数か月しか部署で働いていないというのに、従業員の子どものために社内に託児所を設けるという案をさらりと出してきたのだ。さらに、彼はその資金を作るために翻訳の外部委託の量を専用のソフトウェアとフリーランスの翻訳者を使って削減するという計画を出した。彼の計画によると、それによって我が社は年間6000万円以上の節約ができ、託児所を運営するのに十分になるという予測だ。6000万円とは！　こんなのは見たことがない。一般的な改善案は小規模に生産性を向上させて、そこここで何円か節約するようなものだ。一方、新渡戸の提案はドキュメンテーション課の日常的な業務の運び方にアプローチしている。彼の提案書はやや穴が多いし、予算も少々大きく見積もりすぎているが、その提案していることのスケールはそれだけで度肝を抜かれるものだ！

　私は昨日その提案書を社長に転送し、同じ日にさらに電話をかけてその件について話し合った。社長も私と同じくらい驚いていた。私は社長に新渡戸と話して少し自信を与えてやること、さらにその会話を録音しておいて追加の宿題として彼にそれを書き起こさせて英語に翻訳させてほしいと頼んだ。ポール・ウィンストンが新渡戸の上達具合を定期的に報告してくれているが、彼の出す宿題は少し簡単すぎるような気がする。もう少し歯ごたえのあるものが役立つかもしれない。

米澤

32

e-mailed me a copy ►

添付ファイル付きメールを書いてみよう!

From: Masami Fujiwara <mfujiwara@tomizawais.co.jp>
Sent: Tuesday, October 04, 4:04 PM
To: Mr. Yonezawa <yonezawa@tomizawauk.com>
Subject: Shinnosuke Nitobe's Kaizen Proposal

KaizenNitobe.zip
72 KB

Dear Mr. Yonezawa,

I hope you are enjoying your sojourn in London. Everything is running
smoothly over here, and we are all looking forward to welcoming you back
to Tokyo.

As requested, I am sending you a copy of Shinnosuke Nitobe's Kaizen
proposal (attached). It's a big proposal, and I think you'll agree that it is
very impressive. He has tackled a subject that nobody has ever thought
of before, setting up a nursery school inside the company, and he has
suggested that we pay for it by cutting costs in a very unique manner. I
have been running the Kaizen Competition for more than ten years now,
and I have never seen a proposal suggesting a new project while providing
a method for financing it. I think this young man will go far in the company.

Please don't hesitate to let me know if there is anything else you want.

Fujiwara

POINT

添付ファイルがあることを示す表現は、このメールのように文尾に（attached）を付ける以外にも複数あります。
例：Attached is a copy of... / Please find attached a file of...など。

差出人: 藤原正美 <mfujiwara@tomizawais.co.jp>
送信: 10月4日（火曜日）午後4:04
宛先: 米澤様 <yonezawa@tomizawauk.com>
件名: 新渡戸慎之助の改善提案書

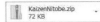
KaizenNitobe.zip
72 KB

米澤様

ロンドンご滞在を楽しまれていることと存じます。こちらではすべてが円滑に進んでおり、私たちは皆、部長が東京にお戻りになることを楽しみにしています。

ご要望の通り、新渡戸慎之助の改善提案書のコピーをお送りします（添付）。大きな提案で、とても印象的なものと思われると存じます。新渡戸は社内託児所の設置という今までだれも考えつかなかったテーマに取り組み、とても独特の方法でコストを削減することでそのための費用を出すと提案しています。私もこれまで10年以上改善コンペに携わっていますが、資金捻出の方法を提供しながら新しいプロジェクトを提案している提案書は見たことがありません。この若者は社内で成功していくと思います。

もし他に何か必要なものがあれば、ご遠慮なくお知らせください。

藤原

32

クイックQ&A

Q 〉 **What is included in the e-mail attachment?**
（このメールの添付ファイルの内容は何ですか）

POINT

本文1行目にあるsojournは「期間が不特定の一時的な滞在」を意味し、始まりと終わりさえあれば数日の場合にも数年の場合にも使えます。よって、例えば日本人がロンドンに永住する場合、その人は日本に帰る予定がないので、それはsojournではありません。以下はこの語を使った例文です。

- I had a sojourn in the Sales Department when I first started working here. (私はここで働き始めた頃、一時的に営業部にいたことがあります)
- She had a twenty-year sojourn in Malaysia, but has since returned to Japan. (彼女はマレーシアに20年間滞在しましたが、その後日本に戻ってきました)
- I learned much during my sojourn in the Toronto office. (私はトロント支社での滞在の間に多くを学びました)

A 〉 Nitobe's Kaizen proposal（新渡戸の改善提案書）

forwarded it onto the president ►

転送Eメールを読んでみよう!

From: O Yonezawa <yonezawa@tomizawauk.com>
Sent: Wednesday, October 05, 11:31 AM
To: Mr. H. Tomizawa <htomizawa@tomizawais.co.jp>
Subject: Kaizen Competition

KaizenNitobe.zip
72 KB

Dear Mr. Tomizawa,

Just a brief note to ask you to take a look at the attachment I am sending.
It is a proposal submitted for the Kaizen Competition by one of my young
protégés named Shinnosuke Nitobe. He is currently undergoing English
training in the Global Logistics Department.

I recruited him into the department earlier this year, and so far, he has
shown excellent progress. The proposal he has come up with is extremely
interesting, and if possible, I would like to discuss it with you. I'll call you
tonight (local time), so please expect my call at around 11 a.m. your time.

I look forward to speaking to you then.

Regards, O Yonezawa

差出人: 米澤 <yonezawa@tomizawauk.com>
送信: 10月5日（水曜日）午前11:31
宛先: 富沢様<htomizawa@tomizawais.co.jp>
件名: 改善コンペ

KaizenNitobe.zip
72 KB

富沢様

取り急ぎ、お送りしている添付をご覧いただきたくご連絡しております。新渡戸慎之助という私の若い部下の1人から改善コンペに提出された提案です。彼は現在、海外事業部で英語研修を受けております。

彼は私が今年初めに当部署にスカウトし、これまで秀でた成長を見せています。彼が出してきた提案は極めて興味深く、もし可能であればこれについて検討させていただきたいと思います。今夜（現地時間）お電話いたしますので、そちらの時間で午前11時頃に私の電話をお待ちくださいますか。

それではお話しするのを楽しみにしています。

よろしくお願いいたします。
米澤

32

クイックQ&A

Q \ If Tokyo is nine hours ahead of London, what time will Yonezawa call?
（東京がロンドンより9時間進んでいるとすると、米澤が電話をかけるのは何時ですか）

POINT

本文1行目にある形容詞briefは、shortの代わりによく使われます。ほとんどの場合、これは物理的な長さではなく時間を表すのに用いられ、メッセージや報告書などに対して使うときは、それら自体の長さではなく読むのにかかる時間を指します。以下はその使用例です。
・She was asked to give a brief speech at the end of the meeting. （彼女は会議の最後に簡単なスピーチをするよう頼まれました）
・He visited a client on his way home from the office for a brief visit. （彼は会社からの帰りに短い訪問のため取引先に立ち寄りました）
・He was so busy that he only had time for a brief lunch. （彼はあまりに忙しかったので手早く昼食をとる時間しかありませんでした）

A \ 20:00 (8 p.m.) (20時 (午後8時))

called him to discuss the matter ► CD 1-03

実際の会話を聞いて話してみよう!

SETTING:

Yonezawa calls President Tomizawa from the London office.

Yonezawa: Good morning. London calling!

Tomizawa: Osamu! Nice hearing from you. How's everything on your side of the world?

Yonezawa: Fine, thank you. Did you read the proposal I sent you?

Tomizawa: Yes, I did. It's very impressive. Where do you find these smart young people?

Yonezawa: They're all around you if you take the time to look. I was also impressed by the proposal. There are some obvious things that he has overlooked, but the fact that he saw what the company was lacking and then tried to fix it was extremely eye-opening. He's right! We don't do enough for employees with young children.

Tomizawa: Do you think it's a viable proposition?

Yonezawa: In its present state, no. He has assumed that all translations are in English, which they are not. Employing staff to handle freelance translators in all languages required would cost considerably more than we save. He has also overlooked the fact that there are very strict laws governing the operation of nurseries. Additional sprinkler systems, emergency exits, and many other facilities would need to be installed, so I don't believe a nursery would be possible. But even if we could save only a quarter of what he suggests, we could still use it to make things easier for employees with young children. A monthly allowance, for example, to help them pay nursery fees.

Tomizawa: Yes, I see your point. I'll leave the details up to you and Fujiwara. In the meantime, what do you want me to do?

Yonezawa: I want you to speak to him. Just to let him know that he has attracted the attention of top management. Praise him a little. Give him some encouragement. He is going to be an enormous asset to the company in the future.

Tomizawa: Okay, no problem. Anything else?

Yonezawa: If you don't mind, I'd like you to record the meeting, and then ask Nitobe to translate it into English and send a transcription to me directly.

called him to discuss the matter

場面：

米澤がロンドン支社から富沢社長に電話をかける。

Y：おはようございます。こちらロンドンです！

T：修！　声が聞けてうれしいよ。地球のそっち側では全部順調か。

Y：ええ、ありがとうございます。そちらに送った提案書は読まれましたか。

T：ああ、読んだぞ。あれは素晴らしいな。君はあんな優秀な若者をどこから見つけてくるんだ？

Y：時間をかけて見れば周り中にいるものですよ。私もその提案書に感心したんです。いくつか明らかな見落としをしてはいますが、彼がこの会社に足りないものを見つけて、さらにそこを直そうとしたという事実には目を見張りました。彼の指摘はその通りですよ！　我が社は小さな子どもがいる従業員に対して十分に手を尽くしていません。

T：新渡戸の案は実行可能だと思うか。

Y：現在のままの形ですと、無理ですね。彼はすべての翻訳が英語だと想定していますが、実際は違います。必要とされる言語すべてのフリーランス翻訳者に対応するだけのスタッフを雇うとなると、節約できるのよりもかなり多くの費用がかかります。それから彼は、託児所の運営に関してとても厳しい法律があるという点を見逃しています。追加のスプリンクラー設備、非常口、その他の多くの設備を導入する必要があるので、託児所は無理だと思います。ですが彼が示す4分の1ほどしか節約できないとしても、小さな子どものいる社員がもっと楽になるようにするのに浮いた費用を使うことはできます。例えば、保育所費用の支払いの援助としての月々の手当などですね。

T：ああ、もっともだな。詳細は君と藤原に任せる。それで俺には何をしてほしいんだ？

Y：新渡戸と話してくれませんか。ただ彼が経営陣の関心を引いたと知らせてやってくれればいいんです。少しほめて、自信を持たせてやってください。彼は将来、我が社の大きな財産になるでしょうから。

T：わかった、任せとけ。他には？

Y：よろしければ、その会話を録音しておいて、新渡戸にそれを英語に翻訳して文字にしたものを私に直接送るよう言ってください。

KEY WORDS & PHRASES

CD 1-04

キーワードやフレーズをチェック!

be sad for 〜　　〜を気の毒に思う、〜に同情する

I **was sad for** Peter when he failed to pass the examination, but he didn't seem to mind.
私はピーターが試験に落ちたのを気の毒に思ったが、彼は気にしていないようだった。

Everybody in the department **was sad for** Mary when she lost her husband.
メアリーが夫を亡くしたことには部署のみんなが同情した。

feel a sense of 〜　　〜の感じがする

She **felt a sense of** achievement after having successfully completed the project.
彼女はそのプロジェクトを成功させて達成感を味わった。

I always **feel a sense of** irritation whenever a new e-mail arrives.
私は新しいメールが来るたびにいつもイライラする。

anything like 〜　　〜のようなもの

I've never seen **anything like** the sales figures he achieved in just one month.
彼がたった1か月で達成した売上高は、私が今まで見たことがないようなものだ。

No other product the company produces has received **anything like** the popularity of this product.
この会社が製造してきた中でこの製品に及ぶほどの人気があったものはない。

some small way　　ささやかな方法

She wanted to contribute in **some small way** to the company's prosperity.
彼女は会社の繁栄に少しずつでも貢献したいと思った。

He offered his services as a volunteer to repay her kindness in **some small way**.
彼は彼女の親切にささやかながら報いるため、進んで無償で協力した。

here and there　　あちこちで

The company has branches located **here and there** throughout the country.

その会社は全国のあちこちに支社を置いている。

The use of artificial intelligence is becoming apparent **here and there** throughout the industry.

人工知能の活用はその業界全体のあちこちで目立つようになってきている。

mind-boggling　　形 仰天する、度肝を抜かれる

32

The amount of money the company spends on entertainment is **mind-boggling**.

その会社が娯楽に費やす予算の量には仰天する。

The speed at which she was promoted through the company is **mind-boggling**.

彼女がその会社で昇進したスピードには度肝を抜かれる。

マナーのヒント

　海外のオフィスにいる人に電話をかけるときは、当然ながら時差に配慮する必要がありますが、そのときに相手の一日のスケジュールも考慮に入れることをお勧めします。欧米やその他の多くの地域の会社は9時－5時、つまり勤務時間は午前9時から午後5時までという基準で回っているので、午後5時以降に会社にいる人はほとんどいないでしょう。また、一日の仕事をメールの確認などの決まった日課で始める人が多いため、相手が朝に仕事を始めてすぐのタイミングで電話をかけるのは不躾とされています。相手が会社から帰宅する予定の時刻の直前に連絡するのもお勧めできません。もう1つの注意点は昼休みの違いです。日本では正午から午後1時が普通ですが、例えばイギリスでは12時半から13時半が一般的な昼休みの範囲です。従って、緊急以外の電話は午前中半ば、もしくは午後半ばのタイミングでするのが望ましいでしょう。

OCTOBER 17TH (THURSDAY)

I was **invited to the presentation** (p.36) at the German e-commerce company, Rhein Gourmet Food & Confectionary, today. I attended the initial sales pitch last month, and today's meeting was for presenting the system concept and quotation. Everything went as planned. On the way back to the office, the salesmen seemed confident that we would win the contract.

I also had a very strange experience earlier this week. I was called into the president's office! I received a phone call from his secretary asking me to go up to the 8th floor immediately. I had no idea what the summons was about, so I was extremely nervous as I traveled up in the elevator. The president's office was smaller than I had expected, but it was very tastefully decorated. A large wooden desk in dark wood, with matching bookcases around three of the walls. Four comfortable chairs with a coffee table were placed in front of the desk. The president, who I was meeting for the first time, told me to sit down, and his secretary served us coffee. He told me that he was going to record the meeting (huh?!?), and then went on to say how impressed he was with my Kaizen proposal! He said that the company was very serious about the wellbeing of employees, and that my idea to help the parents of young children meshed closely with company policy.

We spoke for a few minutes, and he then stopped the recorder and handed me the memory chip, telling me to translate our conversation into English and send the transcription directly to Mr. Yonezawa in London.

I might have known that Mr. Yonezawa was involved. But, it was very nice to be recognized by the president (the PRESIDENT!!!), and to receive so much praise. I spent the rest of the day walking around with a big smile on my face... ☺

This week's English lessons are good fun. Mr. Winston has been **teaching us about word selection** (p.40). He told us that we have to select the most appropriate words in the target language (English) without relying on the actual meaning of the source language (Japanese). He also set us a **homework assignment** (p.38) for selecting the most suitable words for the Japanese [うるさい] in different situations.

Nitobe

１０月１７日（木曜日）

今日、僕はドイツのＥＣ企業、ライン・グルメ食品製菓会社でのプレゼンテーションに招かれた。先月の初回売り込みにも参加したのだけど、今日の打ち合わせはシステムのコンセプトと見積りを提示するためのものだった。すべては予定通りに進み、会社への帰り道で営業マンたちは、これは契約を獲得できるぞと自信に満ちた様子だった。

それから、今週の初めはとても珍しい経験をした。なんと社長室に呼ばれたのだ！社長の秘書からすぐに８階に来てほしいという電話がかかってきて、なぜ呼び出されたのか見当もつかなかったので、エレベーターで昇りながら僕はひどく緊張していた。社長室は想像していたよりも大きくなかったけれど、とても上品な感じにコーディネートされていた。大きな濃い色の木のデスクと、３方向の壁にそろいの本棚。デスクの前には座り心地のいい椅子が４つ、コーヒーテーブルと一緒に置いてあった。初めて会った社長は僕に座るよう促し、秘書がコーヒーを出してくれた。社長はこの会話を録音すると僕に伝えてから（これには「え！？」と驚いた）、なんと僕の改善案にとても感心したと話し始めた！　社長によると、我が社は社員の福利にとても真剣に取り組んでいて、小さい子どもの親を手助けするという僕のアイデアは会社の方針によく合っているのだそうだ。

何分か話をした後、社長はレコーダーを止めて僕にそのメモリーカードを渡し、今の会話を英語に訳して、それを書き起こしたものをロンドンの米澤部長に直接送るように言った。

やっぱり米澤部長が関わっているんだろうと思った。でも、社長に認められて（社長だぞ！！）あんなにほめられたのはすごくうれしかったな。そのあと僕は一日中どこへ行っても顔がニヤニヤしっぱなしだった… ☺

今週の英語の授業はとても楽しい。ウィンストン先生は僕たちに言葉選びについて教えてくれている。元の言語（日本語）での文字通りの意味にとらわれず、目的の言語（英語）で最も適切な単語を選び出さなければならないと教わった。それから、いろんな状況における日本語の「うるさい」に一番合った語句を選ぶという宿題を出された。

新渡戸

invited to the presentation ▶

プレゼンへの招待Eメールを書いてみよう!

From: Taiki Ishibashi <tishibashi@tomizawais.co.jp>
Sent: Thursday, October 17, 10:26 AM
To: Shinnosuke Nitobe <snitobe@tomizawais.co.jp>
Subject: Rhein Gourmet Food & Confectionary

Nitobe,

The concept plan and quotation for Rhein Gourmet e-commerce system is ready, and we are giving them a presentation at 2:30 this afternoon. Do you want to attend? Ms. Ota will be acting as interpreter, but you are welcome to join her if you have time.

Owing to the short development period, we have come up with a plan for splitting the system into two. The first stage, consisting of the basic system, will be ready for cutover by April next year so that they can accept online orders, and the second stage, consisting of all value-added functions, will be cutover in mid-June.

We will be leaving the office at around 1:45. Let me know if you want to come.

Taiki Ishibashi

POINT

相手の意思や都合を思いやる語句(Do you want to attend?、if you have timeなど)を要所に使います。

差出人: 石橋大樹<tishibashi@tomizawais.co.jp>
送信: 10月17日（木曜日）午前10:26
宛先: 新渡戸慎之助<snitobe@tomizawais.co.jp>
件名: ライン・グルメ食品製菓会社

新渡戸様

ライン・グルメのECシステムの基本計画と見積りが用意できたので、今日の午後2時30分に先方にプレゼンを行います。新渡戸さんも出席しませんか。太田さんが通訳として参加する予定ですが、もしお時間があれば同行を歓迎します。

開発期間が短いため、システムを2つに分けるプランを考えました。第1段階は基本的なシステムから成り、来年4月までにカットオーバーのための準備ができますので、オンラインでの注文を受けることができるようになります。そして、第2段階はすべての付加価値付きの機能から成り、6月半ばにカットオーバーされる予定です。

1時45分頃にオフィスを出発する予定です。もし来られるならお知らせください。

石橋大樹

33

クイックQ&A

Q How long does it take to travel from Tomizawa to Rhein Gourmet?
（富沢からライン・グルメまで移動するのにかかる時間はどれくらいですか）

POINT

英語には時刻の書き方がいくつかあり、基本的に個人がそれぞれ好きなスタイルを使うことになります。以下はその例です。
・o'clock: I will call you at two o'clock this afternoon. （今日の午後2時に電話します）
・つづり通り: I will call you at four-thirty this afternoon. （今日の午後4時30分に電話します）
・a.m.／p.m.: I will call you at 10 a.m. / at 4 p.m. （午前10時に／午後4時に電話します）
・12時制: I will call you at 1:45. （1時45分に電話します）
・24時制: I will call you at 13:45. （13時45分に電話します）

A Approximately 45 minutes（約45分）

「うるさい」の様々な英訳を読んでみよう！

Homework: English Translations of [うるさい] by Situation

- [(声が)うるさい] → Shut up. / Keep quiet. / Be quiet.
  When somebody is shouting or speaking in an uncomfortably loud voice, and when somebody has said something insulting.

- [(音が)うるさい] → noisy / what a racket / what a noise
  When a machine or other inanimate object is making an uncomfortably loud noise.

- [(要求などが)うるさい] → hard to please / finds fault
  When somebody constantly complains about things, such as a manager who always finds fault with people's work or is very demanding.

- [(虫／電話などが)うるさい] → annoying / irritating / nuisance / bothersome
  When animate objects (people, insects, animals) and inanimate objects (e-mail, telephone calls) are overly persistent.

- [(こだわりが)うるさい] → particular / stickler / finicky
  When people have their own ideas about something and refuse to accept anything less.

宿題：状況による「うるさい」の英訳

- 「(声が)うるさい」→ Shut up. / Keep quiet. / Be quiet.
  誰かが叫んでいたり、不快なくらい大きな声で話しているときや、侮辱するようなことを言ったとき。

- 「(音が)うるさい」→ noisy / what a racket / what a noise
  機械や他の無生物のものが不快なくらい大きな音を出しているとき。

- 「(要求などが)うるさい」→ hard to please / finds fault
  常に部下の仕事のあら探しをしたり、とても要求が厳しい上司のように、誰かが物事について絶えず文句を言っているとき。

- 「(虫／電話などが)うるさい] → annoying / irritating / nuisance / bothersome
  生物(人、虫、動物)や無生物(Eメール、電話の着信音)が過度にしつこいとき。

- 「(こだわりが)うるさい」→ particular / stickler / finicky
  人が何かについて独自の考えを持っていて、それ以外のものを受け入れるのを拒むとき。

33

クイックＱ＆Ａ

Q Somebody who is hard to please is overly persistent. True or false?
(hard to pleaseな人とは過度にしつこい人のことです。正しいですか、誤りですか)

POINT

次のページの会話でウィンストン先生が指摘している通り、日常の場面で使われる言葉はその国の文化によって違います。普通の一般的な名詞、動詞、形容詞の他に、英語と日本語の最大の違いの1つが、英語は人物を指すときに年齢に基づいた名詞をほとんど使わないということです。つまり、「先輩・後輩」、「兄・弟」、「おじさん・おばさん」のような言葉はほとんど使われません。elder brother「年上の兄弟」やmiddle-aged lady「中年の女性」というような言い回しをすることはありますが、これはその人物の年齢が話の中で重要な場合に限られます。そうでない場合は、単にbrother「兄弟」やlady「女性」と言います。また、「大学の先輩」については、例えばWe attended the same university.「同じ大学に通っていた」と説明し、年齢の違いには触れません。

A False (誤り)

39

CD
1-05

実際の会話を聞いて話してみよう!

SETTING:

> Nitobe and Ichiro Misaki are listening to Paul Winston during their English lesson.

Winston: We must always remember the limitation of dictionaries. For example, if you looked up the word [うそ] in the dictionary, what would you get?

Nitobe: Lie.

Winston: Exactly! Now, imagine that you receive an internal memo saying that this year's bonus has been cancelled. Your first reaction is to say [うそ!]. What would you say in English?

Misaki: "Oh, no!" maybe. Or "Damn!"

Winston: That's right. Well done. Now, how about discovering one day that you have won this year's jumbo lottery? You are amazed and say, [うそ!]. How would you say that in English?

Nitobe: "Oh, my God!" or "Wow!" or "Yippee!"

Winston: Very good. Okay, one more. Your brother tells you that he is getting married. You are delighted and congratulate him, but then he says, [うそだよ!]. What would he say in English?

Nitobe: "I'm lying!"

Winston: No. The word "lie" has a deeper meaning in English. It is an antisocial act that means to deceive somebody for nefarious purposes. Because your brother is immediately owning up to the deception proves that he had no nefarious motive. In this case it would be treated as a joke, not a lie.

Nitobe: So, something like "I'm joking," or "I'm kidding"?

Winston: Exactly! So, there we have three examples in which a single word in a source language uses totally different words in the target language. Remember, the meaning of words is determined by cultural background, not the dictionary.

Misaki: But if the dictionary can't be relied on, how can we learn the correct words?

Winston: By using your powers of observation. Read, listen and learn.

teaching us about word selection

場面：

> 新渡戸と岬一郎が英語の授業でポール・ウィンストンの話を聞いている。

W：辞書がすべてではないということを僕たちはいつも覚えておかなければならない。例えば、「うそ」という単語を辞書で引くと、なんて書いてある？

N：lie です。

W：その通り！　じゃあ、今年のボーナスがなしになったという社内通知を受け取ったと想像してみて。君はとっさに「うそ！」って言う。これを英語で言うとしたら何だい？

M：Oh, no! でしょうか。それか Damn! ですね。

W：正解。上出来だよ。じゃあ、ある日、今年のジャンボ宝くじに当たったって知ったとしたら？　君は驚いて「うそ！」と言う。これを英語で何と言うかな？

N：Oh, my God! か、Wow! か Yippee! です。

W：素晴らしい。それじゃあ、もう1問。君の兄さんが結婚を報告してくる。でも君が喜んでおめでとうと伝えると、彼は「うそだよ！」と言う。彼は英語で何と言うだろう？

N：I'm lying! です。

W：不正解。英語で lie という言葉はもっと重い意味を持つんだ。悪意から人をだます反社会的な行為という意味になる。君の兄さんはうそをすぐに認めているから、悪意のある動機はなかったと証明されるよね。この場合、これは「うそ」ではなく「冗談」とされるんだ。

N：では、I'm joking や I'm kidding のような感じですか。

W：その通り！　さて、元の言語では1つの言葉なのに目的の言語では全く別の言葉になってしまう例がこれで3つ出てきたわけだ。言葉の意味は辞書ではなく文化的背景によって決まるってことを覚えておいてほしい。

M：ですが、辞書に頼れないなら、どうやって正しい言葉を覚えればいいんですか。

W：観察力を使うんだよ。読んで、聞いて、学ぶんだ。

KEY WORDS & PHRASES

CD
1-06

キーワードやフレーズをチェック!

☐ **sales pitch**　売り込み、セールストーク

His **sales pitch** lacked details, so he had to return for another meeting.

彼のセールストークには詳細が足りなかったため、彼はもう一度別の打ち合わせを行わなければならなかった。

She gave a tremendous **sales pitch** that fascinated her audience.

彼女は素晴らしいセールストークで聞き手の心をとらえた。

☐ **go as planned**　計画通りに進む

He had intended to visit six clients during his trip to Bangkok, but things did not **go as planned**.

彼はバンコクへの出張の間に6社の顧客を訪問するつもりだったが、物事は予定通りには進まなかった。

The product's release included lots of advertising, and everything **went as planned**.

その製品の発売はたくさんの宣伝とともに行われ、すべて計画通りに進んだ。

☐ **tastefully decorated**　上品に装飾された

Her aim was to ensure the store was **tastefully decorated** to attract customers.

彼女の目的は客を引き寄せるために店をおしゃれにデザインすることだった。

The reception was the only part of the building that was **tastefully decorated**.

フロントは建物内で唯一、趣味のいい内装になっているところだった。

☐ **go on to say ～**　続けて～と言う

He outlined this year's targets in his speech, and then **went on to say** that he was very optimistic about achieving them.

彼はスピーチで今年の目標の概要を説明し、続けてその達成について非常に前向きに考えていると述べた。

He thanked his hosts for their hospitality before **going on to say** how much he loved visiting Sydney.
彼はもてなしてくれた人たちのやさしさへの感謝を伝え、それからどんなにシドニーを訪れるのが好きかを話した。

mesh closely　ぴったり合う

The company's ideas on hiring overseas workers **meshes closely** with government policy.
その会社の外国人社員の雇用に関する考えは、政府の方針と一致している。

I was pleased to know that my manager's views on overtime **meshed closely** with mine.
私はうちの部長の残業についての意見が私のものと合っていると知ってうれしかった。

33

might have known (that) 〜　〜ではないかと思った

I **might have known** that it would rain on the day of the company's softball game.
会社のソフトボールの試合の日に限って雨が降るなんて。

I didn't expect her to quit, but I **might have known** that she would.
彼女が辞めるとは予想していなかったが、思い当たる節はあった。

マナーのヒント

　英語では大文字で書くのは大声で叫ぶことに相当するとされ、非常に失礼なこととみなされます。なのでメールを送るときやSNSなどでメッセージを投稿するとき、文頭や固有名詞の語頭などを除き、大文字で書くことは絶対に避けなければなりません。一般的に、そのようなタイプのメッセージをよく投稿する人は極端または過激な考えを持っていることが多いので、すべて大文字で書かれたメッセージを読もうとさえしない人もたくさんいます。1つの単語を強調のために大文字で書くことはありますが、それも私的なメールやメッセージの中だけで、正式な文書やビジネス文書では決して使われません。

OCTOBER 22ND (TUESDAY)

I attended a barbecue hosted by one of the Japanese managers on Sunday. There are three Japanese managers in the London office, Nobuo Akashiya, Junko Yamaguchi and Takeo Miyazaki, all of whom were transferred over here from the Tokyo office for three-year periods. Nobuo Akashiya, our host, lives in Finchley, northwest London, and has a large garden, hence the barbecue. His wife and two small children accompanied him to London, and he told us about the preparations they were making for **this year's Halloween (p.46)**. I always thought that Halloween was an American invention, but **Junko Yamaguchi told me (p.50)** that it is a two-thousand-year-old pagan festival, very similar to Japan's Obon festival, that originated with the Celts of Scotland.

Apparently, it is only in the past decade or so that the American style of Halloween has become popular in the United Kingdom, and already the popularity is on the wane. One of the reasons for this is that the date is so close to another popular annual event, **Guy Fawkes Night (p.48)**, which is held on November 5th. Guy Fawkes was the man who tried to blow up the Houses of Lords in 1605 and kill King James I, and his capture and subsequent execution is still celebrated today with bonfires and fireworks. The British love their history and traditions.

We have a very busy period coming up. The latest edition of the Fleet Suite accounting software is due to be released on November 25th, and the company is buzzing with activity. Fleet Suite is Tomizawa UK's premier commercial product, and the new edition represents its eighth upgrade. It was originally a package containing word-processing software, spreadsheet software and accounting software, but it became impossible to compete against Microsoft Office in the fields of word-processing and spreadsheets, so these products were gradually phased out (although support will continue to be provided for another few years). FS Accounting, however, remains very popular and is a big seller. A large public launch is planned for November 25th, and the sales section and advertising section are currently inundated with work. Salesmen are visiting existing customers, DM is being sent out, and a large advertising campaign, including ads in trade journals, is underway.

Yonezawa

キーワード＆キーフレーズ→p.52

１０月２２日（火曜日）

　日曜日に、日本人の管理職の1人が主催するバーベキューパーティーに参加した。ロンドン支社には明石家信夫、山口順子、宮崎武雄の3人の日本人管理職がいて、全員が東京本社から3年の期間でこちらに転勤してきた。主催者の明石家信夫はロンドン北西部のフィンチリーに住んでいて、大きな庭を持っているので、そこでバーベキューパーティーを開いたというわけだ。彼の妻と2人の小さな子どもも彼と一緒にロンドンまで来ていて、彼は家族でやっている今年のハロウィーンの準備について話してくれた。今まで私はハロウィーンがアメリカでできたものだと思っていたが、実はスコットランドのケルト民族由来の、日本のお盆によく似た、2000年前から続く非クリスチャンの祭りなのだと山口順子に教わった。

　どうやら、アメリカ式のハロウィーンがイギリスで広まったのはほんの10年くらい前からで、その人気もすでに下火になり始めているようだ。その理由の1つが、11月5日に行われるもう1つの人気の年中行事、ガイ・フォークス・ナイトと日にちが近すぎることらしい。ガイ・フォークスは1605年に貴族院を爆破してジェームズ1世を暗殺しようとした男で、彼の逮捕とそれに続く処刑は現代でもかがり火や花火で祝われている。イギリス国民は自分たちの歴史や伝統に愛着を持っているのだ。

　我々は非常に忙しい時期に差しかかろうとしている。会計ソフトウェア「フリートスイート」の最新版が11月25日に発表される予定で、社内ではみんながせっせと動き回っている。フリートスイートは富沢UKの最高級の商用製品で、今回の最新版はその8回目のアップグレードだ。もとはワープロソフト、表計算ソフト、会計ソフトを含むパッケージだったが、ワープロと表計算の分野でマイクロソフトオフィスとの競合が不可能になり、そっちの製品は段階的に廃止されていった（ただし、あと数年はサポートが提供されることになっている）。しかしFS会計のほうは依然として大人気で、売れ筋商品になっている。11月25日に大々的な公開が計画されていて、営業課と宣伝課は現在仕事に追われている。販売員が既存顧客を訪問したりDMが送られたりしており、業界誌に載せる広告を含む大規模な広告キャンペーンも進行中だ。

米澤

this year's Halloween ►

ハロウィーンの起源を書いてみよう!

Origins of Halloween

Halloween was originally the Samhain festival celebrated by the Celts in Scotland and Ireland over two thousand years ago. The arrival of Christianity in the Celtic lands resulted in the word "Samhain" being substituted for "Halloween." November 1st is Hallow's Day in the Christian calendar, so October 31st became "Hallow's Eve," which later became "Halloween."

October 31st is the night on which the Celts believed the connection between this world and the next world to be at its thinnest, which allows the dead to return to earth. The Celts feared the spirits of the dead, and had many customs to placate them, most of which are still observed in modern-day Halloween celebrations.

Costumes: The custom of dressing up as scary creatures was known as "guising," and it was carried out to mock the spirits by indicating that the wearer could not be intimidated.

Trick-or-treat: This custom originated with the Celts leaving food and other gifts at the entrance to their houses for the spirits who wandered the countryside. It was thought that the spirits would break into the house to find food if this was not observed.

Pumpkin lanterns: The Celts made lanterns out of pumpkins, known as jack-o'-lanterns, for people to carry when walking at night on Halloween to keep the ghosts and spirits at bay.

ハロウィーンの起源

ハロウィーンは2000年以上前にスコットランドとアイルランドのケルト人によって祝われたサウィン祭が起源です。ケルト人の土地へのキリスト教の伝来によって「サウィン」という言葉が「ハロウィーン」に結果的に変わりました。11月1日はキリスト教暦で「神聖（ハロー）」の日なので、10月31日が「神聖の前夜（ハロー・イブ）」となり、これが後に「ハロウィーン」となりました。

10月31日はケルト人がこの世とあの世の間が最も薄くなると信じていた夜で、死者が地上に戻って来られるとされています。ケルト人は死者の霊魂を恐れ、それらを慰めるたくさんの慣習を持っていて、そのほとんどは現在のハロウィーンのお祝いでいまだに見られます。

衣装：怖い生き物の格好をする慣習は「ガイジング」として知られ、その格好をしている人たちを怖がらせることはできないということを示すことによって霊魂をまねてあざけるために行われました。

トリック・オア・トリート：この慣習は、その地方をさまよう霊魂のためにケルト人が食べ物やその他の贈り物を家の玄関に置いたことが起源です。もしこれが行われないと、霊魂が食べ物を見つけるために家に入り込んでくると考えられていました。

パンプキンちょうちん：「ジャックオーランタン」として知られており、ハロウィーンの夜歩くときに幽霊や霊魂を寄せつけないように人々が持ち運ぶよう、ケルト人がカボチャからちょうちんを作りました。

34

クイックQ＆A

Q 〉 **What triggered the change in name from Samhain to Halloween?**
（サウィンからハロウィーンに呼び名が変わったきっかけは何ですか）

POINT

Costumesの説明にあるscaryという単語は英語で「恐ろしい」という感覚を表すたくさんの形容詞の1つに過ぎません。同義語としては以下のようなものがあります。
alarming bloodcurdling chilling creepy eerie frightening hair-raising horrendous horrifying intimidating shocking spine-chilling spooky terrifying

A 〉 The arrival of Christianity（キリスト教の伝来）

Guy Fawkes Night ►

ガイ・フォークス・ナイトの説明を読んでみよう！

Guy Fawkes Night

On November 5th, 1605, a catholic named Guy Fawkes stockpiled a large quantity of gunpowder in an area directly beneath the House of Lords in an attempt to blow up the House and kill the protestant King James I, who was attendant on that day. The authorities were warned of this plot by an anonymous letter and searched the building, where Fawkes was discovered guarding the gunpowder.

Known as the Gunpowder Plot, Fawkes was questioned and tortured until he confessed, and he was sentenced to death by hanging for treason. People lit bonfires around London in celebration of the fact that King James I had survived the attempt on his life, and this day was later designated as an annual public day of thanksgiving.

The custom of lighting bonfires is still observed today on November 5th in events known as either Guy Fawkes Night or Bonfire Night. Local organized events are held by churches or on public land in which effigies of Guy Fawkes are burned on large bonfires against a background of extravagant firework displays. In addition to organized events, individual households also hold small celebrations in their own gardens with bonfires and fireworks.

ガイ・フォークス・ナイト

1605年11月5日にガイ・フォークスというカトリック教徒が大量の火薬を貴族院の真下の地点に蓄え、貴族院を爆破して、その日議会に出席していたプロテスタントのジェームス1世を殺害しようと企てました。当局は匿名の手紙でこの陰謀を警告され、建物を捜索し、火薬を隠し持っていたフォークスを発見しました。

火薬陰謀事件として知られ、フォークスは自白するまで尋問と拷問をされて、反逆罪として絞首刑の判決を受けました。ジェームス1世が暗殺を免れたという事実を祝うため人々はロンドン中に大かがり火をつけ、後にこの日は毎年行われる感謝祭の祝日に指定されました。

大かがり火をつけるという慣習は今日でも、ガイ・フォークス・ナイトあるいはボーンファイヤー・ナイトとして知られるイベントで11月5日に行われます。地元で組織されたイベントが、教会のそばや、膨大な花火の打ち上げを背景にガイ・フォークスの像が大かがり火で燃える公有地で開催されます。組織的なイベントに加え、個人の家庭も各々の庭でかがり火や花火でささやかなお祝いを行います。

34

クイックＱ＆Ａ

Q In what century did the Gunpowder Plot take place?
（火薬陰謀事件が起こったのは何世紀ですか）

POINT

1文目にあるstockpileは、特定の目的のために一定期間何かを集めて蓄える行動を表すのによく使われる動詞です。従って例えば、切手を収集している人は最終的に切手を特定の目的のために使うわけではないので、切手をstockpileしているとは言えません。以下はこの単語を使った例文です。
・They are stockpiling wine for their Christmas party.（彼らはクリスマスパーティーのためにワインを買いだめしています）
・We stockpile food and water to make sure we are ready for earthquakes.（私たちはいつ地震が来てもいいように食糧と水を備蓄しています）
・The company has stockpiled portable generators for use in emergencies.（その会社には非常時に使用するためポータブル発電機が備蓄してあります）

A 17th century（17世紀）

Junko Yamaguchi told me ▶

実際の会話を聞いて話してみよう!

SETTING:

> Yonezawa and Junko Yamaguchi are sitting in Nobuo Akashiya's garden with plates of grilled meat and vegetables on their laps and glasses of wine by their side.

Yonezawa: I didn't know that Halloween was celebrated in England. I always thought that it was an American festival.

Yamaguchi: Actually, Halloween originated in Scotland. It's an old pagan festival similar to Japan's Obon festival. October 31st is supposed to be the day on which the veil between this world and the afterworld is the thinnest, which allows the dead to return to earth.

Yonezawa: Really? That's fascinating.

Yamaguchi: Traditionally, it was not celebrated in England, but it became popular during the 90s due to the influence of American culture arriving via the Internet and SNS sites. In fact, a few years ago, Halloween overtook Valentine's Day to become the third largest annual event after Christmas and Easter.

Yonezawa: So, you're saying that a festival that originated in the UK was ignored until it was introduced back here from America? That sounds sort of crazy.

Yamaguchi: The reason why it was not celebrated here was because it is too close to another annual event that is celebrated by nearly every household throughout the country.

Yonezawa: Another festival, you mean?

Yamaguchi: I wouldn't really call it a festival. November 5th is the anniversary of the day that a man named Guy Fawkes tried to kill the King of England by blowing up the House of Lords at the beginning of the 17th century. He failed, and this failure is still celebrated every year with bonfires and fireworks.

Yonezawa: Ah, yes. I think I've heard of that. That also explains why I've been seeing large displays of fireworks in the shops.

Yamaguchi: Yes, that's right. Guy Fawkes Night, as it is called, is still incredibly popular. So much so that the novelty of Halloween is already beginning to wear off. Fewer and fewer people bother to celebrate it now.

Junko Yamaguchi told me

場面：

> 米澤と山口順子が明石家信夫の家の庭で、膝の上に焼肉や野菜の載った皿、自分たちの横にワインの入ったグラスを置いて座っている。

ＹＮ：イギリスでもハロウィーンが祝われているとは知らなかったよ。今までずっとアメリカの祭りだと思っていた。

ＹＭ：実は、ハロウィーンはスコットランド発祥なんですよ。古くからのクリスチャンでない人々の祭りで、日本のお盆に似ています。10月31日はこの世とあの世の境界線が最も薄くなって、死者が地上に戻って来られる日とされているんです。

ＹＮ：そうなのかい？　それは興味深いね。

ＹＭ：伝統的にはイングランドでは祝われていなかったのですが、インターネットやＳＮＳサイトを通して伝わったアメリカ文化の影響で、1990年代に広まったんです。それどころか、数年前にはバレンタインデーを追い抜いてクリスマスとイースターに次ぐ3番目に大きな年中行事になりました。

ＹＮ：つまり、イギリスで生まれた祭りなのに、アメリカから逆輸入されるまでこっちでは意識されていなかったということかい？　なんだかおかしな話だね。

ＹＭ：こっちでハロウィーンが祝われていなかったのは、全国のほとんどの家庭で祝われている別の年中行事と日にちが近すぎるからでした。

ＹＮ：別の祭りということかい？

ＹＭ：祭りとは少し違う気がします。11月5日は17世紀初めにガイ・フォークスという男が貴族院を爆破してイギリス国王を殺害しようとした記念日です。フォークスの企ては失敗したので、その失敗が今でも毎年かがり火や花火で祝われているんです。

ＹＮ：ああ、そうそう。それは聞いたことがあるように思う。最近、店で花火が大きく陳列されているのを見かける理由もそれだね。

ＹＭ：ええ、そうです。その日はガイ・フォークス・ナイトと呼ばれていて、いまだに非常に人気で、ハロウィーンの目新しさがもう薄れてきてしまっているくらいですよ。今はあえてハロウィーンを祝う人がどんどん減っています。

34

KEY WORDS &
PHRASES
CD
1-08

キーワードやフレーズをチェック!

☐ hence　副 だから、そのために

He graduated from a very prestigious university; **hence** his superior attitude.
彼はとても有名な大学を卒業していて、彼の傲慢な態度はそこから来ている。

Sales increased by an enormous sixty percent this year; **hence** the big winter bonus.
今年は売上が大きく60%も伸びた。この多額の冬のボーナスはそのおかげだ。

☐ accompany *one*　〜と一緒に行く

I **accompanied her** to the airport to meet a very important client.
私は非常に重要な顧客に会うため、空港まで彼女に同行した。

He asked me to **accompany him** to the meeting to take notes.
彼は私に、メモを取るために会議に一緒に来てほしいと頼んだ。

☐ on the wane　衰えかけて

The company was stricken with a virulent form of influenza, but it's **on the wane** now.
その会社では感染力の強いタイプのインフルエンザが流行っていたが、今は収まってきている。

Land prices have been **on the wane** for years, but are recently making a comeback.
地価は何年も下がり続けていたが、最近になって回復し始めている。

☐ try to 〜　〜しようと試みる

The company **tried to** enter the nursing care business, but couldn't attract investors.
その会社は介護事業に参入しようと試みたが、投資家を引き付けることができなかった。

His problem is that he doesn't even **try to** understand the difficulties his staff face.
彼の問題は社員の苦労を理解しようともしないことだ。

buzz with activity　　活気にあふれる

The office was **buzzing with activity** when I returned from my business trip.

私が出張から帰ったとき、オフィスではみんな忙しく動き回っていた。

The hall **buzzed with activity** when the president announced the restructure.

社長が改革を宣言するとホール内は活気にあふれた。

phase out ～　　～を徐々に消滅させる

Phasing out the use of fossil fuels will help to decelerate global warming.

化石燃料の使用を徐々に減らしていくことは地球温暖化の抑制に役立つだろう。

Support for my cellphone will be **phased out**, so I need to get a new one.

私の携帯電話のサポートが段階的に廃止される予定なので、新しいものを入手しなければ。

34

マナーのヒント

　個人の家で催されるパーティーには大きく3つのタイプがあります。比較的大人数が招待されビュッフェスタイルの食事がふるまわれるホームパーティー、少人数が夕食に招待されるディナーパーティー、そしてその時々で招かれる人数が異なるバーベキューパーティーです。パーティーの形式に関わらず、客は贈り物、たいていはボトルのワインを1、2本持っていくのが一般的です。普通ホームパーティーやバーベキューパーティーの招待状にはワインや、それに加えてもしくは代わりに、ビュッフェのための食べ物を1品持ってきてほしいというリクエストがついていますが、マストではありません。食べ物について何も言われていなければ、ワインだけで十分です。ディナーパーティーに招かれた場合は、花もふさわしい贈り物になります。

DAY

35

OCTOBER 30TH (WEDNESDAY)

Work on the release of the upgrade for the Fleet Suite accounting software is heating up. The first of the advertisements were released in several newspapers and trade journals this week, and the sales department is working overtime to make sure that all existing users are aware of the new version. So far, interest has been very encouraging. I accompanied the sales manager on several courtesy calls to existing clients over the course of the past week, and next week we are planning on visiting potential new clients who have inquired about it after seeing it advertised.

I thought it might be worthwhile advertising it on TV and mentioned this to Stephen Jones, the managing director, but he explained that the people with decision-making capabilities in small- to medium-sized companies are more susceptible to Internet advertising than TV advertising. Thinking about it, I'm sure he is right. I rarely have the time for watching TV when in Tokyo, and even if I do, it is purely for recreational purposes. Never once have I decided to purchase something for the company based on a TV commercial. Internet advertisements, on the other hand, are much more likely to catch my eye when I'm browsing the web while sitting at my desk.

I received an e-mail from Nitobe (p.56) today. He sent me the **translation of his meeting** (p.60) with the president. He did a very good job, although the meeting was a little shorter than I was hoping. I realize that Mr. Tomizawa is a very busy man, but I'm sure he could have spared a few more minutes to chat with Nitobe. Oh, well, never mind. I can see from the lack of mistakes that Nitobe's English is coming along fine. In a way, I'm rather proud of him, as I am of all my protégés.

Actually, I have decided that I want him to come to London for his overseas training. It has been seven months since he started his intensive English training in the Global Logistics Department, and I want to check his progress for myself. His transcription of his chat with the president indicates that he can write English proficiently, but can he speak it? I need to check this for myself. I therefore **e-mailed the president** (p.58) to ask him to send him to London.

Yonezawa

キーワード&キーフレーズ→p.62

１０月３０日（水曜日）

　会計ソフト「フリートスイート」のアップグレードの発表に向けた作業はどんどん進んでいる。今週、広告の第１弾がいくつかの新聞や業界誌に載せられ、営業部はすべての既存顧客がこの最新版を認知していることを確実にするため時間外勤務をしている。今のところ、顧客の反応はとてもいい感じだ。先週の間、私は営業部長のいくつかの既存顧客への挨拶訪問に同行したが、来週は２人で、広告を見た後に問い合わせてきた新規の顧客候補を訪問する予定だ。

　テレビでの宣伝もやる価値があるかもしれないと思い、そのことを取締役のスティーブン・ジョーンズに話してみたのだが、中小企業で意思決定の力を持つ人間はテレビ広告よりもネット広告の影響を受けやすいと説明された。考えてみれば、彼の言う通りだろう。私は東京にいるときにテレビを見る時間なんてほとんどないし、見るとしても純粋に娯楽としてだ。テレビＣＭを見て会社のために何かの購入を決めたことは一度もない。その点、ネット広告のほうが執務中にウェブを見ているときに私の目に留まる可能性がずっと高い。

35

　今日、新渡戸からメールが届いた。彼の社長との会話の訳文を送ってきたのだ。課題の出来はとてもよかったが、会話は私が期待していたのよりも少々短かった。富沢社長が非常に忙しい人だとはわかっているが、あと数分くらい新渡戸との会話に割いてくれることもできただろうに。まあいいか、仕方ない。翻訳に間違いが見当たらないことから新渡戸の英語は順調に上達していることがわかる。彼のことは、私の他の教え子たち同様、なかなかよくやっていると思っている。

　実は、新渡戸の海外研修のときにはロンドンに来てもらおうと決めた。彼が海外事業部で英語の集中訓練を始めてからもう７か月になることだし、彼の成長を自分で確認しておきたいのだ。彼の社長との会話の書き起こしは彼が英語で堪能に書くことができると示しているが、話すほうはどうだろう。これに関しては私が自ら確かめるしかない。なので、社長に新渡戸をロンドンに送ってほしいと頼むメールを送った。

I received an e-mail from Nitobe ►

上司への報告Eメールを書いてみよう！

From: Shinnosuke Nitobe <snitobe@tomizawais.co.jp>
Sent: Wednesday, October 30, 04:13 AM
To: Mr. Yonezawa <yonezawa@tomizawauk.com>
Subject: Meeting with the president

MeetingTranscription.zip
19 KB

Dear Mr. Yonezawa,

I hope you are well. Mr. Winston mentioned that he is in constant contact
with you and said that you appeared to be enjoying your stay in London. I
hope the food agrees with you.

I was called into the president's office on October 17th with regard to
my Kaizen proposal, and he asked me to send you a translation of our
conversation. I have attached the translation here in a zip file, together with
a transcription of the meeting in Japanese.

Best regards, Nitobe

POINT

ご機嫌うかがいや気遣いの言葉、こちらの近況などを初めにさらっと入れるとよいです。

差出人: 新渡戸慎之助 <snitobe@tomizawais.co.jp>
送信: 10月30日（水曜日）午前04:13
宛先: 米澤様 <yonezawa@tomizawauk.com>
件名: 社長との打ち合わせ

 MeetingTranscription.zip
19 KB

米澤様

お元気でいらっしゃることと思います。ウィンストン先生が、米澤部長とは定期的に連絡を取っており、ロンドンでの滞在を楽しまれているようだとおっしゃっていました。食べ物もお口に合っているといいですね。

10月17日に私の改善案に関することで社長室に呼ばれ、社長との会話の翻訳をお送りするように申しつかりました。日本語での打ち合わせの書き起こしと一緒に、圧縮ファイルでその翻訳を添付いたしました。

よろしくお願いいたします。
新渡戸

クイックQ&A

Q 〉 **What has Nitobe included in the attachment?**
（新渡戸はメールに何を添付しましたか）

POINT

第1段落にあるagree with youという表現はgo to your taste「あなたの口に合う」の別の言い回しですが、以下のように食べ物とは関係ないものにも使うことができます。
・The winter agrees with me more than the summer. （夏よりも冬のほうが私の体に合っています）
・I suggest you buy a blue coat, as blue agrees with you better than any other color. （青はあなたに一番似合う色だから、青いコートを買うことを勧めます）
・The hotel we stayed in was very luxurious and it agreed with me perfectly. （私たちが泊まったホテルはとても豪華で、この上なく快適でした）

A 〉 Translation of his conversation with the president and the original Japanese transcription（彼とそれぞれの社長の翻訳文とその日本語の書き起こしです）

社長へのお願いEメールを読んでみよう!

From: O Yonezawa <yonezawa@tomizawauk.com>
Sent: Wednesday, October 30, 05:26 PM
To: Mr. H. Tomizawa <htomizawa@tomizawais.co.jp>
Subject: Shinnosuke Nitobe

Dear Mr. Tomizawa,

Thank you very much for having a word with Nitobe. He sent me the translation of your conversation today.

I now have another favor. Nitobe is scheduled for overseas training in December, and I want him to be assigned to London. I have high hopes for this young man, and I want to check out the level of progress he is making in his English studies. His writing abilities have improved greatly (as can be seen from the transcription of the conversation you had with him), but I would also like to check out his comprehension and speaking abilities. I would therefore appreciate it if you could arrange for the Personnel Department to send him to the UK.

Thanking you in advance.

Regards, O Yonezawa

POINT

頼み事をするときの表現(I have a favor、I would appreciate it if you could ～など)を身につけましょう。

差出人: 米澤 <yonezawa@tomizawauk.com>
送信: 10月30日（水曜日）午後05:26
宛先: 富沢様 <htomizawa@tomizawais.co.jp>
件名: 新渡戸慎之助

富沢様

新渡戸と話してくださり、誠にありがとうございました。新渡戸から本日、会話の翻訳を送ってもらいました。

もう1つ別のお願いがございます。新渡戸は12月に海外研修に行く予定になっているのですが、私は彼をロンドンへ来させたいと思っています。私はこの若者に大変期待しており、英語学習における彼の進展度を確認したいのです。彼のライティング能力は非常に進歩していますが（社長との会話の書き起こしからもわかるように）、彼の理解力とスピーキング力も確認したいと思っています。従いまして、もし社長から人事部のほうに彼をイギリスに派遣するようお取り計らいいただけましたらありがたく存じます。

どうぞよろしくお願いいたします。

米澤

35

クイックQ&A

Q 〉 **What favor does Yonezawa ask the president?**
（米澤は社長に何を頼んでいますか）

POINT

第2段落にあるhigh hopesはhigh expectations「高い期待」のより一般的に使われる表現で、hopeは常に複数形になります。以下はその用例です。
・I'm going fishing tomorrow, and I have high hopes for a good catch.（明日私は釣りに行くが、大漁を強く期待している）
・She has high hopes for a big return on her investment in cybercurrency.（彼女は仮想通貨への投資から大きな利益を得るという期待を膨らませている）
・The company has high hopes for increased profits this quarter.（その会社は今四半期の増益を大きく期待している）

A 〉 To send Nitobe to London（新渡戸をロンドンに来させること）

translation of his meeting ► CD 1-09

実際の会話を聞いて話してみよう!

SETTING:

Nitobe enters president Tomizawa's office and is asked to sit down. After the president's secretary has served coffee, the conversation starts.

Tomizawa: First of all, I ought to tell you that I am recording this conversation. I hope you don't mind.

Nitobe: No, of course not, sir.

Tomizawa: I have called you in here today to tell you how impressed I was with your Kaizen proposal.

Nitobe: My Kaizen proposal?

Tomizawa: Yes, your proposal. What induced you to come up with such an adventurous plan?

Nitobe: I hadn't been working in the Global Logistics Department for very long when I started it, so I didn't have the confidence to come up with anything to improve operations. Instead I decided to focus on a project that would improve things for employees. I realized that employees with young children were having daily-life problems, so I came up with the idea for a nursery. Then I realized that it needed to be financed, so I looked around for a method of doing that.

Tomizawa: Well, you did an excellent job. The company is very serious about the wellbeing of employees, and your proposal fits in very well with our internal policies. Everybody who has read it was deeply impressed.

Nitobe: Thank you very much, sir.

Tomizawa: Okay, you can return to your work now. I just wanted to let you know that we appreciate the thought that you have put into your proposal.

Nitobe: Thank you, sir.

Tomizawa: Oh, and one more thing. I'll give you the memory card containing the recording of this meeting. I want you to transcribe it, and then translate it into English. When you've done that, send it directly to Mr. Yonezawa in London.

Nitobe: Yes, sir, I understand.

translation of his meeting

場面:

> 新渡戸が富沢の社長室に入り、座るよう促される。社長の秘書がコーヒーを出した後、会話が始まる。

T：まず初めに、私はこの会話を録音していると言っておかなければならないな。構わないかい。

N：ええ、もちろんです、社長。

T：今日ここに呼んだのは、君の改善案に感心したと伝えるためだ。

N：私の改善案ですか。

T：そう、君の提案書だ。何がきっかけであんな大胆な計画を思いついたんだね。

N：改善案に取りかかったとき、海外事業部でそんなに長く働いていなかったので、業務を改善するようなものを考えつく自信はありませんでした。なので代わりに、従業員の環境を改善する企画に重点を置こうと決めました。小さな子どものいる従業員が日常生活で困っていることに気づいて、それで託児所というアイデアを思いつきました。そのあと企画に資金が必要だと気がついたので、それを調達する方法を探しました。

35

T：ふむ、君は素晴らしい仕事をしたな。うちの会社は従業員の福利にとても真剣に取り組んでいるのだが、君の案は我々の社内方針に非常によく合っている。提案書を読んだ者は皆深く感銘を受けていたよ。

N：どうもありがとうございます、社長。

T：よし、もう仕事に戻って構わないぞ。君が改善案に注いだ努力を我々は高く評価していると伝えたかっただけだからな。

N：ありがとうございます、社長。

T：ああ、それともう1つ。この会話の録音の入ったメモリーカードを渡す。会話を書き起こしてから英語に翻訳してほしいんだ。それが終わったら、完成したものをロンドンの米澤部長に直接送ってくれ。

N：はい、社長、承知しました。

キーワードやフレーズをチェック!

☐ heat up　活発になる

The labor union's dispute with management over this year's pay rise is **heating up**.

今年の給料引き上げに関する労働組合と経営側との議論はヒートアップしてきている。

Sales of air-conditioners are beginning to **heat up** now that summer is nearly here.

夏が目前に近づいている今、エアコンの売上の伸びが加速し始めている。

☐ courtesy call　表敬訪問

It is his policy to pay **courtesy calls** to his customers when he has the time.

時間があれば顧客を表敬訪問するのが彼のポリシーだ。

In my experience, most people dislike **courtesy calls** unless they are contacted in advance.

私の経験では、ほとんどの人は事前に連絡されていない場合、表敬訪問を快く思わない。

☐ worthwhile　形 価値のある

Mary is a **worthwhile** addition to the sales team.

メアリーは営業チームへの価値ある追加メンバーだ。

The president told us that it would be **worthwhile** to come up with a strategy for solving the issue.

社長は我々に、その問題の解決のための戦略を考えつくのは価値のあることだと言った。

☐ decision-making capability　意思決定能力

Individuals should not have **decision-making capabilities**. All decisions should be made by the Board of Directors.

個人が意思決定をする権限を持つべきではない。すべての決定は役員会によって下されるべきだ。

The project manager has been given **decision-making capabilities** for all required purchases.

そのプロジェクトマネージャーは必要なすべての仕入れに関する決定権を与えられている。

small- to medium-sized company 中小企業

She worked for a **small- to medium-sized company** before we headhunted her.

彼女はうちにスカウトされる前は中小規模の会社に勤めていた。

The recession is hurting **small- to medium-sized companies** more than large companies.

この不景気は大企業よりも中小企業に打撃を与えている。

come along fine 順調に進む

He had trouble familiarizing himself with the work at the beginning, but he is **coming along fine** now.

彼は初めのうちこそ仕事に慣れるのに苦労したが、今はうまくやっている。

Progress on restructuring the procurement system is **coming along fine**.

調達システムの改革の進み具合は順調だ。

35

マナーのヒント

　人差し指を使って物や人を指し示すのは日本人の多くにとって普通の習慣ですが、海外ではこのジェスチャーを攻撃的に感じる人も多いので避けたほうがよいと覚えておきましょう。代わりに、特に人を指す場合は、全部の指を伸ばした状態で手全体を使うとよいでしょう。また、「私ですか?」という問いの意味で自身を指す場合、日本ではよく自分の鼻の辺りを指さしますが、英語圏では人差し指を胸に当てるのが一般的です。

NOVEMBER 11TH (MONDAY)

I transcribed and translated the conversation I had with the president and sent it to Mr. Yonezawa in London at the end of last month. He replied with a short "thank you" message and said that I had done very well with my Kaizen proposal, but he made no mention of the transcription. I forgot to get it checked by Mr. Winston, so I hope there were not too many mistakes.

And while I am on the subject of Mr. Yonezawa, it looks as if I am going to be seeing him again sooner than I expected. Misaki and I were called into the Personnel Department (where I used to work!) today and given our **itineraries for the overseas study tours (p.66)** in December. I am being sent to **London! (p.68)** My original hope was to be sent to the New York office, but since Mr. Yonezawa is in London, I'm quite happy with the posting. Misaki will be going to the New York office, and he is over the moon.

I'm really looking forward to it. I haven't been overseas since a visit to Hawaii with some friends after we graduated from university. It will also be my first trip to Europe, a place that I have always wanted to visit. I sometimes watch the documentaries about Europe on the BS television channels, and the scenery and sense of history is very appealing. All of my travel arrangements, including visa, flights, accommodation, etc., are being arranged by Aiko Furukawa in the section I currently work in, the Customer Support Section. She has promised to treat me like a VIP, although when I asked if that meant first-class air tickets, she raised an eyebrow and laughed as if I had said something humorous. I guess that means I'll be flying in economy…

I had **lunch with a couple of our overseas workers (p.70)** today. There are about twenty foreign workers in the company, most of whom are programmers. I rarely get the chance to speak to them, but I saw an empty chair beside these two in the canteen and asked if I could join them. One of them is from the Philippines and the other is from Brazil. They were very nice and told me about their lives in Japan.

Nitobe

キーワード＆キーフレーズ→p.72

１１月１１日（月曜日）

　先月末、社長との会話を書き起こして翻訳し、それをロンドンの米澤部長に送った。部長からは短いお礼のメッセージが返ってきて、僕の改善案はとてもよくできていたと書いてあったが、書き起こしについては全く触れられていなかった。ウィンストン先生に翻訳を見直してもらうのを忘れていたから、あまりミスが多くないといいのだけど。

　で、米澤部長と言えば、僕は思っていたよりも早く部長と再会することになりそうだ。今日、岬と僕は人事部に呼ばれて（僕が以前働いていたところだ！）12月の海外研修の旅程表を受け取った。僕はロンドンに送られることになったのだ！　もともとはニューヨーク支社がいいなと思っていたのだが、米澤部長がロンドンにいるので、この割り当てに結構満足している。岬はニューヨーク支社に行くことになり、有頂天になっている。

　本当に楽しみだ。大学卒業後に1回、友達何人かとハワイに行って以来、海外には行っていないからな。それに、これは僕がずっと訪れたいと思っていたヨーロッパへの最初の旅になる。時々、テレビのBSチャンネルでヨーロッパについてのドキュメンタリーを見るけど、景色や歴史を感じる雰囲気にとても心を惹かれる。僕の旅行の準備は、ビザ、フライト、宿泊先などを含め、僕が現在働いている顧客サポート課の古川愛子さんがすべて手配してくれている。彼女が僕にVIP扱いにしてあげると請け負ったので、ファーストクラスの航空券を手配してくれるということかと聞いたら、彼女は驚いた顔をして、僕が面白いことを言ったかのように笑った。つまり、僕はエコノミークラスに乗るということだろうね…。

　今日、僕は2人の外国人社員と一緒に昼食をとった。我が社には約20人の外国人社員がいて、そのほとんどがプログラマーだ。彼らと話す機会は滅多にないが、社員食堂でこの2人の横に空いた席を見つけたので、一緒に座ってもいいかと尋ねたのだ。1人はフィリピン出身で、もう1人はブラジル出身。2人はとても感じがよくて、自分たちの日本での暮らしについて話してくれた。

　　　　　　　　　　　　　　新渡戸

海外研修の旅程表を書いてみよう!

Itineraries for the Overseas Study Tours

Name: Shinnosuke Nitobe
Department: Global Logistics Department
Section: Customer Support Section
Subject: Study Trip to London (UK)
Approved by: Yuko Haraguchi

Your flights to and from London have been confirmed as follows:

Date	Flight	Depart	Arrive	Remarks
Nov. 30	XX807	NRT 12:35	LHR 16:10	Economy
Dec. 25	XX045	LHR 19:00	NRT 15:55+1	Economy

- Flight departure/arrival at Terminal 2 Narita International Airport.
- Luggage limited to one bag/suitcase (max. 25kg) and one item of carry-on luggage.
- A Passenger Service Facility Charge (PSFC) of ¥2,090 and a Passenger Security Service Charge (PSSC) of ¥520 is to be paid at Narita Airport upon departure (not required for arrivals).
- Accommodation details to be advised.

海外研修の旅程表

名　　前：　新渡戸慎之助
所属部署：　海外事業部
所属課：　顧客サポート課
件　　名：　ロンドン（イギリス）への研修旅行
決裁者：　原口裕子

ロンドンへの往復のフライトは下記の通りです：

日にち	フライト	出発	到着	備考
11月30日	XX807	NRT 12:35	LHR 16:10	エコノミー
12月25日	XX045	LHR 19:00	NRT 15:55+1	エコノミー

- フライトの出発・到着は成田国際空港第2ターミナル。
- 手荷物は1つのバッグまたはスーツケース（最大25キロ）、機内持ち込み手荷物は1つに限る。
- 旅客サービス施設使用料（PSFC）2090円と国際線旅客保安サービス料（PSSC）520円は出発時に成田空港支払い（到着時には不要）。
- 宿泊施設の詳細は追って通知。

36

クイックQ&A

Q > **What do you think "+1" listed by the arrival time in Japan means?**
（日本への到着時間の横に書いてある「＋1」はどういう意味だと思いますか）

POINT

この旅程表にあるPSFCとPSSCという料金は日本からの国際線にのみ適用されるものですが、世界中の多くの空港が違う名称で同様にいくらかの料金を徴収しています。これらはまとめて「空港税」と呼ばれ、それにあたる料金は日本を出国する前に調べておくことを勧めます。一部の空港ではチケット代にすべての料金が含まれており、追加で空港税を取らないことも覚えておきましょう。空港税を取るのは出発便と一部の乗り継ぎ便だけです。なので、日本に帰国する際は、出発時にこれらの料金を支払うため、現地通貨で十分な金額を残しておく必要があります。

A > "+1 day," meaning that the flight leaving London on December 25 arrives in Japan on December 26 owing to the difference in the time zone（「＋1日」、つまり12月25日にロンドンを出発する便は、時差のため12月26日に日本に到着するという意味）

London ►

ロンドンの紹介文を読んでみよう!

London

London is the capital city of the United Kingdom of Great Britain and Northern Ireland. It is located on the River Thames in southeastern England, 80km upstream from its estuary on the North Sea. It was originally a Roman settlement named Londinium established in the year 47 AD. It had the largest population of any city in the world between 1831 and 1925, but has since dropped to around 25th with a population of approximately 8.8 million people. It currently covers a total area of 1,583 square kilometers.

In addition to being a global financial center and one of the world's most popular destination for international tourists, the elements that Londoners are most proud of include its diverse range of people and cultures, its World Heritage Sites, the largest concentration of higher education institutes in Europe, and its proximity to natural wildlife. London is known as one of the world's "greenest" cities, with 40 percent of the city consisting of parkland or open water. Two thousand species of flowering plants, 120 species of fish, more than 60 species of birds, and a wide range of other wildlife can be found within the city limits. This includes red foxes, hedgehogs, rabbits, squirrels, voles, hares, badgers and shrews, to say nothing of various amphibians and reptiles.

POINT

都市の由来と簡単な歴史、基本データなどを初めに説明するとよいです。

ロンドン

ロンドンはグレートブリテン及び北部アイルランド連合王国の首都です。北海の河口から上流80キロ、イングランド南東部にあるテムズ川沿いに位置しています。もともとは紀元後47年に建設されたロンディニウムというローマ人の入植地でした。1831年から1925年まで世界の都市の中で最大の人口を擁していましたが、それ以降は880万ほどの人口で約25位に順位を下げました。現在の総面積は1583平方キロメートルに及びます。

国際的な金融の中心地であることや海外の観光客にとって世界で最も人気の渡航先の1つであることに加え、ロンドン市民が最も誇らしく思っている要素は、その人種と文化の多様性、世界遺産、ヨーロッパの中でも高等教育施設が最も集中していること、そして自然の野生動物が身近であることです。ロンドンは世界で「最も環境に優しい」都市の1つとして知られており、街の40%が公園に適した地域や自然の水域から成っています。2000種の植物や120種の魚、60種以上の鳥やその他の幅広い種類の野生動物を市内で見ることができます。これには様々な両生類や爬虫類は言うまでもなく、アカギツネ、ハリネズミ、ウサギ、リス、ハタネズミ、野ウサギ、アナグマ、トガリネズミなどが含まれます。

36

クイックＱ＆Ａ

Q 〉 **How far is London located from the ocean?**
（ロンドンは海からどれくらいの距離のところにありますか）

POINT

最終文にあるto say nothing ofはin addition toのもっとドラマチックな言い方で、よく使われるフレーズです。以下のように、同じ意味を表すのに使える表現は他にもあります。
let alone:
・This includes red foxes, hedgehogs, rabbits, squirrels, voles, hares, badgers and shrews, <u>let alone</u> various amphibians and reptiles.

not to mention:
・This includes red foxes, hedgehogs, rabbits, squirrels, voles, hares, badgers and shrews, <u>not to mention</u> various amphibians and reptiles.

A 〉 Eighty kilometers from the North Sea（北海から80キロメートル）

lunch with a couple of our overseas workers ► [CD 1-11]

実際の会話を聞いて話してみよう!

SETTING:

Nitobe is looking for a seat in the staff canteen, and sees an empty position beside two overseas employees; Nicolas Regaldo and Cesar Santos.

Nitobe: Excuse me, do you mind if I join you?

Regaldo: Not at all. Please sit down.

Nitobe: I hope I'm not disturbing you. My name is Shinnosuke Nitobe. I work in the Global Logistics Department.

Regaldo: You're not disturbing us in the least. I'm Nicolas Regaldo and this is Cesar Santos. We work in the Systems Development Department.

Santos: Your English is very good. Not many people can speak English in our department. Did you study abroad?

Nitobe: No. Everybody in my department has to speak English. It's part of our job description. We receive intensive training, although some people lived overseas when they were young. How about you? Can you speak Japanese?

Santos: My Japanese is not very good yet, but Nicolas speaks it fluently.

Nitobe: Really? Where did you learn it?

Regaldo: I went to university in Japan, and my wife is Japanese. I've lived here for nearly fifteen years.

Santos: I've only been here for eighteen months. I originally came to study martial arts, but I have a background in software development, and a friend introduced me to one of the Tomizawa managers. I had an interview and was offered a job, and the company then arranged for me to receive a working visa.

Nitobe: Do you like it here?

Santos: Very much. The people are friendly, and the work is interesting.

Nitobe: How about you, Nicolas?

Regaldo: I sometimes get a little homesick for the Philippines, but I am quite happy, I suppose.

Nitobe: That's good. I'm glad to have had the chance to chat with you.

lunch with a couple of our overseas workers

場面：

> 新渡戸が社員食堂で席を探しており、2人の外国人社員、ニコラス・レガルドとセザール・サントスの横に空いている場所を見つける。

N：すみません、相席してもいいですか。

R：構いませんよ。どうぞ座ってください。

N：お邪魔じゃないといいんですけど。僕は新渡戸慎之助といいます。海外事業部で働いています。

R：全然邪魔ではありませんよ。私はニコラス・レガルドで、こちらはセザール・サントス。私たちはシステム開発部で働いています。

S：英語がとても上手ですね。僕たちの部署には英語を話せる人はあまりいないんです。海外に留学していたんですか。

N：いえ。僕の部署では全員英語を話さないといけないんです。そこでの職務の一部なので。みんな英語の集中訓練を受けるのですが、若い頃海外に住んでいた人もいます。あなたはどうですか。日本語は話せるんですか。

S：僕の日本語はまだそんなにうまくありませんが、ニコラスはペラペラですよ。

36

N：そうなんですか。どこで覚えたんです？

R：日本の大学に通っていて、妻が日本人なんです。もう15年近く日本に住んでいます。

S：僕はまだ18か月しかこちらにいません。最初は武道を学ぶために来日したのですが、ソフト開発の経験があって、友達が富沢のマネージャーの1人に僕を紹介してくれたんです。面接を受けて内定をもらったので、会社が就労ビザの手配をしてくれました。

N：ここは気に入っていますか。

S：とっても。みんな親切ですし、仕事も面白いです。

N：ニコラスさんは？

R：たまにフィリピンがちょっと恋しくなりますが、かなり楽しく過ごせていると思います。

N：それはよかったです。お2人と話す機会を持ててうれしかったです。

KEY WORDS & PHRASES

CD
1-12

キーワードやフレーズをチェック！

☐ ## make no mention of ～　　～については何も言わない

He told me to be at the station by 9 a.m., but **made no mention of** the meeting place.

彼は私に午前9時には駅に着いているようにと言ったが、待ち合わせ場所については何も言わなかった。

She invited me to the meeting, but **made no mention of** who else would be attending.

彼女は私を会議に招いたが、他に誰が出席するのかについては何も触れなかった。

☐ ## sooner than expected　　思ったよりも早く

She finished preparing for the meeting **sooner than expected**.

彼女は思ったよりも早く会議の準備を終えた。

The mid-term targets were achieved **sooner than expected**.

中期目標は予定より早く達成された。

☐ ## over the moon　　有頂天で

He was **over the moon** when told that he was being transferred to the head office.

彼は本社へ転勤になると知らされ、天にも昇る心地だった。

The president was **over the moon** when the company was showcased in a TV documentary.

社長は会社がテレビのドキュメンタリー番組で紹介されて有頂天だった。

☐ ## haven't ～ since...　　…以来～していない

Yesterday I was contacted by a client I **haven't** heard from **since** summer last year.

昨日、私は去年の夏以来音沙汰がなかった顧客から連絡を受けた。

She **hasn't** met her sales target **since** January.

彼女は1月からずっと売上目標を達成できていない。

72

☐ treat *one* like 〜　（人を）〜のように扱う

The manager is a power freak who **treats everyone** in the section **like** dirt.

その課長は課内の人みんなをゴミのように扱うパワハラ上司だ。

She was **treated like** royalty after her advertising campaign turned out to be a huge success.

彼女の広告キャンペーンが大成功を収めてから、彼女はまるで王族のような扱いを受けた。

☐ raise an eyebrow　驚く、眉をひそめる

His announcement that he was quitting the company failed to **raise an eyebrow**.

彼の会社を辞めるという宣言に周囲はあまり驚かなかった。

His consistent lack of punctuality **raised an eyebrow** in the personnel department.

彼のいつも時間を守らない態度は人事部で問題視された。

36

マナーのヒント

　他人との会話では、相手が失礼と感じるような質問はしないようにする必要があります。これには相手の年齢、結婚歴、その他すべての個人的な質問を含みます。特に、人の宗教や政治的思想は絶対に尋ねるべきではないことをしっかり覚えておきましょう。ただ、多くの場合、まずこちらから自分の個人的な情報を伝えれば、相手もそれに対して自分の情報を教えてくれます。以下はその１例です。

　　A：I'm thirty-two years old and married with two children. （私は32歳で、結婚していて2人の子どもがいるんです）

　　B：Really? I'm thirty-six, and still a bachelor. （そうなんですか。私は36歳で、まだ独身ですよ）

　相手がこのような返答をしない場合、その人は自分の個人的な情報を明かさないでおきたいということです。

37

NOVEMBER 14TH (THURSDAY)

My young protégé Shinnosuke Nitobe is due to arrive in London at the beginning of next month. The president arranged for him to be sent here as per my request. I'm sure he will learn much while he is here. I especially want to get him accustomed to the British accent. All of his learning so far has concentrated on American English, so a few weeks in a non-American culture will add another string to his bow. Not that there is much difference between the two. The widespread access to movies, TV dramas and the Internet has resulted in both countries beginning to share the same expressions and idioms, etc., so it's now almost impossible to differentiate between British English and American English. The only real difference is the accent, although that is an extremely minor difference.

Anyway, I think a first-hand experience of British culture will benefit young Nitobe. I have decided that I want him to attend one of the **motivational courses for businesspeople (p.76)** that are all the rage over here right now. The course I chose is called the Merryweather Motivational Business Course; a one-day course targeting section chiefs, supervisors and junior managers. **I visited the company earlier this week (p.80)** to make sure that it was suitable for him, and I received a very favorable impression. If all goes well, I may suggest to Kenneth Lewis that a similar course is tailor-made for all of the junior staff in Tomizawa UK. The PR manager mentioned that they are able to design courses specifically for individual companies and dispatch instructors and consultants to carry them out.

I have now been in London for four months, and I have mostly gotten used to everything about life here. There is only one thing that still confuses me, and that is the **payment of tips (p.78)**. Tips are expected when you eat in a restaurant, ride in a taxi and stay in a hotel, but I never know how much I should leave. I have questioned several British people about this, and even they admit that sometimes they don't know how much to leave. One saving grace is the fact that even if you leave a small tip, nobody complains.

Yonezawa

キーワード＆キーフレーズ→p.82

１１月１４日（木曜日）

　私の若い部下、新渡戸慎之助は来月初めにロンドンに来ることになっている。社長が私の頼み通り、彼がこちらに派遣されるように手配してくれたのだ。ここでの滞在中に新渡戸が学ぶことは多いだろう。特に私は彼にイギリスのアクセントに慣れてほしいと思っている。彼のこれまでの学習はすべてアメリカ英語を中心としてきたので、数週間アメリカ系以外の文化に触れることで能力の幅を広げられるだろう。ただ、イギリスとアメリカの英語にそんなに違いがあるわけではない。映画やテレビドラマ、インターネットの広範な普及の結果、両国は同じ表現や慣用句などを共有するようになり始め、現在ではイギリス英語とアメリカ英語はほとんど区別がつかなくなっている。唯一の明確な違いはアクセント（なまり）だが、これも極めて小さな違いだ。

　いずれにせよ、イギリス文化を直に体験することは若い新渡戸のためになるだろう。こちらで今大人気になっている経営者向けのモチベーション講座の１つに彼を出席させようと決めた。私が選んだ講座はメリーウェザー・モチベーショナル・ビジネスコースといって、課長、係長、下級管理職に向けた１日コースだ。今週初めに講座が彼に適したものかを確認するためにその会社を訪問して、かなり良い印象を受けた。順調に行ったら、富沢ＵＫの若手社員全員に向けて同じようなコースを設計してもらうことをケネス・ルイスに提案してみようかと思う。その会社の広報担当者によると、彼らは個別の企業に専用のコースをデザインして、それらを行う講師や顧問を派遣することができるという。

37

　私はロンドンに滞在してもう４か月になり、ここでの生活のあれこれにはほとんど慣れた。でもいまだに戸惑うことが１つだけあって、それがチップの払い方だ。チップはレストランで食事をしたり、タクシーに乗ったり、ホテルに泊まったりするときに払うものだが、私はいつもいくら渡すべきかわからないのだ。このことについて何人かのイギリス人に尋ねてみたが、彼らでさえいくら渡すべきなのかわからないときがあると言っていた。唯一の救いはチップが少額だったとしても誰も文句を言わないことだ。

米澤

motivational courses for businesspeople ▶

モチベーション講座のコース説明を書いてみよう!

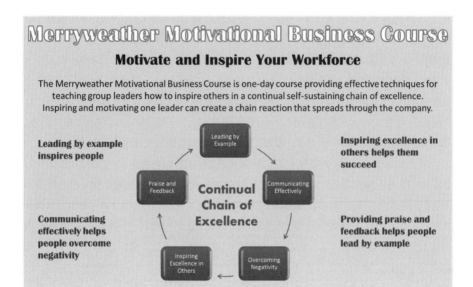

Merryweather Motivational Business Course

Motivate and Inspire Your Workforce

The Merryweather Motivational Business Course is one-day course providing effective techniques for teaching group leaders how to inspire others in a continual self-sustaining chain of excellence. Inspiring and motivating one leader can create a chain reaction that spreads through the company.

Leading by example inspires people

Communicating effectively helps people overcome negativity

Leading by Example

Praise and Feedback

Continual Chain of Excellence

Communicating Effectively

Inspiring Excellence in Others

Overcoming Negativity

Inspiring excellence in others helps them succeed

Providing praise and feedback helps people lead by example

POINT

図表など（ここでは好循環のサイクル）を効果的に用いてアピールしましょう。

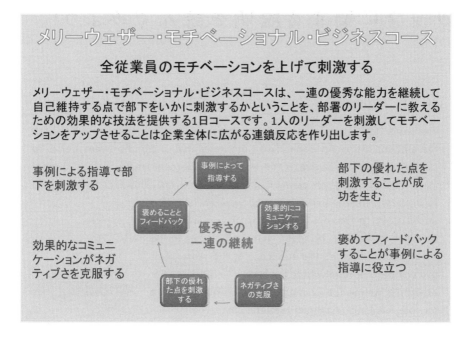

メリーウェザー・モチベーショナル・ビジネスコース

全従業員のモチベーションを上げて刺激する

メリーウェザー・モチベーショナル・ビジネスコースは、一連の優秀な能力を継続して自己維持する点で部下をいかに刺激するかということを、部署のリーダーに教えるための効果的な技法を提供する1日コースです。1人のリーダーを刺激してモチベーションをアップさせることは企業全体に広がる連鎖反応を作り出します。

事例による指導で部下を刺激する

事例によって指導する

褒めることとフィードバック

優秀さの一連の継続

効果的にコミュニケーションする

部下の優れた点を刺激することが成功を生む

効果的なコミュニケーションがネガティブさを克服する

部下の優れた点を刺激する

ネガティブさの克服

褒めてフィードバックすることが事例による指導に役立つ

37

Q 〉 **What is the suggested starting point for the above circle?**
（上記のサイクルの起点として示されているものは何ですか）

POINT

本文2行目にあるself-sustainingという形容詞は会社のパンフレットや広告で、いったん連鎖が始まれば外からの干渉がなくても自立して機能し続ける活動やサービスを表すのによく使われます。以下はその用例です。

・Our goal is to create a system of quality control that is self-sustaining. （我が社の目標は独立した品質管理システムを作ることです）

・Biodynamic farming is a self-sustaining method of raising crops. （バイオダイナミック農法は作物を育てる自律的な方法です）

・Advertising on travel blogs provides us with a self-sustaining level of growth. （旅行ブログに広告を出すことは我が社に自動的な成長レベルをもたらします）

A 〉 Leading by example（事例によって指導すること）

payment of tips ►

チップに関する説明を読んでみよう!

Tipping

The word "tip" is an acronym of the phrase "to insure perfection." Although the amount of the tip depends on the individual, a common yardstick is to pay approximately between ten and twelve percent of the cost of a meal in a restaurant, and ten percent of the fare for a taxi. However, a tip is paid as a reward for receiving good service, so it is also acceptable to leave a smaller tip if you were not satisfied. Remember, however, that the tip goes to the person who provides the service, not the restaurant, taxi company or hotel where the service is received. So, blaming a waiter, for example, for being made to wait for your meal in a restaurant is a little unfair.

In addition to restaurants and taxis, it is also customary to pay tips in hotels when a hotel worker provides an individual service for you. For example, concierges, bellboys, the people who deliver items to your room (room service, etc.), and the people who clean your room. Usually the equivalent of a few hundred yen is sufficient for this, although any loose change that is less than this is also acceptable. Tips for the people who clean your room only need to be paid once at the end of your stay, not every day. The equivalent of a few hundred yen per day is usually okay for this. This is to be left on the pillow or on the bedside cabinet on the day you check out. It is not necessary to leave tips for the people who work on the reception.

チップ

tip「チップ」という言葉はto insure perfection「完璧を保証する」というフレーズの頭文字です。チップの額は個人によりますが、一般的な基準はレストランでは食事代の10〜12%程度、タクシーでは料金の10%程度の支払いになります。しかし、チップは良いサービスを受けたことに対する報酬として支払われるので、もし満足いかなかったら少なめのチップを渡しても大丈夫です。しかし、覚えておきたいことは、チップはレストランやタクシー会社、ホテルといったサービスを受けるところではなく、サービスをしてくれる個人に支払われるということです。そのため、例えば、レストランで食事を待たされたといってウェイターを責めることは少し不公平です。

レストランやタクシーに加えて、ホテルの従業員が個人的なサービスをしてくれたとき、ホテルでチップを払うこともしきたりです。例えば、コンシェルジュ、ベルボーイ、部屋に物を持ってきてくれる人（ルームサービスなど）や部屋を掃除してくれる人です。これにはたいてい数百円程度に相当する額で十分ですが、これより少ない額の小銭でもOKです。部屋を掃除してくれる人へのチップは毎日ではなく、宿泊の最後に一度支払うだけで構いません。これには1日につき数百円程度に相当する額でたいてい大丈夫です。チェックアウトする日に枕の上かベッド脇のキャビネットの上に置いておきます。フロントで働く人にチップをあげる必要はありません。

37

クイックＱ＆Ａ

Q 〉 **When is it acceptable to leave a small tip.**
（払うチップが少額でもよいのはどんな時ですか）

POINT

2文目にあるyardstickは、参考として一般に認められている「基準」という意味で、benchmarkと同義です。以下はこの語の使用例です。
・IQ tests are used as a yardstick for measuring intelligence. （IQテストは知能を測る目安として使われています）
・An effective yardstick for gauging the health of the economy is stock prices. （経済の健全性を判断する有効な基準が株価です）
・He judged people against a yardstick of honesty and integrity. （彼は正直さと誠実さという尺度に照らして人を評価しました）

A 〉 When you are not satisfied with the service（サービスに満足していないとき）

I visited the company earlier this week ► CD 1-13

実際の会話を聞いて話してみよう！

SETTING:

Mr. Yonezawa has a meeting with Glenda Harlow, the PR manager.

Harlow: Thank you for visiting us, Mr. Yonezawa. It's a pleasure to meet you.

Yonezawa: Thank you for inviting me. I wish to enroll a young Japanese man into your one-day Motivational Business Course. English is his second language, so I wanted to check with you to make sure the course was suitable for him.

Harlow: Well, the suitability of the course will depend heavily on the level of his English proficiency. The course is carried out in English, naturally, and a relatively high level of comprehension is required.

Yonezawa: That should be no problem. The person I have in mind has good comprehension skills.

Harlow: In which case, there should be no problem. The course contains a total of four sessions, with each session lasting for one-and-a-half hours. In addition to classroom studies, the participants will be required to take an active part by engaging in debates, giving presentations, and acting out skits.

Yonezawa: And the ultimate aim of the course is?

Harlow: In a nutshell, improved communication skills. The one element common to all leaders is their ability to communicate with the people around them. The overall aim of the course is to trigger a cycle of improved communications. A leader capable of communicating well is able to overcome negativity within the workplace and inspire excellence in the staff, who will then be encouraged to follow the leader's example. In other words, a good leader inspires other people to also become good leaders, which is the start of a cycle that will benefit the company over the course of time.

Yonezawa: I see. That's very interesting. It sounds perfect for the person I have in mind. Actually, it sounds perfect for everybody else in the company.

Harlow: We are able to design programs based on your individual requirements and dispatch instructors and consultants to your premises if needed.

Yonezawa: Okay, I'll think about that. In the meantime, thank you for your help.

Harlow: It's a pleasure, Mr. Yonezawa. I'll look forward to hearing from you.

I visited the company earlier this week

場面：

> 米澤部長が広報担当者のグレンダ・ハーロウと打ち合わせをしている。

H：この度はお越しいただきありがとうございます、米澤様。お目にかかれて幸いです。

Y：お招きいただきありがとうございます。若い日本人男性をそちらの1日モチベーショナル・ビジネスコースに参加させたいのですが、英語は彼の第2言語なので、その講座が彼に適切かどうか確認するためにご相談したかったんです。

H：そうですね、コースがその人に合っているかどうかはその人の英語力に大きく左右されます。当然ながら、講座は英語で行われるので、比較的高い理解力が必要とされます。

Y：そこは心配ないでしょう。私が考えている人物には英語の理解力は十分あります。

H：それでしたら、問題ありません。この講座は全部で4つのセッションで構成されていて、1つのセッションは1時間半の長さです。参加者は教室形式の学習に加え、討論やプレゼンテーション、寸劇を行うことで積極的に参加するようになっています。

37

Y：それで、講座の最終的な目標とは？

H：一言でいうと、コミュニケーション能力の向上です。あらゆるリーダーに共通する1つの要素が周りの人間とコミュニケーションを取る能力です。このコースの全体的な目標はコミュニケーションの改善のサイクルを引き起こすことです。うまくコミュニケーションを取れるリーダーは職場のマイナスの空気を打開して社員の能力を引き出すことができ、社員はそのリーダーを見習うよう促されます。つまり、良いリーダーは他の人たちを刺激し、その人たちも良いリーダーになり、やがて会社に利益をもたらすサイクルが始まるのです。

Y：なるほど。それはとても興味深いですね。おそらく私が考えている人物にはぴったりですよ。それどころか、他の社員全員にも最適に聞こえます。

H：もし必要でしたら、お客様の個別の条件に基づいたプログラムをデザインし、そちらの会社に講師や顧問を派遣することもできますよ。

Y：ええ、それも考えておきます。とりあえず、今日はありがとうございました。

H：お役に立てて幸いです、米澤様。ご連絡をお待ちしております。

キーワードやフレーズをチェック!

☐ as per ～　　～により

The details were announced in a press release **as per** the president's request.
その詳細は社長の要望によりプレスリリースで発表された。

He set up the system **as per** the instructions, but it still failed to work properly.
彼は指示通りにそのシステムを立ち上げたが、それでもちゃんと作動しなかった。

☐ string to *one's* bow　　（有益な）手段

Learning how to use spreadsheet software added another **string to her bow**.
表計算ソフトの使い方を覚えることで彼女の能力の幅は広がった。

Expanding into the property market has added another **string to the company's bow**.
不動産市場に進出したことでその会社の選択肢は1つ増えた。

☐ differentiate between ～　　～を区別する

We are hoping that the new product will allow consumers to **differentiate between** our company and rival companies.
我々はその新製品によって、顧客が我が社をライバル社と識別できるようになることを期待している。

Smartphones are so similar nowadays that it is difficult to **differentiate between** them.
最近のスマートフォンは皆似通っているので、区別するのが難しい。

☐ first-hand experience　　直接の経験

The meeting gave him **first-hand experience** in high-level negotiations.
その会議で彼は高度な交渉の直接経験を得た。

He has **first-hand experience** in sales and is a valuable addition to the team.
彼は営業の直接的な経験があり、チームにとって有益な追加メンバーだ。

all the rage　　大流行して

Fashion styles from the past are **all the rage** recently.
最近、過去のファッションスタイルが大ブームだ。

Interactive video games in which players compete against strangers are **all the rage**.
プレーヤーが他人と戦う双方向のビデオゲームが大人気だ。

saving grace　　救われる点

The product is very expensive, and its one **saving grace** is that it is environmentally friendly.
その製品はとても高価で、唯一の利点は環境にやさしいことだ。

The new manager's only **saving grace** is that he doesn't demand overtime work.
新しい部長の唯一の取り柄は残業を要求しないところだ。

37

マナーのヒント

　会話で相手の名前を呼ぶことは話し手の信頼感を高め、聞き手を安心させることに効果がありますが、これはビジネスの場、特に初対面の人に会うときにおける一般的な戦略でもあります。以下はその例です。
　・Ah, Mr. Greenwood. How nice to meet you.（ああ、グリーンウッドさん。お会いできてうれしいです）
　・I have been looking forward to meeting you, Mr. Greenwood.（お会いできるのを楽しみにしておりました、グリーンウッドさん）
　・And so, I finally get to meet the famous Mr. Greenwood.（あなたが有名なグリーンウッドさんですね）
　ただし、相手の名前を言いすぎると若干必死な印象になるので、1つの会話中に多くても2、3回にとどめるようにしましょう。

DAY 38

NOVEMBER 17TH (SUNDAY)

It has been uncommonly warm recently, despite it being November. I stayed over at my parents' home in Yokohama on Saturday. I was hoping to see some autumn colors, but it is still too early. My father said that we'll have to wait until early December, although if we get any strong winds, the gingko trees may lose their leaves before they get the chance to turn yellow.

It was a very relaxing weekend. I went over there to borrow a suitcase and some other things for my trip to London. We went out to a local restaurant for dinner and then brought a couple of bottles of wine home with us to drink while we watched an action movie on TV (instead of *One Flew Over the Cuckoo's Nest*, which is usually the movie my father wants to watch). I really enjoyed myself. Time seems to move more slowly when I am at home.

Tomizawa won the contract for the German food company. **Mr. Ishibashi from the Sales Department e-mailed me** (p.86) to let me know.

Mr. Winston is going through another "list" period. One item of our (Misaki's and my) homework last week was to make a **list of our five favorite proverbs**, (p.88) together with their meanings. This was more difficult than I expected. I've never really thought about what proverbs I like best, so it took me ages to complete.

I went out for a drink with Kenta Uehara on Friday night. We have become quite friendly, and often have lunch together. He was headhunted into the department by Mr. Yonezawa in the same way as I was, and he also went through one year of intensive English training. When I told him that I was being sent to London for my overseas training, he surprised me by saying that he had also been sent to London for his training. So, I spent most of the evening gathering information on what I can expect next month.

His advice was very encouraging (p.90). I was a little worried over whether the local staff would welcome me. I'm sure they are fed up with taking care of trainees. But Uehara said that everybody was very friendly, so I needn't worry.

I can't wait to arrive in London now...

Nitobe

キーワード＆キーフレーズ→p.92

１１月１７日（日曜日）

　この頃は11月だというのに珍しく暖かい日が続いている。土曜日に両親のいる横浜の実家に泊まった。紅葉が見られるのを期待していたのだけれど、まだ早すぎたみたいだ。父が、紅葉には12月初めまで待たないといけないが、その間に強風があったらイチョウの葉は黄色く染まる前に落ちてしまうだろう、と言っていた。

　とてもくつろいだ週末だった。実家に行ったのは、ロンドンへの旅のためのスーツケースやその他のものを借りるためだ。僕たち家族は地元のレストランに夕食を食べに行き、それからボトルのワインを2本ほど家に持ち帰って、それを飲みながらテレビで（父がたいてい見たがる映画の『カッコーの巣の上で』ではなく）アクション映画を見た。実に楽しく過ごした。実家にいるときはいつもより時間がゆっくり流れているように感じる。

　富沢はドイツの食品会社との契約を勝ち取った。営業部の石橋さんがメールで知らせてくれた。

　ウィンストン先生はまた「リスト」期間に入っている。先週の僕たちの（岬と僕の）宿題の1つは、好きなことわざ5つをそれらの意味と一緒に書いたリストを作ることだった。これは思ったよりも難しかった。どんなことわざが一番好きかなんて今まで特に考えたことがなかったから、出来上がるまですごく時間がかかった。

　金曜日の夜、上原健太さんと飲みに行った。僕たちはかなり仲良くなっていて、よく一緒に昼食を食べる。彼は僕と同じ方法で米澤部長にうちの部署に引き抜かれて、1年間の英語の集中訓練も受けた。僕が海外研修でロンドンに送られると伝えたら、彼も研修ではロンドンに送られたのだと言うので驚いた。そこで、その夜はほとんど来月のために行き先のことを教えてもらって過ごした。

38

　彼のアドバイスはとても心強かった。地元の社員が僕を快く迎えてくれるかどうか少し心配だったからだ。彼らはきっと研修生の面倒を見るのに飽き飽きしていることだろう。でも上原さんは、みんなすごくフレンドリーだから心配ないと言ってくれた。

　今はロンドンに行くのが待ち遠しいな…。

　　　　　　　　　　　　　　　新渡戸

Mr. Ishibashi from the Sales Department e-mailed me ▶

他部署間のEメールを書いてみよう!

From: Taiki Ishibashi <tishibashi@tomizawais.co.jp>
Sent: Thursday, November 15, 10:26 AM
To: Shinnosuke Nitobe <snitobe@tomizawais.co.jp>
Subject: Rhein Gourmet Food & Confectionary

Nitobe,

Just a brief note to let you know that the concept plan and quotation for Rhein Gourmet e-commerce system have been accepted. I have contacted Ms. Ota separately to let her know.

The plan for splitting the system into two parts was also accepted, and we will begin work on the first stage, which will commence operations next April, immediately.

Thanks for all your help.

Taiki Ishibashi

POINT

実際には特に大きな役に立たなかったとしても、結語にThanks for all your help.などと述べておくと、今後何かあったときに快く手伝ってもらえることにもつながるので、good。

差出人: 石橋大樹<tishibashi@tomizawais.co.jp>
送信: 11月15日（木曜日）午前10:26
宛先: 新渡戸慎之助<snitobe@tomizawais.co.jp>
件名: ライン・グルメ食品製菓会社

新渡戸様

ライン・グルメのEコマースシステムの基本計画と見積りが承諾されましたので、取り急ぎお知らせします。太田さんにも別途ご連絡してお知らせしました。

システムを2部に分けるという計画についても認められ、まずは第1段階の作業に取りかかり、来年4月にすぐに運用が始められるようにしようと思います。

お力添えありがとうございました。

石橋大樹

クイックQ&A

Q > The scheduled cutover date for the entire system is scheduled for April next year. True or false?
（全システムの切り替え予定日は来年の4月に予定されています。正しいですか、誤りですか）

38

POINT

このメールのように、justという単語を文頭部に置くと、1つの用件を述べるだけの短いメッセージを、その簡潔さを詫びる必要もなくしっかり伝えるのに役立ちます。これはEメール、テキストメッセージ、グリーティングカードやお悔やみカードにもよく使われています。以下はその例です。

・Just a short message to say how much I enjoyed your presentation during yesterday's seminar. （昨日のセミナーでのあなたのプレゼンテーションは大変勉強になりました。取り急ぎご連絡まで）
・Just a quick "thank you" for dinner last night. （昨夜は夕食をごちそうになりまして、ありがとうございました。取り急ぎご連絡まで）
・I just wanted to let you know that I received your letter. I'll reply when I have the necessary information. （あなたの手紙を受け取りました。必要な情報がそろいましたらお返事いたしますので、取り急ぎご報告まで）

A > False（誤り）

好きなことわざリストを読んでみよう!

My Five Favorite Proverbs
—Shinnosuke Nitobe

1. The pen is mightier than the sword.

This means that convincing people by explaining your standpoint is more effective than trying to force your beliefs onto them.

2. When in Rome, do as the Romans do.

This means to act in the way that the people around you are acting. It is especially meaningful with regard to different cultures.

3. Hope for the best, but prepare for the worst.

This is an excellent proverb for business affairs, and it means that not everything may go according to plan, so preparations for failure must be made.

4. Necessity is the mother of invention.

I love this proverb. It means that when you're really in need, creative solutions will save the day.

5. Two heads are better than one.

I have discovered that this is true from personal experience. It means that two people cooperating with each other can achieve better results than a person working alone.

クイックQ&A

Q 〉 **Which proverb best explains the development of solar power and wind power as a deterrent to global warming?**
（地球温暖化の対策としての太陽光発電や風力発電の開発を最もよく表していることわざはどれですか）

僕の好きなことわざベスト5

新渡戸慎之助

1. ペンは剣よりも強し。

これは、自分の立場を説明することで人を納得させることは、自分の信念を押し付けようとするよりも効果的だという意味です。

2. 郷に入っては郷に従え。

これは、自分の周りにいる人がしているように振る舞うことを意味しています。異なる文化への配慮について特に意味のあることです。

3. 最善の状態を望み，最悪の事態に備えなさい。

これはビジネス全般にとって優れたことわざで、何事も計画通りに行くとは限らないので、失敗したときのための準備がなされていなければならないという意味です。

4. 必要は発明の母。

大好きなことわざです。本当に困った状況にあるとき、創造的な解決策が危機を救ってくれるという意味です。

5. 3人寄れば文殊の知恵。

個人的な経験からこれは本当だとわかりました。2人で互いに協力すれば1人で取り組むよりも良い結果を達成できるという意味です。(注：英語はtwo headsになっていますが、日本語訳は日本の元々のことわざを採用しました)

38

POINT

会話の中でことわざを引用するとき、聞き手が自然と理解してくれるだろうという認識に基づいて、そのことわざを丸ごとではなく最初の数語だけ言う場合がよくあります。例えば、このリストの2番目のことわざはよくWhen in Rome「郷に入っては何とやら」とだけ言われます。その他には以下のようなものがあり、カッコ内はしばしば口に出されない部分です。

- Birds of a feather (flock together). 「類は友を呼ぶ」
- A fool and his money (are soon parted). 「愚か者の金はすぐにその手を離れる」
- A problem shared (is a problem halved). 「悩みも分かち合えば半減する」
- An eye for an eye (, a tooth for a tooth). 「目には目を、歯には歯を」
- Don't bite the hand (that feeds you). 「恩を仇で返すな」
- Once bitten (twice shy). 「あつものに懲りてなますを吹く」

A〉Necessity is the mother of invention.（必要は発明の母）

89

His advice was very encouraging　►　

実際の会話を聞いて話してみよう!

SETTING:

Nitobe and Uehara are sitting in a bar after work on Friday night.

Nitobe: Did you hear about my overseas training being fixed? I'm going to London!

Uehara: You're kidding! I was sent to London for my training, too.

Nitobe: Really? That's great! You can give me some information, then!

Uehara: What do you want to know?

Nitobe: Just general stuff, I guess. What the people are like, what the food is like, what the accommodation is like. You know, that sort of thing.

Uehara: Okay, well, the people are fine. Very friendly, in fact. The food was okay, although the fast food isn't very good. The accommodation was okay, too. I stayed in a small private hotel and had my own room. It was small, but it had a television, a refrigerator and Internet access, so I had nothing to complain about. The owner also served me breakfast every morning.

Nitobe: Don't the people in the office get fed up with trainees?

Uehara: What do you mean?

Nitobe: I'm a little worried as to whether they'll welcome me. I'm sure they get many trainees, which must distract them from their work. I don't want to arrive to hear everyone saying, "Oh, no! Not another one!"

Uehara: Ha, ha, ha… You're being paranoid. They'll treat you like royalty. I made many friends during my visit. They took me out to lunch in the local pub, took me drinking at night, invited me to their homes. They are extremely friendly! You worry too much. Relax! Just enjoy yourself.

Nitobe: Really? That sounds encouraging. What about the British accent? Is it difficult to understand?

Uehara: At first, but you'll soon get used to it. Somebody once told me that the difference between British English and American English is similar to the difference between Kanto Japanese and Kansai Japanese. You just have to get used to it. It doesn't take long.

Nitobe: Thanks for the information. You've set my mind at rest.

His advice was very encouraging

場面：

新渡戸と上原が金曜日の夜、仕事の後に居酒屋で座っている。

N：僕の海外研修の予定が決まったことは聞きましたか。ロンドンに行くことになったんです！

U：嘘だろ！ 僕も研修でロンドンに送られたんだ。

N：本当ですか。よかった！ じゃあ、向こうについて教えてもらえますね！

U：何が知りたいんだい？

N：ただ一般的なことです。向こうの人のこととか、食べ物のこととか、宿泊施設のこととか。ほら、そんな感じのことです。

U：なるほど、そうだね、向こうの社員は感じがいいよ。むしろとてもフレンドリーだ。食べ物も普通においしかったけど、ファストフードはいまいちだね。宿泊施設もいい感じだった。僕は小さいプライベートホテルに泊まって、個室をもらったよ。部屋は小さかったけど、テレビと冷蔵庫、インターネット接続が付いていたし、何の不満もなかったな。あと、毎朝オーナーが朝食を出してくれた。

N：支社の人たちは研修生にうんざりしないんですか。

U：どういう意味だい？

N：僕を快く迎えてくれるかどうか少し心配なんです。向こうには研修生がたくさん来るでしょうし、そうすると仕事の邪魔になると思うんです。向こうに行ってみんなに「おいおい！ また研修生かよ！」とか言われたくないですし。

U：ははは…それは考えすぎだよ。みんな至れり尽くせりにしてくれるさ。僕は滞在中にたくさん友達ができたよ。みんな地元のパブにランチに連れて行ってくれたり、夜は一緒に飲みに行ったり、家にも招待してくれたりして、すごくフレンドリーなんだ！ 君は心配性だよ。リラックスして！ ただ楽しんで来ればいいさ。

N：そうなんですか。それを聞いて心強いです。イギリスのアクセントはどうなんですか。理解しづらいのでしょうか。

U：最初のうちはね、でもすぐに慣れるさ。誰かに聞いたことがあるんだけど、イギリス英語とアメリカ英語の違いは関東弁と関西弁の違いに似ているって。慣れればいいだけだ。長くはかからないよ。

N：情報をありがとうございます。おかげで安心できました。

38

KEY WORDS & PHRASES

CD
1-16

キーワードやフレーズをチェック!

☐ **despite it 〜**　　〜にかかわらず

Beer sales are up, **despite it** being a cool summer.
冷夏をよそに、ビールの売上は伸びている。

The product failed to sell, **despite it** being discounted.
割引されたにもかかわらず、その製品は売れなかった。

☐ **stay over**　　宿泊する

Our flight was cancelled so we had to **stay over** in Seattle.
私たちのフライトがキャンセルになったので、シアトルに泊まらなければならなかった。

I will be **staying over** in Melbourne for one night to see a client during my trip to Australia.
私はオーストラリアへの出張中、顧客と会うためにメルボルンで1泊するつもりだ。

☐ **hope to 〜**　　〜したいと思う

We **hope to** expand sales by establishing a long-term vision.
我々は長期的なビジョンを確立することによる売上の拡大を望んでいる。

He **hoped to** motivate the workers with his speech, but it didn't work out.
彼は自分のスピーチが社員の意欲を高めることを期待したが、そうはならなかった。

☐ **go through**　　（苦労などを）経験する、経る

She **went through** hell trying to persuade her boss to stop harassing her.
彼女は上司を説得して嫌がらせをやめさせようと大変な苦労をした。

The company is **going through** a period of sluggish growth.
その会社は低成長の時期に入っている。

☐ gather information　情報を集める

She spent the morning **gathering information** on the revisions to the law.

彼女はその法改正に関する情報収集に午前中を費やした。

The first step to expanding overseas is to **gather information** on the local markets.

海外進出のための最初の一歩は進出先の市場に関する情報を集めることだ。

☐ fed up with ～　～に飽き飽きして、うんざりして

He has a short temper, and gets **fed up with** people asking the same questions.

彼は気が短く、同じ質問を繰り返す人にはイライラする。

Consumers appear to be **fed up with** high smartphone communication rates.

消費者はスマートフォンの通信料の高さにうんざりしているようだ。

マナーのヒント

　相手のアクセント（なまり）が理解しづらいときは、聞き取るのに苦労していると丁寧に伝えましょう。とがめているように聞こえるI can't understand your strange accent.（あなたのアクセントが理解できません）やI don't understand what you are saying.（あなたの話していることがわかりません）のような言い方はせず、自分の力不足という言い回しをします。以下はその例です。

- ・I'm sorry, but I'm afraid I am not yet used to your accent.（すみませんが、まだあなたのアクセントに慣れていないようなんです）
- ・Would you mind speaking a little slower until I get accustomed to your accent?（私があなたのアクセントに慣れるまでもう少しゆっくり話していただけませんか）
- ・I studied American English, so I'm not yet used to your accent. Would you mind speaking a little slower?（私が学んだのはアメリカ英語なので、まだあなたのアクセントに慣れていません。もう少しゆっくり話していただけますか）

38

39

NOVEMBER 27TH (WEDNESDAY)

The past two weeks have been a hectic rush to launch the upgrade to the **Fleet Suite software package (p.96)**. The Sales Department and Advertising Department have been frantically contacting existing users and potential users with their sales pitches, and as many people as can be spared from the other departments have been press-ganged into preparing press packages and filling envelopes with promotional sheets for sending out as direct mail.

Fleet Suite is an extremely important product for Tomizaka UK, and alone it generates more than sixty percent of the company's annual revenue. Everybody in the company is fully aware of this, and they all pull together to make sure that nothing goes wrong. It is this sense of comradery that I find most endearing about the London office. The total number of employees is still small enough to ensure that everybody feels as if they are part of one big family. This is lost as a company grows larger, which is sad. I try to maintain this sense of comradery within my department in Tokyo, and from what I can see, I think I have been successful.

But finally, Fleet Suite has been successfully launched, and interest among users appears to be favorable. The **press release was sent out on Monday (p.98)**, and we held a reception in a classy hotel in the evening to celebrate the launch. The reception was attended by nearly sixty people in total, including some of our major customers and suppliers, representatives from the local Chamber of Commerce and Industry, a few guests from the Japanese Embassy, and several editors and reporters from various trade magazines. I got into **a conversation with the chief editor (p.100)** of a trade magazine known as *IT Personified*. Apparently, he is an old friend of Kenneth Lewis, and regularly runs articles on Tomizawa. He asked me if I would submit to an interview, and I agreed. He promised to send a reporter round to the office next week.

Shinnosuke Nitobe arrives in London for his overseas training on Sunday. I have asked Takeo Miyazaki, one of our Japanese managers, to pick him up at the airport. I'm looking forward to getting first-hand information from the Tokyo office.

Yonezawa

1 1 月 2 7 日（水曜日）

　この2週間は「フリートスイート」ソフトのアップグレードの発売に向けててんてこ舞いだった。営業部と宣伝部はせっせと既存ユーザーや見込顧客に連絡を取って売り込みをしていたし、他の部署からも割くことのできる人員は皆、宣伝用資料の準備やダイレクトメールとして送るチラシを封筒に入れる作業に駆り出されていた。

　フリートスイートは富沢UKにとって非常に重要な製品で、それのみでこの会社の歳入の60％以上を生み出している。社内の誰もがこのことを十分心得ていて、すべて滞りなく進むように協力している。私がロンドン支社で最も大切に思っているのがこの仲間意識だ。ここの全社員の数はまだ、皆が1つの大きな家族の一員だと感じることができるくらいに小さい。残念なことに、これは会社が大きくなるにつれて失われてしまうものだ。私は東京本社の部署内でこの仲間意識を維持しようと努めており、私が見る限り、それはうまくいっているようだ。

　何はともあれ、いよいよフリートスイートは首尾よく発売され、ユーザーの反応もいい感じだ。月曜日にプレスリリースが発行され、その夜は一流のホテルで発売を記念するパーティーを開いた。パーティーには主要な顧客や供給業者、地元の商工会議所からの代表者、日本国大使館からの招待客数名、様々な業界誌の編集者や記者を含めて、合計60人ほどが出席した。そこで『ITパーソニファイド』という業界誌の編集長と会話をした。どうやら、彼はケネス・ルイスの昔からの友人で、富沢に関する記事をよく載せるらしい。彼に取材を受けてくれないかと聞かれたので、承諾した。彼は来週、記者をオフィスに向かわせると約束した。

39

　日曜日に新渡戸慎之助が海外研修のためにロンドンに着くので、こちらの日本人の管理職の1人の宮崎武雄に、空港まで彼を迎えに行ってくれるよう頼んだ。東京本社の生の情報を聞くのが楽しみだ。

Fleet Suite software package ►

ソフトウェアパッケージの宣伝文を書いてみよう!

Tomizawa Integrated Solutions

Fleet Suite Ver.8 Accounting Software

Used by 350,000 small-to-medium businesses throughout the UK!

Online accounting software covering all accounting requirements, including invoicing, expense management, payroll, VAT and tax-return filing.

- Manages cashflow, income, expenditures and payments
- Manages accounts receivable and accounts payable
- Manages VAT and submits online returns
- Manages standing orders and direct debits

Supports Foreign Currencies!

POINT

　一番の人目を引くキャッチコピーを上段に大きく入れ、次に具体的な内容の紹介→詳細情報という流れにすると効果的。キャッチコピーは「文」にはせずに、過去分詞などを冒頭に用いた「句」にして、簡潔にしましょう。

富沢インテグレーテッド・ソリューションズ

フリートスイート Ver.8 会計ソフト

イギリス全国の中小企業35万社で利用！

請求書、経費管理、給与、VAT（付加価値税）、確定申告などすべての会計要件をカバーするオンライン会計ソフトです。

- キャッシュフロー、所得、経費、支払いの管理
- 売掛金と買掛金の管理
- VAT（付加価値税）の管理とオンライン申告の提出
- 自動振替の依頼と口座引き落としの管理

外国通貨にも対応！

クイックQ＆A

Q "Tax-return filing" means the "submission of tax papers." True or false?

（tax-return filingは「確定申告書の提出」という意味です。正しいですか、誤りですか）

39

POINT

VATはvalue-added tax「付加価値税」の略で、日本の消費者が払う「消費税」と同等のものです。消費者が物を買うときに付加される税を支払う制度は世界の多くの国にありますが、それぞれ違う名称で呼ばれています。最も一般的な名称はvalue-added tax／VAT「付加価値税」、consumption tax「消費税」、goods and services tax／GST「商品サービス税」の3つです。多くの場合、この税金は購入された商品が在外者によって国外に持ち出されるときは返金可能なので、返金を希望するなら事前に訪れる国の制度を個別に確認しましょう。

A　True（正しい）

プレスリリース文を読んでみよう!

Tomizawa IS (UK), PLC.

Press Release
(For Immediate Release)

Re: Tomizawa Fleet Suite Ver.8 Accounting Software Released

On November 25th, Tomizawa IS (UK), PLC (president: Kenneth Lewis, acting president: Osamu Yonezawa) released the latest edition of its popular Fleet Suite accounting software targeting small- to medium-sized business concerns.

Fleet Suite was first released onto the market in 1990, and has remained popular ever since. It is currently used by approximately 350,000 firms throughout the UK. Version 8 represents the eighth upgrade. In addition to all conventional functions, the upgrade also includes instant graph display, bill tracking, automatic payment reminder issuance and many other new functions.

Inquiries: Peter Drew, Advertising Department
Contact Peter for a full press package and all other inquiries.

Osamu Yonezawa (Acting President)
November 25th

富沢IS(イギリス)株式会社

プレスリリース
(即日発表用)

Re: 富沢フリートスイートVer.8会計ソフトのリリース

11月25日、富沢IS(イギリス)株式会社(代表取締役社長：ケネス・ルイス、代表取締役社長代理：米澤修)は、中小企業を対象とした人気商品「フリートスイート」会計ソフトの最新版をリリースしました。

フリートスイートは1990年に初めて市場に投入され、以来人気を博してきています。現在イギリス全国でおよそ35万社の企業にご利用いただいております。バージョン8はその8回目のアップグレードになります。従来のすべての機能に加え、簡易グラフ表示、請求書の追跡、自動支払い通知の発行、その他多くの新しい機能が搭載されています。

お問い合わせ先: ピーター・ドリュー(宣伝部)
完全な広報資料とその他のご質問はピーターにご連絡ください。

米澤修(代表取締役社長代理)
11月25日

クイックQ&A

Q In whose name was the press release issued? : Kenneth Lewis / Osamu Yonezawa / Peter Drew
(このプレスリリースは誰の名前で発行されましたか。ケネス・ルイス、米澤修、ピーター・ドリューの中から選んでください)

39

POINT

第1段落にあるactingという形容詞は役職の前に付けられると「代理」という意味になり、ここでは現在は休職していて将来復帰する予定である実際の支社長の職務を一時的に引き受けている人物を指します。しばしば誤ってactingと同じように使われる語にinterimがありますが(例:interim president)、実際には、interimは役職の前に付けられているとき、前任の人物はもう会社を辞めていて、将来は別の人がその立場を引き継ぐ予定だという意味になります。つまり、interim presidentとは、新しい支社長が任命されるまでの間、すでに会社を去った支社長の職務を一時的に引き受けている人物のことです。actingもinterimもacting/interim manager、acting/interim directorなどのように、どんな役職の前にでも置くことができます。

A Osamu Yonezawa(米澤修)

99

a conversation with the chief editor ►

実際の会話を聞いて話してみよう!

SETTING:

> The chief editor of the *IT Personified* trade magazine, Gregory Fisher, approaches Yonezawa at the Fleet Suite launch reception.

Fisher: Mr. Yonezawa? My name is Gregory Fisher. I'm the chief editor of *IT Personified*. I have been looking forward to meeting you. I have known Kenneth Lewis for many years, and he told me that you would be taking over while he underwent treatment.

Yonezawa: Ah, yes, Mr. Fisher. Stephen Jones told me to look out for you. It is a pleasure to meet you. Can I get you a drink?

Fisher: No, I'm fine, thank you. I'm not much of a drinker. Congratulations on the launch of the new version of Fleet Suite, by the way.

Yonezawa: Thank you very much.

Fisher: So, tell me, how are you getting on in London? It must be a very different environment to the one you are used to.

Yonezawa: I'm getting along very well, thank you. The environment is not as different as you would imagine. Corporate life is very much the same no matter what nation you are in. The only real difference I have noticed so far is that London seems to have fewer sunny days than Tokyo.

Fisher: Oh, isn't that the truth! London probably has fewer sunny days than every city in the world. That's part of its charm.

Yonezawa: Ha, ha. Yes, you're right, of course. I must admit, I find the city very charming.

Fisher: May I ask you a favor, Mr. Yonezawa?

Yonezawa: Yes, of course. Fire away.

Fisher: Would you mind if I sent one of our reporters to your office next week for an interview? We're running a story about the release of Fleet Suite in next week's edition, but I'd like to follow that up with a story about the relationship between the Tokyo company and London branch. Would that be possible?

Yonezawa: Yes, of course. I'd be delighted. Shall we say Wednesday next week at 2 p.m.?

Fisher: That's perfect! Thank you very much.

a conversation with the chief editor

場面：

> 業界誌『ITパーソニファイド』の編集長グレゴリー・フィッシャーが、フリートスイートの発表記念パーティーで米澤に話しかける。

F： 米澤支社長代理ですよね。私は『ITパーソニファイド』の編集長のグレゴリー・フィッシャーと申します。お目にかかれるのを楽しみにしておりました。実はケネス・ルイス氏とは何年も前から知り合いでして、彼が治療を受けている間あなたが職務を引き継ぐと聞かされています。

Y： ああ、はい、フィッシャー編集長ですね。スティーブン・ジョーンズにあなたを探すように言われていたんですよ。お会いできてうれしいです。何か飲みますか。

F： いえ、お気持ちだけいただきます。お酒はあまり飲めないんです。遅くなりましたが、フリートスイートの最新版の発表おめでとうございます。

Y： どうもありがとうございます。

F： それで、ロンドンでの暮らしはいかがですか。あなたの慣れ親しんだ環境とはずいぶん違うでしょう。

Y： とてもうまくいっていますよ、お気遣いありがとうございます。環境は想像するほど違いませんよ。国によらず、会社生活はどこでもほとんど変わりませんね。今までで唯一気づいた大きな違いといえば、ロンドンは東京より晴れの日が少ないということでしょうか。

F： ああ、確かに！ ロンドンはおそらく世界のどの都市よりも晴れの日が少ないでしょうね。そこもまた魅力の1つなんですけどね。

Y： はは。ええ、本当にそうですね。実は私もこの町がとても気に入っているんですよ。

F： 米澤支社長代理、1つお願いしてもよろしいでしょうか。

Y： はい、もちろんです。ご遠慮なくどうぞ。

F： 来週、インタビューのためにそちらのオフィスに弊社の記者を1人行かせてもよろしいでしょうか。来週の号でフリートスイートの発表に関する記事を掲載するのですが、それに加えて東京本社とロンドン支社との関係についての記事を載せたいんです。よろしいでしょうか。

Y： ええ、もちろんです。喜んで。来週の水曜日の午後2時でどうですか。

F： いいですね！ どうもありがとうございます。

39

キーワードやフレーズをチェック！

☐ **hectic rush**　大忙し、てんてこ舞い

Making sure our booth was ready for the trade fair was a **hectic rush**.
見本市のために私たちのブースの準備を整えるのにてんてこ舞いした。

With the staff shortage, this summer is sure to be a **hectic rush**.
人員不足のため、今年の夏は大忙しになること間違いなしだ。

☐ **frantically**　副 必死に

The last time I saw him, he was **frantically** trying to meet this month's sales target.
彼を最後に見たとき、彼は今月の売上目標を達成しようと必死だった。

The company is **frantically** recruiting factory workers to meet demand.
その会社は需要を満たすため、熱心に工場労働者を募集している。

☐ **press-gang**　他 ～を駆り出す

The entire section has been **press-ganged** into working on Saturday this week.
今週は課内全員が強制的に土曜日に働かされた。

I was **press-ganged** into organizing the company's annual trip to a hot spring.
私は毎年恒例の温泉への社員旅行の企画に駆り出された。

☐ **pull together**　協力する

The entire department has vowed to **pull together** to increase sales.
部署内全員が売上を上げるため協力することを決意した。

Everybody in the company **pulls together** when needed.
必要なときは社員全員が協力する。

be attended by ～ 　～が出席する

The General Meeting **was attended by** more than one hundred stakeholders.

株主総会には100人以上の株主が出席した。

We are hoping that the press conference will **be attended by** as many media representatives as possible.

我々は、この記者会見にできるだけ多くのマスコミ関係者が出席してくれることを期待している。

known as ～ 　～として知られる

The company is **known as** a leader in its field.

その会社はその分野でのリーダーとして知られている。

The new CEO is **known** in the industry **as** the "innovator."

新しいCEOはこの業界では「革新者」として知られている。

マナーのヒント

　手紙やEメールの冒頭に書く敬辞（頭語）は、以下のように、相手に関して持っている情報によって変わります。

・受取人の名前がわかっている場合：

Dear Mr. Greenwood, 　または　Dear Ms. Greenwood,

このようなとき、肩書は決して使われないので注意してください。つまり、グリーンウッド氏が社長であっても、President Greenwoodと書く必要はありません。Mr. Greenwoodだけで十分です。また、女性には、その人が結婚しておりMrs.と呼ばれるほうを好むとわかっているとき以外、Mrs.ではなくMs.を使うことをお勧めします（もちろん未婚女性にもMs.が使われます）。

・特定の人物（社長、営業部長など）宛てだが、その人の名前がわからない場合：

Dear Sir,（相手が男性だとわかっている場合）

Dear Madam,（相手が女性だとわかっている場合）

Dear Sir/Madam,（相手の性別がわからない場合）

・特定の人物宛てではない場合：

To whom it may concern,

39

DAY

NOVEMBER 29TH (FRIDAY)

I received the **itinerary for my trip (p.106)** to London earlier this week, together with **details of the guesthouse (p.108)** I will be staying at. I have to be at the airport tomorrow morning by 9:30 to catch my flight. The flight doesn't leave until 12:35, but I have to check in three hours early. I'm really looking forward to it, although I have a few butterflies in my stomach. Mr. Miyazaki, one of the Japanese managers in the London office, will be picking me up at the airport and taking me to my guesthouse, which is a big relief. I was a bit worried about being able to find it in an unfamiliar city while carrying heavy luggage.

The guesthouse seems quite nice. My room has Wi-Fi and a television, and a buffet breakfast is available every morning. It is located in a district called Finchley in northwest London, and apparently it is quite convenient for traveling into central London. It seems strange to think that this time tomorrow night I will actually be sleeping in that room.

Misaki is also looking forward to his visit to New York. He leaves from Narita an hour or so after me. I guess he will also be checking in three hours early, so maybe we can meet up in the terminal and have a coffee together. I should have suggested that when we were at work. I'll text him later and see if he is also leaving from Terminal 2. We had our final English lesson for the year with Mr. Winston this afternoon. Our next lesson isn't until next year. **He took us out to a coffee shop (p.110)** near the station and wished us good luck on our trips.

I also went out for a farewell drink with some of the people in the department last night. Kenta Uehara was there, and so was Aya Shibata! We have remained friendly since our split-up, and we still get on really well. Actually, I'm still very fond of her. We sat next to each other for most of the night, and I really enjoyed chatting to her. She is smart and has a great sense of humor. I wonder if I still have a chance...

Nitobe

１１月２９日（金曜日）

　今週初めに、ロンドンへの旅の旅程表と、僕が泊まる予定のゲストハウスの詳細情報をもらった。僕が乗る便に間に合うためには、明日の朝9時30分までに空港に着いていなければならない。飛行機は12時35分発だが、3時間前に搭乗手続きをしなければいけないのだ。とても楽しみだけど、ちょっと緊張でそわそわもしている。ロンドン支社の日本人の管理職の1人の宮崎さんが僕を空港で出迎えてゲストハウスまで連れて行ってくれることになっているので、それにはすごくホッとしている。重い手荷物を運びながら見知らぬ街でそこを見つけられるかどうか少し心配だったのだ。

　ゲストハウスはかなり良いところのようだ。部屋にはWi‐Fiとテレビが付いているし、毎朝ビュッフェ形式の朝食が食べられる。ロンドン北西部のフィンチリーという地区に位置していて、ロンドン中心部までの移動にとても便利らしい。明日の夜のこの時間には本当にその部屋で寝ているんだと思うと不思議な感じだ。

　岬もニューヨークへ行くのを楽しみにしている。彼は成田空港から僕の1時間くらい後に出発する。たぶん彼もその3時間前に搭乗手続きをするだろうから、ターミナルで会って一緒にコーヒーを飲んだりできるかもしれない。仕事中にそう提案すればよかったな。後で携帯のメールで岬も第2ターミナルから出発するのかどうか聞いてみよう。今日の午後、僕たちはウィンストン先生に今年最後の英語の授業を受けた。次の授業は来年からになる。ウィンストン先生は僕たちを駅の近くのコーヒーショップに連れて行って、僕たちの旅がうまくいくことを願うと言ってくれた。

　昨夜は部署の社員何人かと壮行会として飲みに行った。上原健太さんも参加したし、柴田彩さんもいた！　僕たちは別れた後も仲が良く、今でもとても馬が合う。むしろいまだに彼女には好感を持っている。その夜はほとんど隣同士に座っていたし、彼女としゃべるのは本当に楽しかった。彼女は聡明で、素晴らしいユーモアのセンスの持ち主だ。まだ僕にチャンスはあるだろうか…。

40

新渡戸

itinerary for my trip　►

海外研修の旅程表を書いてみよう！

Itinerary for the Overseas Training

Name: Shinnosuke Nitobe
Department: Global Logistics Department
Section: Customer Support Section
Subject: Study Trip to London (UK)
Approved by: Yuko Haraguchi

The itinerary for your study trip to London is as follows:

Date	Flights	Details
Nov. 30	Leave Narita Airport aboard flight XX807 at 12:35	Terminal 2. Check in by 09:30.
	Arrive London Heathrow Airport at 16:10	London manager Miyazaki will meet you upon arrival and take you to the High Grove Guesthouse, Finchley.
		Accommodation: High Grove Guesthouse
	November 31st 〜 December 25nd Free itinerary Accommodation: High Grove Guesthouse	
Dec. 25	Leave London Heathrow Airport aboard flight XX045 at 19:00	Take taxi to London Heathrow Airport. Terminal 3, Zone D. Check in by 16:00.
Dec. 26	Arrive Narita Airport at 15:55	Free upon arrival.

Bon voyage...

◼ クイックQ&A

Q〉**What mode of transport will Nitobe use to go to the airport upon departure?**
（新渡戸が帰国の際、空港へ行くのに使う交通手段は何ですか）

海外研修旅程表

名前：　　　新渡戸慎之助
所属部署：海外事業部
所属課：　顧客サポート課
件名：　　ロンドン（イギリス）研修旅行
決裁者：　原口裕子

ロンドンへの研修旅程は以下の通り：

日付	搭乗便	詳細
11月30日	12時35分 成田空港発。XX807便	第2ターミナル。9時30分までに搭乗手続き。
	16時10分 ロンドン・ヒースロー空港着	ロンドンの宮崎部長が到着時に出迎え、フィンチリーのハイ・グローブ・ゲストハウスへ同行。 宿泊先：ハイ・グローブ・ゲストハウス
	11月31日～12月25日 自由行動 宿泊先：ハイ・グローブ・ゲストハウス	
12月25日	19時 ロンドン・ヒースロー空港発。 XX045便	タクシーでロンドン・ヒースロー空港へ。 第3ターミナル、Dゾーン。 16時までに搭乗手続き。
12月26日	15時55分　成田空港着	到着後自由。

良い旅を…

40

---

details of the guesthouse ►
ゲストハウスの詳細を読んでみよう!

High Grove Guesthouse
16 Clifton Avenue, Finchley, N3
Tel: 020-3111-3111

Family-run Bed & Breakfast

Five spacious guestrooms in a large Victorian redbrick house. The High Grove Guesthouse has been family-run since its establishment in 1953. It is conveniently located for shopping, recreation and entertainment, and it is just ten-minutes' walk to Finchley Central tube station, from which it is a 25-minute journey into central London on the Northern Line. All rooms have high-speed Internet connections (Wi-Fi). Suitable for single-night stays and long-term stays. Breakfast included in the rate.

Accommodation: £65.00 per room per night for short-term stays
(1 week or less)
£50.00 per room per night for long-term stays

* High-speed Wi-Fi   * Buffet breakfast (07:00 to 09:00)
* All rooms with double bed   * Shared bathroom
* Television in all rooms
The High Grove Guesthouse is a no-smoking facility!

ハイ・グローブ・ゲストハウス

N3 フィンチリー 16クリフトンアベニュー
電話：020-3111-3111

家族経営のベッド＆ブレークファスト

大きなビクトリア朝風の赤レンガの家に、広々としたゲストルームが5部屋あります。ハイ・グローブ・ゲストハウスは1953年に建てられて以来、家族経営されています。買い物やレクリエーション、エンターテインメントに便利なロケーションで、ノーザン線でロンドン中心部まで25分のフィンチリー・セントラル地下鉄駅へはわずか徒歩10分です。す全室に高速インターネット接続（Wi-Fi）があります。1泊にも長期滞在にも最適です。料金には朝食が含まれています。

宿泊料： 65ポンド／短期滞在（1週間以下）1泊1部屋
　　　　 50ポンド／長期滞在1泊1部屋

    *高速Wi-Fi　　　　　　*朝食バイキング(7:00 ～ 9:00)
    *全室ダブルベッド付き　*バスルーム共用
    *全室テレビ付き
    ハイ・グローブ・ゲストハウスは全室禁煙です！

クイックQ＆A

Q In how many of the guesthouse rooms is smoking permitted?
（このゲストハウスに喫煙が許されている部屋はいくつありますか）

40

POINT

英語は時々紛らわしいことがあり、例えば、本文3行目にあるrecreationとentertainmentという名詞は微妙に違う意味を持ちます。recreationは体を使う参加型のアクティビティ（ゴルフ、ハイキング、水泳など）ですが、entertainmentは体を動かさず目や耳で楽しむ知覚的なアクティビティ（映画・音楽鑑賞など）です。しかし、これらの語は両方とも形容詞（recreationalとentertaining）になると同じ意味を持ち、参加型のアクティビティと知覚的なアクティビティのどちらを表すのにも使えます。以下はその例です。
・I like to watch TV dramas for recreational purposes. （私は娯楽としてテレビドラマを見るのが好きです）
・I had a very entertaining game of tennis on Saturday. （私は土曜日にとても楽しいテニスの試合をしました）

A None（なし）

He took us out to a coffee shop ► CD 1-19

実際の会話を聞いて話してみよう!

SETTING:

Mr. Winston, Nitobe and Misaki order coffees from the self-service counter and find a table to sit at.

Winston: Have you finished packing yet?

Nitobe: Nearly. I've just got a few more things to add, and I'll be ready.

Misaki: Lucky you! I haven't even started yet!

Winston: You'd better hurry up. And don't forget to pack warm clothes. New York is very cold at this time of the year.

Nitobe: Have you ever been to London, Mr. Winston?

Winston: No, unfortunately not. I have never visited any country in Europe. I have always wanted to go, though. European history is fascinating.

Misaki: My father was stationed in Rome a few years ago. He became very interested in European history after that. He said that living in Rome was like living in a museum.

Winston: Your father gets around, doesn't he? Didn't you live in Australia when you were young?

Misaki: New Zealand, actually. My father is a civil engineer. He gets transferred abroad on big projects quite often.

Winston: Well, now it's your turn to be transferred abroad. Are you looking forward to it?

Misaki: Yes, very much. I've always loved American culture, and I'm really looking forward to experiencing it first-hand.

Winston: What about you, Shinnosuke? Happy to be sent to England?

Nitobe: Oh, yes. I can't wait! I just hope that I am able to keep up with the work. I have no idea what sort of job I will be assigned, so I'm a little nervous.

Winston: Don't worry. I'm sure they won't give you anything too difficult to do. Anyway, I wish you both good luck and I'll see you again at the beginning of next year. Enjoy your trips!

He took us out to a coffee shop

場面:

> ウィンストン先生、新渡戸、岬がセルフサービスのカウンターでコーヒーを注文し、席を見つけて座る。

W：荷造りはもう終わったのかな？

N：大体は。あといくつか持ち物を詰めれば準備完了です。

M：うらやましい！　僕なんてまだ始めてさえいないのに。

W：急いだほうがいいよ。あと、暖かい服を持っていくのを忘れないように。今の時期のニューヨークはとっても寒いからね。

N：ウィンストン先生はロンドンに行ったことはありますか。

W：いや、残念ながらないな。ヨーロッパの国はどこも訪れたことがないんだ。ずっと行きたいとは思っているんだけどね。ヨーロッパの歴史はすごく興味深いから。

M：僕の父は数年前ローマに赴任していました。それ以来ヨーロッパの歴史に強く興味を持つようになったみたいです。ローマでの暮らしは博物館に住んでいるみたいだったって言っていました。

W：君のお父さんはあちこちに行っているんだな。君は子どもの頃オーストラリアに住んでいたんだろう？

M：ニュージーランドですよ。父は土木技師なんです。大規模なプロジェクトのためにかなり頻繁に海外へ渡っています。

W：なら、今度は君が海外へ渡る番だね。楽しみかい？

M：はい、とても。アメリカ文化は以前から大好きだったので、実際に体験するのがすごく楽しみです。

W：君はどうだい、慎之助。イギリスに送られることになってうれしいかい？

N：ああ、はい。待ちきれません！　ただ仕事にちゃんとついていけることを願ってます。どんな仕事を割り当てられるか見当もつかないので、少し緊張しています。

W：心配ないさ。向こうの人も君にそんなに難しいことはやらせないと思うよ。とにかく、君たち2人とも頑張ってきなさい。来年の初めにまた会おう。旅を楽しんでおいで！

40

KEY WORDS & PHRASES

CD 1-20

キーワードやフレーズをチェック！

☐ butterflies in *one's* stomach　そわそわ、ドキドキした感覚

She had **butterflies in her stomach** while waiting to give her presentation.

彼女は自分のプレゼンテーションの順番を待つ間、緊張でそわそわしていた。

The television cameras at the press conference gave him **butterflies in his stomach**.

記者会見のテレビカメラを見て、彼はドキドキして落ち着かなかった。

☐ pick *one* up　（人を）迎えに行く、途中で乗せる

I have arranged for a taxi to **pick me up** at 11:45.

私はタクシーが11時45分に迎えに来るように手配した。

Her boss **picked her up** on the way to the airport.

彼女の上司は空港へ向かう途中で彼女を車で拾った。

☐ big relief　多大な安心

Winning the licensing contract was a **big relief** for the company.

ライセンス契約を勝ち取ってその会社は肩の荷が下りた。

It was a **big relief** to know that I wasn't going to be made redundant.

クビにされないと知って私はとてもホッとした。

☐ convenient for ～　～に便利な

The location of the new office is very **convenient for** access to other parts of the city.

新しいオフィスの立地は市内の他の場所と行き来するのにとても便利だ。

There are many restaurants in the area, which is **convenient for** lunch.

この地区には飲食店が多くあり、ランチに便利だ。

☐ wish *one*　（人に）願う

She **wished me** good luck as I left for the conference.
私が会議に向かう際、彼女は「頑張ってね」と言ってくれた。

His boss **wished him** success for the future during his farewell party.
彼の上司は送別会で、彼のこれからの成功を願っていると言った。

☐ sense of humor　ユーモアのセンス

She has a reputation within the company for having a **sense of humor**.
彼女はユーモアのセンスがあると社内で評判だ。

Working in the complaints department has nearly destroyed his **sense of humor**.
クレーム対応係の業務は彼のユーモア感覚を破壊しかけた。

40

マナーのヒント

　もしあなたが喫煙者なら、海外を訪れる前にそこの喫煙マナーを確認する必要があります。一部の国では法律が日本よりも厳しく、違反は場合によっては逮捕にもつながります。しかし、例えばドイツは喫煙者に比較的やさしく、公共施設、病院、レストランなどは禁煙ですが、公園などの場所に灰皿を設置したエリアがあります。また、一部の国ではバーやレストランの特定のエリアで喫煙が許可されていますが、灰皿が用意されていても、たばこに火をつけるのは一緒にいる人に吸っても構わないかどうか聞いてからにしましょう。

UNIT

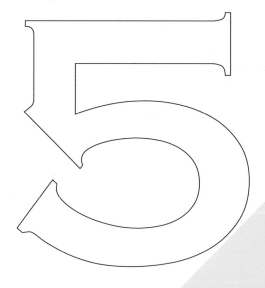

ロンドン
武者修行

DECEMBER 3RD (TUESDAY)

Well, here I am in London! I arrived on Saturday, and yesterday was my first day in the office. The weather is slightly overcast, but about the same temperature as Tokyo. Mr. Miyazaki picked me up at the airport and drove me to my guesthouse, which was very nice of him. He was transferred to London about eighteen months ago, and he is expecting to be here for about four years in total. He said that it took him a few months to acclimatize himself to working in a different environment, but he enjoys it now. I asked him if he misses Japanese food, but he said no. Apparently, there are quite a lot of supermarkets in London that sell Japanese ingredients, so his wife has no trouble with cooking. The staff at the office (mostly the Japanese staff, I guess) also eat out quite regularly in the Japanese restaurants that are relatively common here.

My first day in the office went very well. Mr. Yonezawa (who seemed genuinely pleased to see me) **introduced me during the morning meeting (p.122)**, and everybody gave me a warm welcome. I was even handed an invitation to the **office Christmas party (p.118)** due to be held on the Friday before my return to Tokyo. I have been allocated a desk equipped with a computer, but so far, I haven't been assigned any work. I have been given several documents explaining the operations of the office and the office rules, etc., so my first two days have been spent simply learning about the company. I took the opportunity to write and send an **e-mail to Mr. Winston (p.120)** this afternoon (I promised to let him know that I had arrived safely).

My room at the High Grove Guesthouse is very comfortable. The owner and his wife are very pleasant, and they told me to ask them if there is anything I need. The trip into the office from Finchley is also quite easy. It takes about fifty minutes door-to-door, so it's quite convenient. There is also a pub on the corner of the street. I tried it out on Sunday night, and really enjoyed myself. I sat at the bar and chatted with the barman for a while. He was very friendly, and even served me with a free drink to welcome me to London.

I think I am going to enjoy this trip…

Nitobe

キーワード＆キーフレーズ→p.124

１２月３日（火曜日）

　さて、僕は今ここロンドンにいる！　到着したのは土曜日で、昨日は支社での最初の日だった。天気は曇り気味だけど、気温は東京とほぼ同じだ。すごくありがたいことに、宮崎さんが空港まで僕を迎えに来て、ゲストハウスまで車で送ってくれた。彼は約18か月前にロンドンに転勤してきて、全部で4年ほどこちらにいる予定。今までと違う環境で働くことに慣れるのには数か月かかったけれど、今は仕事を楽しんでいる、と言っていた。日本食が恋しくならないかと彼に尋ねたら、答えはノーだった。どうやら、ロンドンには日本の食材を売っているスーパーマーケットが結構たくさんあるらしく、彼の妻も料理をするには困らないそうだ。オフィスの社員も（大半は日本人社員だと思う）ここでは比較的よく見られる日本食レストランでかなり頻繁に外食している。

　僕の支社での初日はとてもうまくいった。米澤支社長代理（僕と会えたことを心から喜んでくれたようだ）が朝礼のときに僕を紹介してくれて、皆が暖かく迎え入れてくれた。僕が東京に帰る前の金曜日に開かれる予定の社内クリスマスパーティーの招待状までもらったし。僕はコンピュータの付いたデスクを割り当てられたけど、今のところは何の仕事も与えられていない。オフィスの業務や社内のルールなどを説明したいくつかの書類を渡されたので、僕の最初の2日間はただ会社について学ぶことに費やされた。この時間を利用して、今日の午後、ウィンストン先生にメールを書いて送った（無事到着したら知らせると約束したのだ）。

　ハイ・グローブ・ゲストハウスの僕の部屋はとても居心地がいい。オーナーと奥さんはすごくいい人で、必要なものがあったら何でも聞いていいよと言ってくれた。フィンチリーからオフィスへの道のりもかなり楽だ。ドア・ツー・ドアで50分ほどなので、結構便利。街角にはパブもあって、日曜日の夜に試しに行ってみたら、とても楽しく過ごせた。バーのカウンターに座ってバーテンダーとしばらく会話したのだけれど、彼はとてもフレンドリーで、ロンドンへの歓迎の印だと無料で一杯ごちそうさえしてくれた。

　楽しい旅になりそうだ…。

新渡戸

117

office Christmas party ▶

社内クリスマスパーティーの案内を書いてみよう!

It's Christmas!

Annual Tomizawa Christmas Party!

This year's theme is: Santa's Little Helpers
(...so don't forget to dress up as an elf!)

Date: Friday December 20th, 19:00 to 23:00
Place: Three Oaks Hotel, 2nd Floor Banquet Room

You and one guest (wife, husband, girlfriend, boyfriend or partner: no children please) are cordially invited to this year's Tomizawa Christmas Party on December 20th at the Three Oaks Hotel. It starts at 7 p.m., so don't be late!

Food, unlimited drinks, party games and dancing! Everyone gets a gift, and the person in the best elf costume will receive an all-expenses-paid weekend trip for two in Paris!

Contact Pauline Foster in General Affairs if you intend to bring a guest.

POINT

(so don't forget to dress up as an elf!)など、随所にユーモアを交えて、全体的に楽しい雰囲気を出し、参加を促すようにしましょう。

クリスマス!

年に一度の富沢クリスマスパーティー!

今年のテーマは：サンタの小さなお手伝いたち
（…だから、エルフの仮装をするのを忘れずに!）

41

日時: 12月20日（金曜日）19:00 〜 23:00
場所: スリーオークス・ホテル　2階宴会場

1人のゲスト（奥様、旦那様、彼女、彼氏かパートナー：お子様はご遠慮ください）とご一緒に、
12月20日にスリーオークス・ホテルで開かれる今年の富沢クリスマスパーティーへ謹んでご招待
いたします。午後7時から始まりますので遅れないように!

食べ物、飲み放題の飲み物、パーティーゲームにダンス!　全員がプレゼントをもらえ、エルフ
のコスプレが最も良かった人はパリへの週末ペア旅行にご招待!

ゲスト同伴予定の方は、総務部のポーリーン・フォスターにご連絡ください。

クイックQ&A

Q 〉 To what country will the person who wins the costume
competition go?
（仮装コンペで優勝した人が行ける国はどこですか）

POINT

本文第2段落のall-expenses-paidのように、ハイフンを使って単語をつなげた独自の形容詞（また
は名詞）を作ることができます。do-it-yourself、balance-of-payments、mother-in-lawなどの
ようにすでに定着しているハイフン付きの語もありますが、短い単語ならどんなものでもハイフンでつな
げて形容詞として使うことができます。以下はその例です。
- He counted the rings of the cut-down cedar and discovered that it was a three-hundred-year-old tree. （彼はスギの切り株の年輪を数えて、それが樹齢300年の木だと知った）
- She returned from the meeting with a don't-talk-to-me-now look on her face. （彼女は会議から戻ってきたとき「今は話しかけるな」という顔をしていた）
- He wrote the report in a I-wish-I-didn't-have-to-do-this style. （彼は面倒くさそうに報告書を書いた）

A 〉 France（フランス）

e-mail to Mr. Winston ▶

語学の先生へのEメールを読んでみよう!

From: Shinnosuke Nitobe <nitobe@tomizawauk.com>
Sent: Monday, December 02, 5:17 PM
To: Mr. Winston <paulwinston@wmail.ne.jp>
Subject: Arrived in London…!

Dear Mr. Winston,

I arrived in London safely, and am enjoying my visit so far. The flight was very smooth, and the cabin attendants were pretty (except the men, of course). My guesthouse is very comfortable and has Wi-Fi, so I can use my laptop. This is my first day of work, so it's a bit too early to give you a report on what I'm doing. I'll send you more details when I have settled in.

The e-mail address that I have been assigned during my visit is as follows: nitobe@tomizawauk.com

I hope you are enjoying your freedom from teaching me and Misaki English. I will write again soon.

Best Regards, Nitobe

POINT

目的地に着いてすぐのとりあえずの連絡は、フライトのことや宿泊先の第一印象などを、簡潔にユーモア
を交えて書くとgood。

41

差出人: 新渡戸慎之助<nitobe@tomizawauk.com>
送信: 12月2日(月曜日)午後5:17
宛先: ウィンストン先生<paulwinston@wmail.ne.jp>
件名：ロンドンに着きました…！

ウィンストン先生

無事にロンドンに着き、今のところ楽しくやっています。フライトはとてもスムーズで、CAの方々もきれいでした（もちろん男性を除いて）。僕のゲストハウスはとても快適でWi-Fiがあるので、ノートパソコンが使えます。今日が仕事の初日なので、僕が何をしているかをご報告するにはまだ少し早すぎますね。落ち着いたらもう少し詳しいお話ができるでしょう。

滞在期間中に割り当てられたEメールアドレスは次の通りです：
nitobe@tomizawauk.com

僕と岬の英語指導からの解放感をお楽しみのことと思います。また近いうちにご連絡しますね。

ごきげんよう。
新渡戸

クイックQ＆A

Q 〉 **What will Nitobe do after he has settled in?**
（新渡戸は落ち着いてから何をするつもりですか）

POINT

関係代名詞のthatとwhichは、その使い方がよく混同されますが、ルールは意外と簡単です。thatはその後に続く情報が文にとって重要な場合に使われますが、whichはそれに続く情報が補足的な場合に使われます。この新渡戸のメールでは、第2段落にあるI have been assignedというフレーズは文の重要な部分（これがないと、誰のメルアドかがはっきりしない）なので、thatが正解です。The e-mail address which I have been assigned...は誤りになります。

A 〉 Send more details of London to Mr. Winston
（ウィンストン先生にロンドンのことをもっと詳しく書いて送る）

121

実際の会話を聞いて話してみよう!

SETTING:

> Mr. Yonezawa introduces Nitobe to the other people in the office during the morning meeting.

Yonezawa: Good morning, everybody. You will all be pleased to know that sales of the new Fleet Suite package are doing very well. More than sixty percent of existing users have committed to purchasing the upgrade, and sales to new customers have exceeded even our own expectations. Anything to add to that, Mr. Jones?

Jones: Yes, thank you. I'd just like to say that Mr. Lewis will be discharged from hospital next weekend. His treatment appears to have been successful, and he is looking forward to returning to his own bed. He will recuperate at home for about a month, and should be back in the office sometime in January. And, back to you, Mr. Yonezawa.

Yonezawa: Thank you. That is excellent news! It also means that you'll only have to put up with me for another month or so.

(Laughter)

Yonezawa: The only other thing I have to report is that we have a new trainee with us from today. Allow me to introduce you to Shinnosuke Nitobe from our Tokyo office. He will be with us until Christmas, so I hope you will take good care of him during his visit. Would you like to introduce yourself, Mr. Nitobe?

Nitobe: Good morning, everyone. My name is Shinnosuke Nitobe, but I hope you will call me Shin-chan, which, I'm sure you'll agree, is a lot easier to remember.

(Laughter)

Nitobe: I am really looking forward to working with you all, and I hope to learn a lot from my visit. Please don't hesitate to tell me if I get under your feet or ask too many questions. Thank you.

Yonezawa: Mr. Nitobe's main task while he is in London will be to polish his English. He already speaks quite well, but it is your job to make sure he returns to Tokyo fluent. And that's all for today. Thank you.

introduced me during the morning meeting

場面:

> 米澤支社長代理が朝礼の際に新渡戸をオフィスの他の社員に紹介する。

Y：皆さん、おはようございます。喜ばしいことに、新しいフリートスイートのパッケージの売上は非常に順調に伸びています。既存ユーザーの60％以上がこのアップグレードの購入を確約しており、新規顧客への売上は我々自身の予想をも上回っています。ジョーンズ取締役、何か付け加えることは？

41

J：ええ、ありがとうございます。ルイス支社長が来週末に退院されることになったとだけお知らせしたいと思います。彼の治療は成功したようで、自分のベッドに戻れるのが楽しみだとのことです。1か月ほど自宅で療養し、1月中にはオフィスに復帰できるでしょう。では、米澤支社長代理、どうぞ。

Y：ありがとう。それは素晴らしい知らせだ！　皆、あと1か月ほどで私のことを我慢しなくてよくなるということでもあるね。

　　（笑い声）

Y：もう1つお知らせしなければならないことは、今日から新しい研修生を迎えることになったということです。紹介しましょう、東京本社から来た新渡戸慎之助君です。彼はクリスマスまでここにいる予定なので、彼の滞在中、気にかけてやってください。新渡戸君、自己紹介してくれますか。

N：皆さん、おはようございます。新渡戸慎之助と申します。ですが、慎ちゃんと呼んでもらえるとうれしいです。ご同意いただけると思いますが、そのほうがずっと覚えやすいでしょう。

　　（笑い声）

N：皆さんと働けることをとても楽しみにしています。また、滞在中に多くを学びたいと思っています。仕事の邪魔になっていたり、質問が多すぎたりしたら、遠慮なくおっしゃってください。よろしくお願いします。

Y：新渡戸君のロンドン滞在中の主な課題は英語力を磨くことです。すでにかなり上手に話すことができますが、彼が東京に帰る頃にはペラペラになっているようにすることが皆さんの仕事です。では、本日はこれで以上です。ありがとう。

キーワードやフレーズをチェック！

☐ **expect to 〜**　　〜することを予想する、期待する

She is **expecting to** be assigned to a job involving research.
彼女は自分が調査に関する仕事を任されるだろうと思っている。

We **expect** him **to** do well in his new job.
我々は彼が新しい仕事で好成績を上げることを期待している。

☐ **acclimatize oneself**　　慣れる

She has to **acclimatize herself** to working longer hours every day.
彼女は1日により長い時間働くことに慣れなければならない。

It took him several months to **acclimatize himself** to having less power.
彼は仕事上の権限が少なくなったことに慣れるまで数か月かかった。

☐ **quite regularly**　　かなり頻繁に

I haven't seen any of my old colleagues for many years, but some contact me by e-mail **quite regularly**.
私はもう何年も昔の同僚たちに会っていないが、何人かはかなり頻繁にメールで連絡を取ってくる。

The president visits the factory **quite regularly** to boost morale.
その社長は社員の士気を上げるため、かなり頻繁に工場を訪れる。

☐ **equipped with 〜**　　〜を備えた

The new system is **equipped with** an uninterruptible power supply.
その新しいシステムは無停電電源装置を搭載している。

My office building is **equipped with** a canteen and a fitness room.
私のオフィスの建物には社員食堂とジムが付いている。

be spent　費やされる

The entire afternoon **was spent** trying to fix the problem.
午後は丸々、その問題の解決を試みることに費やされた。

She was surprised to learn that her time would **be spent** in an office without windows.
彼女は自分が窓のないオフィスで過ごすことになると知って驚いた。

door-to-door　副 出発から到着まで、ドア・ツー・ドアで

41

It is only a twelve-minute train ride, but it takes one hour **door-to-door**.
電車に乗るのはたった12分だが、出かけてからそこに着くまでだと1時間かかる。

All products can be delivered **door-to-door** within twenty-four hours.
すべての商品が24時間以内に宅配可能だ。

マナーのヒント

　英語圏で自己紹介を求められることはまれですが、求められた場合、手短なのが望ましいということと、個人的な情報は求められていないということを知っておくとよいでしょう。自分の名前とそこにいる理由、そして締めくくりの言葉があれば十分です。卒業した大学、趣味、その他の個人情報は要りません。以下はその例です。

・My name is Shinnosuke Nitobe, and I was invited here today by Mr. Greenwood. It is very nice meeting you all.（新渡戸慎之助と申します。本日はグリーンウッドさんの招待で来ました。皆さん、初めまして）

・I am Shinnosuke Nitobe, and I will be working in the Personnel Department from today. I look forward to working with you all.（今日から人事部で働くことになりました新渡戸慎之助と申します。よろしくお願いします）

DAY 42

DECEMBER 8TH (SUNDAY)

Nitobe has now completed his first week in London. From what I can see, he is blending in well and appears to be very popular. Some of the younger staff have taken him under their wing and take him out to lunch with them every day. It is not uncommon for people to drink at lunchtime in the UK, and on a couple of occasions he has returned from lunch smelling of beer. As long as he is capable of doing his job, however, this is not a problem. In fact, it indicates that he is assimilating into the local culture, which will provide him with many valuable lessons.

I intend to assign him to the job of answering all incoming calls for a couple of days next week. Tomizawa does not have a switchboard as such and calls are answered by anyone who is free under normal circumstances, but one of the engineers told me that he can rig up the phone system so that all incoming calls can be directed to a single telephone and then be passed manually onto other internal phones. I am hoping that answering all calls will help him improve his hearing skills. Hearing is more difficult when you can't see the speaker's face. I spent this afternoon making up a **list of the phrases** (p.128) that he is likely to need.

I have recently noticed that the people in the office are very fond of coffee mugs bearing humorous phrases. Some even have stickers of these funny phrases pasted to their computers or somewhere else on their desks. Most are tongue-in-cheek messages making fun of work, but they are very amusing, so I started **making a list of them** (p.130).

I was **interviewed for an article** (p.132) in the *IT Personified* trade journal on Wednesday. A very competent-looking reporter named Wendy Freeman did the interview. She spoke in a soft voice and looked deep into my eyes whenever she spoke to me, and after a while I began to feel hypnotized. I'm sure I would have answered any question she asked, even for my bank account number. I guess that is a special technique that reporters have to master. We spoke for an hour, but it felt like only ten minutes.

Yonezawa

キーワード＆キーフレーズ→p.134

１２月８日（日曜日）

　新渡戸がロンドンでの最初の1週間を終えた。私が見る限り、彼は職場にうまく溶け込んで大変人気者になっているようだ。若い社員の何人かは彼をかわいがるようになり、毎日一緒に昼食を食べに連れ出したりしている。イギリスではランチ時に酒を飲むことも珍しくなく、新渡戸も何回かビールのにおいをさせて昼食から帰ってきた。しかし、仕事に支障がない限り、それは問題ない。むしろ、それは彼が地元の文化になじんでいるという証拠であり、そこから彼は多くの貴重な学びを得るだろう。

42

　来週は2日ほど、外からかかってきたすべての電話に対応する仕事を彼に担当させようと思っている。富沢UKには交換台というものはなく、通常の状況では誰でもいいからその時に手が空いている人間が電話に出るが、エンジニアの1人が即席で電話システムをいじって、外からかかってきた電話がすべて1台の電話機につながり、そこから手動で社内の他の電話機につなげるようにできると教えてくれた。電話にすべて対応することが新渡戸の聞き取る能力の向上に役立つことを期待している。話を聞き取るのは話し手の顔が見えないとより難しくなるからだ。今日の午後は彼に必要となるだろうフレーズのリスト作りに費やした。

　最近気づいたのだが、オフィスの社員はユーモアのあるフレーズが書いてあるコーヒーマグをよく好んで使っている。人によってはそのような面白いフレーズのステッカーを自分のコンピュータやデスクのどこかに貼ったりもしている。その多くは仕事をネタにした皮肉の効いた言葉だが、とても面白いので私はそれらを集めたリストを作り始めた。

　水曜日に、業界誌『ITパーソニファイド』の記事のための取材を受けた。取材を行ったのはウェンディ・フリーマンというとても有能そうな記者だ。彼女はやわらかい声で話し、私に話しかけるときは常に私の目をじっとのぞき込むので、しばらくすると催眠術にかかったような気分になり始めた。彼女に尋ねられたことは何でも、たとえ銀行の口座番号でも答えてしまっていただろう。これは記者が身につけなければならない特別なテクニックなのだろうな。私たちは1時間ほど話したが、ほんの10分ほどのように感じられた。

米澤

list of the phrases ►

電話応対フレーズリストを書いてみよう!

List of Telephone Responses

- Tomizawa Integrated Solutions. How can I help you?
- Please hold the line, I'll put you through.
- Mr. XXX is unavailable at the moment. Can I take a message?
- I'm afraid there is no answer from Mr. XXX's phone. Would you mind calling back?
- I'm afraid there is nobody in the company by that name. Are you sure you have the right number?
- I'm sorry, but Mr. XXX has already left the office. He will be available again from nine o'clock tomorrow morning.
- Is your inquiry about software or hardware?
- Can you remember the name of the person you spoke to?
- Mr. XXX left a message to say that he will call you directly this afternoon.

POINT

Please hold the lineはHold on, pleaseと言ったり、Can I take a message?はWold you like to leave a message?と言えるなど、他にも様々な言い方が可能です。

電話応対リスト

- 富沢インテグレーテッド・ソリューションズでございます。どのようなご用件でしょうか。
- しばらくお待ちください。おつなぎいたします。
- XXXはただいま電話に出ることができません。ご用件を承りましょうか。
- 申し訳ありませんが、XXXから何も応答がありません。おかけ直しいただけますか。
- 申し訳ありませんが、弊社にはそのような名前の者はおりません。おかけになった電話番号は確かでしょうか。
- 申し訳ありませんが、XXXはすでに（本日は）退社いたしました。明日の朝9時から出社いたします。
- お問い合わせはソフトウェアに関してでしょうか、ハードウェアに関してでしょうか。
- お話しされた担当者の名前を覚えていらっしゃいますか。
- XXXから、今日の午後直接お電話を差し上げるとの伝言があります。

42

クイックQ&A

Q What is suggested when there is no answer from Mr. XXX's phone?
（XXX氏の電話から応答がないとき、何が勧められていますか）

POINT

4番目と5番目にあるI'm afraidという表現は残念な知らせを伝えるときによく使われますが、Unfortunately／I'm very sorry, but／I regret to say that／I'm sorry to inform you that／Deepest apologies, butなどを代わりに使うこともできます。例えば、「申し訳ありませんが、弊社にはそのような名前の者はおりません」と言いたいときは、Unfortunately, there is nobody in the company by that name.のように言えます。

A That the caller calls back（かけ手が電話をかけ直すこと）

129

making a list of them ►

仕事に関する面白フレーズを読んでみよう!

You don't have to be crazy to work here, but it helps.

To avoid serious injury, don't tell me how to do my job!

Sorry...!
Yesterday was the final deadline for complaints.

I could be wrong, but I doubt it.

Teamwork is great! It lets you share the blame!

The only place where success comes before work is in the dictionary.

Treat me nicely. I know your password!

Don't ask me. I know nothing!

I don't mind coming to work, but I hate waiting eight hours to go home.

あなたがここで仕事に夢中になる必要はありませんが、役には立ちます。	深刻なけがを避けるために、私の仕事のやり方について言わないで！	ごめんなさい…！昨日が苦情の最終期限でした。
間違っているかもしれませんが、疑っています。	チームワークは素晴らしい！責任をみんなで共有できる！	成功が努力より先にくるのは辞書の中だけだ。
私をきちんと扱ってください。あなたのパスワードを知っているのですよ！	私に聞かないで。何も知らないから！	仕事に来るのは構わないが、帰宅まで8時間待つのが嫌なのです。

42

クイックQ＆A

Q ＞ **What is so great about teamwork?**
（チームワーの何がそれほど素晴らしいのでしょうか）

POINT

The only place where success comes before work is in the dictionary.（成功が努力より先にくるのは辞書の中だけだ）は、ヴィダル・サスーンの有名な引用句です。近頃、欧米社会では自己啓発的な引用句がとても人気になっていて、SNSに投稿されていたりバンパーステッカーに貼ってあったり、その他にも様々なところで見られます。以下はそんな人気の引用句です。
・Success is walking from failure to failure with no loss of enthusiasm.（成功とは、失敗を重ねながら意欲を失わずにいることである。—ウィンストン・チャーチル）
・Nothing great was ever achieved without enthusiasm.（情熱なしに成し遂げられた偉業はない。—ラルフ・ワルド・エマーソン）
・There are no shortcuts to any place worth going.（行く価値のある場所に近道などない。—ビヴァリー・シルズ）
・I have not failed. I've just found 10,000 ways that won't work.（失敗ではない。1万通りのうまくいかない方法を発見しただけだ。—トーマス・A・エジソン）
・Yesterday's homeruns don't win today's games.（昨日のホームランで今日の試合は勝てない。—ベーブ・ルース）

A ＞ It lets you share the blame for failure with other people.
（失敗の責任を他の人と共有させてくれます）

131

実際の会話を聞いて話してみよう!

SETTING:

> Mr. Yonezawa ushers the reporter into his office and invites him to sit on the chair in front of his desk.

Freeman: Thank you very much for agreeing to the interview, Mr. Yonezawa.

Yonezawa: It's my pleasure. I hope I can answer all questions to your satisfaction.

Freeman: First of all, allow me to congratulate you on the release of the Fleet Suite accounting package. From what I have heard, it appears to be selling very well.

Yonezawa: Thank you very much. The figures are looking good at the moment, and we are hopeful for the future.

Freeman: Your PR package mentions that you have 350,000 existing users. Are you expecting to expand on this?

Yonezawa: We hope so. Our target is 400,000 users by the end of the fiscal year.

Freeman: I hope you don't mind me saying, but that doesn't sound like a very ambitious target when compared against software marketed by other companies. The package is relatively inexpensive at £248, so an increase of 50,000 users will not generate an enormous sum in revenue. Will you be able to cover development costs?

Yonezawa: A large percentage of our users are small businesses; shops, restaurants, printers, small manufacturers, etc. Our research showed that this type of firm is reluctant to spend excessive amounts on computer software, but they are willing to pay a nominal monthly fee for maintenance and backup purposes. We therefore kept the cost of the software down as much as possible, and rely on the monthly fee, which is reasonable at around £15.

Freeman: Yes, I see. At that rate, a simple calculation based on 400,000 users means that the software generates a monthly income of £6 million. That's very impressive for a company with less than 40 employees. What does the monthly fee include?

Yonezawa: Cloud backup, maintenance, instant updates covering revisions to VAT and other tax laws, etc. It's quite a comprehensive package.

Freeman: I see. Well, now let's move on to the work you handle for your Japanese parent company...

interviewed for an article

場面:

> 米澤支社長代理が記者を支社長室に招き入れ、自分のデスクの前の椅子に座るよう促す。

F： 取材に応じてくださり誠にありがとうございます、米澤支社長代理。

Y： どういたしまして。すべての質問にそちらが満足いくまで答えられたらいいと思っています。

F： まず、「フリートスイート」会計パッケージの発表おめでとうございます。聞くところによると、とてもよく売れているようですね。

Y： どうもありがとうございます。今のところ売上は順調なので、今後にも期待しています。

F： 宣伝用資料には35万の既存ユーザーがいると書いてありますが、ここから拡大するおつもりですか。

Y： そうなることを期待しています。弊社は当事業年度の末までに40万のユーザーを目標としています。

F： 失礼ですが、他社が販売するソフトウェアと比較すると、それはあまり大きな目標ではないように思えます。このパッケージは248ポンドと比較的手ごろな価格なので、5万のユーザーの増加は特別大きな収益にはなりませんよね。開発コストを賄うことはできるのですか。

Y： 弊社の顧客の大部分を占めるのは小売店、レストラン、印刷業者、小規模な製造業者などの小企業です。弊社の調査によると、このタイプの企業はコンピュータソフトにあまり多い額を使うことに消極的ですが、メンテナンスやバックアップのために毎月少額の費用を払うことはためらいません。なので弊社はソフトウェアの価格を可能な限り抑え、約15ポンドと手ごろな月額料金に賭けているのです。

F： なるほど、わかりました。それでしたら、40万のユーザーで単純に計算すると、このソフトウェアは月々600万ポンドの収益を上げることになります。これは社員40人未満の企業としてはかなりの額ですね。月額料金には何が含まれるのですか。

Y： クラウドバックアップ、メンテナンス、付加価値税やその他の税法の改正に即座に対応するアップデートなどです。かなり包括的なパッケージなんですよ。

F： なるほど。それでは、今度は御社が日本の本社に対して担っている役割について聞かせていただきたいのですが…。

CD
1-24

キーワードやフレーズをチェック！

☐ blend in　溶け込む

The new office furniture **blends in** with interior decor.
新しいオフィス家具は内装によくなじんでいる。

He tried hard to **blend in** with the other workers, but they rejected him.
彼は他の社員と打ち解けようと頑張ったが、受け入れられなかった。

☐ take ～ under *one's* wing　～の面倒を見る

She was **taken under the president's wing** from the moment she joined the company.
彼女は入社してすぐに社長にかわいがられるようになった。

My supervisor **took** me **under his wing** and taught me the job.
私の上司は私の面倒を見て、仕事を教えてくれた。

☐ as long as ～　～の限りは

The company should survive **as long as** there are no more scandals.
その会社は、これ以上スキャンダルがない限り生き残るだろう。

We should receive a good bonus this winter **as long as** we keep meeting our targets.
私たちが目標を達成し続けさえすれば今年の冬は多額のボーナスがもらえるだろう。

☐ as such　そのようなものとして

The company does not provide a delivery service **as such**, but it can arrange for goods to be delivered.
その会社は配達サービスそのものはやっていないが、商品が配達されるように手配することはできる。

I don't have an official title **as such**, but I introduce myself as a manager when meeting clients.
厳密には私に役職はないが、顧客に会うときは部長と名乗ることにしている。

rig up 〜　　〜を急ごしらえする

My desk is by the window, so I have to **rig up** a sunshade in summer.

私のデスクは窓際にあるので、夏場は日よけを取り付けなければならない。

A temporary office was **rigged up** in the meeting room for the auditors.

監査役のために、会議室に仮設の事務所が早急に作られた。

tongue-in-cheek　　形 皮肉な

42

She gave a **tongue-in-cheek** answer when asked her age.

彼女は年齢を尋ねられると皮肉を込めた返答をした。

I received a **tongue-in-cheek** e-mail from my boss when on my business trip saying that my desk had been rented out in my absence.

私の出張中、上司が私のデスクを私の留守の間貸し出すことにしたという冗談の効いたメールを送ってきた。

マナーのヒント

　ビジネスの電話におけるエチケットはほとんど世界共通で、国や文化圏による違いはあまりありません。主なポイントは以下の通りです。

　1. かかってきた電話は3コール以内で取ること。

　2. ゆっくり、はっきり話すこと。

　3. 通話の初めはかけ手が名乗るタイミングなので、しっかり注意を向けること。

　4. 自分の周囲で起きていることに気を散らされないこと。

　5. 何かを確認するためにかけ手を待たせる必要があるときは、その旨をかけ手に伝えること。

　6. 常にかけ手からの情報、特に電話番号は復唱すること。

DECEMBER 15TH (SUNDAY)

I met up with some clients the other day, and during general conversation over dinner, one of them asked me to name just one thing about Japan that filled me with the most pride. It seemed like a simple question on the surface, but I had to think about it very hard. There are so many cultural, traditional and historical things that make me proud of Japan, so it was very difficult to narrow it down to just one. In the end I said "manufacturing." When I asked him the same question, he thought about it for a moment, and then said, "the **Magna Carta (p.140)**." Although I have heard of the Magna Carta in the past, I didn't really understand much about it, so I checked it out on the Internet when I got home, and was surprised to discover that it was the world's first written constitution (established over 800 years ago), and that both America's and Japan's constitutions are direct descendants of it. I had no idea that the concept of a constitution to protect the public existed so long ago.

The **interview I had (p.138)** with the reporter from the *IT Personified* trade journal was published on Friday. My jaw dropped when I read how I had been described in the first couple of paragraphs. Apparently, I came across as a competent and honest "gentleman," which is very gratifying. Naturally, the majority of the article concentrated on the technical aspects of Fleet Suite, but I will keep a copy to show my wife when I get back to Japan to remind her how lucky she is to have such a "handsome" and "charismatic" husband.

I **visited Kenneth Lewis at his home (p.142)** yesterday. His recuperation is going well, and he is expecting to be back at work by mid-January. Once this has been confirmed, I will be able to set a date for my return to Japan. As much as I am enjoying my life in London, I still feel like a caretaker and am looking forward to returning to my real job in Tokyo. My final task in London may be setting up a motivational study course for all employees. Kenneth agreed to my suggestion to commission Merryweather PLC to tailor-make a program for us. I'll start checking up on that tomorrow.

Yonezawa

１２月１５日（日曜日）

　先日は何人かの顧客と会い、夕食をとりながら彼らと世間話をしていると、その1人が日本のことで私が最も誇らしく思う点を1つだけ挙げるとしたら何かと聞いてきた。これは一見簡単な質問のように思えたが、私は真剣に答えを考えなければならなかった。日本の文化、伝統、歴史には私が自慢に思えるものが数多くあり、それをたった1つに絞り込むのはとても難しかったのだ。最終的に私は「製造業」と答えた。彼に同じ質問を返したら、彼は少しの間考えてから「マグナ・カルタ」と言った。マグナ・カルタについて以前に聞いたことはあったが、それのことをあまり理解していなかったので、帰宅してからインターネットで調べてみたところ、世界初の成文化された憲法（800年以上前に制定された）であり、アメリカと日本の憲法が両方ともそこから直接派生したものだと知って驚いた。国民を守る憲法という概念がそんな昔に存在していたとは思いもよらなかった。

43

　私が業界誌『ITパーソニファイド』の記者に受けた取材の記事が金曜日に発行された。最初の2つほどの段落にある私に対する描写を読んで唖然としてしまった。どうやら、私は有能で誠実な「紳士」という印象を与えたらしく、これはとてもうれしかった。当然ながら、記事の大部分はフリートスイートの専門的な側面に焦点を当てていたが、日本に帰ったときに妻に見せてこんなに「ハンサム」で「カリスマ的」な夫を持つ彼女はとてもラッキーだと言ってやるために、記事のコピーを取っておくことにした。

　昨日はケネス・ルイスの自宅を訪ねた。彼の回復は順調に進んでおり、1月半ばには仕事に復帰するつもりだそうだ。このことが確定すれば、私は日本への帰国の日取りを決めることができる。ロンドンでの生活を楽しんではいるが、やっぱり留守番役のような気分になるので、東京での本来の仕事に戻るのが楽しみだ。私のロンドンでの最後の仕事は、全社員のためのモチベーション講座を立ち上げることだろう。ケネスはメリーウェザー有限会社に我が社専用のプログラムの設計を依頼するという私の提案に賛成してくれた。明日からこのことについてチェックしてみよう。

interview I had ►

新製品の記事を書いてみよう!

Tomizawa Releases the Latest Version of Fleet Suite

by Wendy Freeman for *IT Personified*

Tomizawa IS (UK) released the latest edition of its popular Fleet Suite accounting package on November 25th. Fleet Suite was first released in 1990, and it remains popular with small- to mid-sized companies throughout the country. I met up with acting president Osamu Yonezawa to discuss the new release.

The moment Mr. Yonezawa walked into the room, I knew that the interview would run smoothly. A handsome, dapper and charismatic gentleman in his mid-fifties, Yonezawa exudes an aura of competence and honesty that is instantly recognizable. He is soft-spoken and answered my questions clearly and concisely with a twinkle of humour in his eyes. Mr. Yonezawa is currently the acting president, having been transferred across to London from the Tokyo head office to take control of UK operations in the absence of president Kenneth Lewis, who is recuperating from an illness.

POINT

まず、誰が、いつ、何を、どうしたかを明確に伝えましょう。

フリートスイートの最新版を富沢がリリース

ウェンディ・フリーマン（ITパーソニファイド）

　富沢IS（イギリス）は11月25日に人気のフリートスイート会計パッケージの最新版をリリースした。フリートスイートは1990年に初めてリリースされ、全国の中小企業で人気を保っている。米澤修支社長代理に会って、この度のリリースについて話を聞いた。

　米澤氏が部屋に入ってきた瞬間、私はインタビューが円滑にいくことがわかった。ハンサムで、着こなしのよいカリスマ性のある50代半ばの紳士である米澤氏は、見てすぐにわかるほど有能さと誠実さのオーラが染み出している。彼は優しい話し方で、目にユーモアの輝きを携えてはっきりと正確に私の質問に答えてくれた。米澤氏は現在支社長代理で、病気から回復中のケネス・ルイス社長の不在の間イギリス支社の運営を担うため東京本社からロンドンに派遣されてきている。

43

クイックＱ＆Ａ

Q ＞ Why did the reporter think that the interview would run smoothly?
（記者がインタビューは円滑に進むだろうと思ったのはなぜですか）

POINT

最終文にあるrecuperateは「健康を取り戻す」という動きを表す動詞です。この語は、経済状態が難局の後に通常に戻るときなどにも使えます。
例：The stock market has recuperated its losses after a 3% plunge.（株式市場は3%の暴落の後その損失を回復した）

以下はrecuperateと同じ意味を表す単語とフレーズの例です。
convalesce　　rally　　recover　　be on the mend　　be out of the woods
get better　　heal well　　perk up　　pull through

A ＞ Because Yonezawa exudes an aura of competence and honesty.
（米澤が有能そうで誠実な雰囲気を表し出しているからです）

Magna Carta ▶

マグナ・カルタの説明文を読んでみよう!

Magna Carta

The Magna Carta is a political charter issued by King John of England and signed at a place called Runnymede beside the River Thames on June 15th, 1215. It established for the first time the principle that everybody in the country, including the king, was subject to the rule of law. The charter contained sixty-three clauses that addressed the grievances of the public with relation to the king's rule. The most famous of these is the 39th Clause, which gave all citizens the right to justice and a fair trial, thereby preventing people from being imprisoned without due cause and without being able to defend the charges against them in a court of law.

Although much of the original charter has been deleted or substantially rewritten over the course of 800 years up to the present day, the basic tenet of protecting the general public from autocracy has survived intact, and some of the Magna Carta's core principles can be seen in many constitutional documents in use throughout the world today, including the United States Bill of Rights, the Universal Declaration of Human Rights, and the European Convention on Human Rights.

POINT

1行目にある動詞issueは「(憲法などを)発布する」以外に、「(雑誌の○○号を)発行する」「(切手などを)発行する」「(招待状を)出す」「(手形を)振り出す」などの意味も表します。

マグナ・カルタ

マグナ・カルタとはイングランド王ジョンによって発布された政治憲章で、1215年6月15日にテムズ川沿いのラニーミードと呼ばれる場所で制定されました。国王を含む全国民が法の支配の下にあるという原則を初めて確立しました。この憲章は国王の統治に対する国民の不平不満に対処する63か条で構成されていました。中でも最も有名なものは第39条で、それはすべての市民に公平な権利と平等な裁判を与え、それゆえ正当な理由および法廷で人々に対する罪を弁護できることなしに彼らが収監されることを防ぐというものです。

今日までの800年の歳月の中で、元々の憲章の多くが削除されたり実質的に書き換えられたりしていますが、専制政治から一般市民を守るという基本的な理念は完全に残っており、マグナ・カルタの核となる原則のいくつかは、アメリカ合衆国の権利章典や世界人権宣言、ヨーロッパ人権条約のような、今日の世界中で有効な多くの定款に見られます。

43

クイックQ&A

Q 〉 **What is the fundamental principle of the Magna Carta?**
（マグナ・カルタの基本理念は何ですか）

POINT

第1段落7行目にあるaddressは住居や職場の場所を表す名詞以外にも、ここでのように動詞としても使われ、その意味が複数あります。以下はその例です（本文でのaddressの意味は最初の例）。
- 「〜に注意を向ける、対処する」
  She addressed the issue by ordering an investigation to be carried out. （彼女は調査命令を出すことでその問題に対処した）
- 「〜と直接コミュニケーションを取る、〜に話しかける」
  He addressed the audience and explained the importance of security. （彼は聴衆に呼びかけてセキュリティの重要性を説明した）
- 「（人を適切な肩書や敬称で）呼ぶ」
  She didn't know that "your honor" was the correct way to address a judge. （彼女は裁判官への正しい呼び方がyour honorだと知らなかった）
- 「（ゴルフでボールを）打とうと構える」
  He waited for the wind to die down before addressing the ball. （彼は風がおさまるまで待ってからボールを打とうと構えた）

A 〉 To protect the public from autocracy（国民を専制政治から守ること）

141

visited Kenneth Lewis at his home　►　CD
1-25

実際の会話を聞いて話してみよう！

SETTING:

> Yonezawa and Lewis are sitting at a kitchen table drinking coffee and looking out at a spacious garden.

Yonezawa: When do you find the time to work on your garden? It's beautiful!

Lewis: It doesn't need too much work in the winter once the autumn leaves have been cleared up. Besides, I've had plenty of time on my hands since I left hospital. Do you have a garden at home?

Yonezawa: A small one, yes. My wife mostly uses it to grow vegetables and herbs for cooking. Anyway, how's the rehabilitation coming along?

Lewis: Very well, thank you. I have another batch of tests coming up next week, and if I pass them, I hope to be back at work by the middle of the month.

Yonezawa: That's excellent news! Congratulations!

Lewis: Which means you'll be able to start preparing for your trip back to Tokyo. Everybody will be sad to see you go. Stephen told me that you have made many fans within the office.

Yonezawa: I'm sure he is exaggerating. I will, of course, be sad to leave, although also a little relieved, I must admit.

Lewis: Yes, I can understand that. But if you want my opinion, you have done an exceptional job since you've been here. You have earned the respect of everyone, and the company is better off for your presence.

Yonezawa: That's very nice of you, Kenneth. I appreciate your kind words. I have tried to rely on the advice of the competent staff you employ and make as few changes as possible. It is fitting that I return to Tokyo without leaving too many ripples. There is no profit in changing something that already operates perfectly.

Lewis: Any suggestions for changes that you'd rather not make yourself?

Yonezawa: No changes, as such, but I have recently had contact with a company that provides tailor-made motivational courses for improving internal communications. The company is called Merryweather PLC, and I was very impressed with them.

Lewis: That sounds great! Maybe you can start the arrangements for that before you return to Japan.

visited Kenneth Lewis at his home

場面:

> 米澤とルイスがキッチンテーブルに座ってコーヒーを飲みながら、家の外の広々とした庭を眺めている。

Y：いつ庭の手入れをする時間を見つけているんだい？　きれいな庭じゃないか！

L：いったん秋の落ち葉を掃除してしまえば、冬はそんなに手入れはいらないんだ。それに、退院してからは時間がたっぷりあったからな。修の家に庭はあるのかい？

Y：ああ、小さいのがある。ほとんどは妻が料理のための野菜やハーブを育てるのに使っているよ。ところで、リハビリの進み具合のほうはどうだい？

43

L：順調だよ、ありがとう。来週また一通り検査があるんだが、それを通れば、来月半ばには仕事に復帰できるはずだ。

Y：それは素晴らしい知らせだ！　おめでとう！

L：つまり修も東京への帰還の準備を始められるということだ。みんな別れをさびしがるだろう。社内に大勢ファンを作ったとスティーブンに聞いているからな。

Y：彼が大げさに話しているんだよ。でも、もちろん別れるのはさびしいさ、ただ少しほっとしているのも事実だけどね。

L：ああ、それはわかるよ。でも私の意見を言わせてもらえば、修はこっちにいる間素晴らしい仕事をしたよ。皆の尊敬を勝ち取ったし、君のおかげで会社はより良い状態になっている。

Y：ありがとう、ケネス。その言葉はうれしいよ。ケネスのところの優秀な社員の助言に従いながらできるだけ何も変えないようにしたんだ。波風立てないまま東京に戻るのがよいだろうからね。もうすでに完璧に回っているものを変えてもいいことはない。

L：自分では手を出したくないけれど改善したいと思う点はあるかい？

Y：改善点とは少し違うけど、最近、社内のコミュニケーションを向上させるためのモチベーション講座を注文に応じて作ってくれる企業を見つけたんだ。メリーウェザー有限会社というんだけど、とても感銘を受けたよ。

L：それはいい！　日本に帰る前にそれの手配を進めておいてくれないか。

キーワードやフレーズをチェック！

☐ fill with pride　誇らしく感じる[感じさせる]

Her eyes **filled with pride** when she was announced Employee of the Month.
月間最優秀社員として自分が発表されると彼女の眼は誇らしげになった。

The advances the company have made in environmental conservation **fill** me **with pride**.
我が社が環境保全の面でしてきた進歩は私を誇らしさでいっぱいにする。

☐ on the surface　表面上は

The company appears prosperous **on the surface**, but it is struggling financially.
その会社は表面上成功しているように見えるが、実際は財政的に苦戦している。

Overall sales look favorable **on the surface**, but we still lack operating revenue.
総売上は見かけでは好調に思えるが、まだ営業利益が不足している。

☐ narrow down　絞り込む

The location of the new office was **narrowed down** to Nagasaki and Miyazaki.
新しいオフィスの場所は長崎と宮崎に絞り込まれた。

We need eight employees in the new sales team, and so far we have **narrowed** this **down** to twelve potential candidates.
新しい営業チームのために8人の社員が必要だが、現時点で我々は候補者を12人まで絞り込んでいる。

☐ jaw drop　びっくり仰天する

My **jaw dropped** when I saw how much tax had been deducted from my summer bonus.
私の夏のボーナスからどれだけの税金が差し引かれているかを見て私は開いた口がふさがらなかった。

The boss's **jaw dropped** when he heard she worked throughout the night.

彼女の上司は、彼女が一晩中働いていたと聞いてひどく驚いた。

---

concentrate on ～　　～に集中する、重点を置く

The company's business strategy for this year is to **concentrate on** after-sales services.

その会社の今年の経営戦略はアフターサービスに重点を置くことだ。

Overseas sales rose by twenty percent last year, **concentrated on** Asian nations.

昨年は海外売上がアジアの国々に集中して20％上昇した。

43

tailor-make　　[他] ～を特注する

The desks and chairs were **tailor-made** for the new office.

これらのデスクや椅子は新しいオフィスのために特注されたものだ。

We tried over-the-counter inventory systems, but in the end had our own system **tailor-made**.

我々は市販の在庫管理システムを試してみたが、最終的にわが社専用のシステムを注文して作ってもらった。

マナーのヒント

　日本ではタクシーや宴席などで座る位置が地位によってあらかじめ決まっていますが、欧米ではそのような習慣は一般的ではありません。ですが、例えば同じ会社の人と一緒にタクシーを使うときは、一番地位の高い人に先に乗り込ませるのがふつうです。その場に2人以上いて、一番地位の高い人が窓際に座りたくない場合は、たいていその人が「お先にどうぞ」というようなことを言い、あとから乗り込みます。覚えておくべきポイントは、座る位置は決まっていない一方、一番地位の高い人が最初に座る場所を選べるということです。

I'm still enjoying myself in London. Commuting is easy, the atmosphere in the office is very pleasant, and I've made many friends. I'm not too keen on the short days, though. It doesn't get light until past eight o'clock in the morning, and it's dark again by around four o'clock in the afternoon, which gets to you after a while. Nobody seems to mind, though. I guess they're used to it.

Last week was a busy week for me. I was assigned to answering all incoming calls from Monday, and I attended a one-day business course last Friday. Actually, it was more of a motivational course teaching people the best way to communicate with work colleagues. It was run by a company called Merryweather, and it was divided into four participatory lessons. There were fourteen people mostly around my own age taking part, and we had to act in skits, form teams for solving various problems, and take part in debates. Most of what we were taught was common sense, but I suppose I learned a few lessons, and I quite enjoyed it.

British people seem quite interested in motivation. The word seems to crop up at regular intervals, and there are signs and posters concerning "initiative" and "motivation" everywhere. There is even a **large poster on being successful (p.148)** hung on the wall of the staffroom where the coffee machine is located. I wonder if anyone takes any notice of them?

I had a very **pleasant evening out with Mr. Yonezawa (p.152)** last night. He took me to a wine bar near Covent Garden. Over a bottle of Merlot, we discussed the differences between Japanese and English, which was quite interesting. There are many phrases in Japanese that are used by rote on a daily basis, but the same phrases are rarely used in English. [頑張ります], for example. This is usually translated as "I'll do my best," but it is not used with the same level of frequency or in the same situations as Japanese. When I returned home, I started **making a list of the phrases (p.150)** that are difficult to use in English (on Mr. Yonezawa's suggestion, of course).

Nitobe

１２月１７日（火曜日）

　現在も僕はロンドンで楽しく過ごしている。通勤は楽だし、社内の雰囲気はとても居心地がいいし、友達もたくさんできた。ただ、日が短いのはあまり好きじゃないかな。朝は８時過ぎまで明るくならないし、午後４時頃にはまた暗くなってしまうので、ずっとこれだとだんだん気が滅入ってくる。でも、誰も気にしている様子はないから、慣れているんだろうな。

　先週は僕にとって忙しい週になった。外からかかってきた電話全部に対応する仕事を月曜日から与えられ、金曜日は１日ビジネスコースに参加したのだ。受けてみると、どちらかというと仕事仲間とのベストなコミュニケーションの取り方を教えるモチベーション講座という感じだった。メリーウェザーという会社が運営するコースで、４つの参加型のレッスンに分けられていた。参加者は14人、主に僕と同じくらいの年齢で、寸劇を演じたり、チームを作っていろんな問題を解いたり、討論に参加したりしなければならなかった。教わったことのほとんどは一般常識だったけど、いくつか学ぶことがあったと思うし、結構面白かった。

44

　イギリスの人はモチベーションにかなり関心を持っているようだ。この言葉はたびたび出てくるし、あちこちに独創力やモチベーションに関する看板やポスターがある。休憩室のコーヒーメーカーが置いてあるところの壁にまで、成功する人に関する大きなポスターが貼ってあるけど、気に留めている人っているのかな。

　昨夜は米澤支社長代理と出かけて、とても楽しい時間を過ごした。コベント・ガーデンの近くにあるワインバーに連れて行ってもらったのだ。ボトルのメルローを飲みながら、日本語と英語の違いについて話したのだけど、すごく興味深かった。日本語には日常的に決まり文句として使われるフレーズがたくさんあるが、同じフレーズが英語でも使われることはほとんどないのだ。例えば「頑張ります」。たいてい I'll do my best と訳されるけど、これは日本語と同じくらい頻繁には使われないし、日本語と同じ場面でも使われない。帰宅してから、そのように英語では使いにくいフレーズのリストを作り始めた（もちろん、米澤支社長代理の提案でね）。

新渡戸

large poster on being successful ►
成功する人のためのポスターを書いてみよう!

Difference Between Successful People and Unsuccessful People

Successful People	Unsuccessful People
Read every day	Watch TV every day
Compliment others	Criticize others
Embrace change	Fear change
Forgive others	Hold a grudge
Talk about ideas	Spread gossip
Continuously learn	Think they know it all
Accept responsibility	Blame others
Show gratitude	Expect gratitude

Which one are you?

POINT

Read every dayとWatch TV every dayのように、左右の文言の意味がうまく対比するように並べると効果的です。

成功する人と成功しない人の違い

成功する人	成功しない人
毎日読書をする	毎日テレビを見る
他人をほめる	他人を批判する
変化を喜んで受け入れる	変化を恐れる
他人を許す	ねたみを抱く
アイデアについて話す	ゴシップを広める
学び続ける	すべてを知っていると思う
責任を受け入れる	他人を責める
感謝を示す	感謝を期待する

あなたはどちら？

44

クイックQ&A

Q What is the opposite of "compliment" as used here?
（ここでは「ほめる」の反対として何が使われていますか）

POINT

英語にはつづりと発音がとても似ている単語がいくつかあるので、注意が必要です。上のQ&Aにも出てきたcomplimentは、よくcomplementと混同されます。complimentは「〜をほめる」という意味ですが、complementは主にgoes well with「〜とよく合う」という意味です。以下の例を確認しましょう。

・She complimented him on his necktie.（彼女は彼のネクタイをほめた）
・Red wine complements red meat, and white wine complements fish or white meat.（赤ワインは赤身肉によく合い、白ワインは魚や白身肉によく合う）

A Criticize（批判する）

使い方の難しい日本語フレーズの説明を読んでみよう!

Japanese Phrases That Are Difficult to Use

- お先に失礼します ／ お疲れさまでした

  When people are leaving the office, they usually just call out "Good night" or "See you tomorrow." Other people respond to this in the same way with either "Good night" or "See you tomorrow." The phrase [お疲れさまでした] after someone has completed a chore is usually expressed as "Well done" or "Good job."

- いただきます ／ ごちそうさまでした

  There are no fixed phrases for these, although something like "Thank you, that was delicious" can be said after a meal. The phrase [いただきます] when receiving a gift, etc., is covered with a simple "Thank you."

- 行ってきます ／ 行ってらっしゃい

  These phrases are usually expressed with "I'm off now" or "I'll be back later," with the response being "Okay" or "See you later / tomorrow / next week."

- ただいま ／ お帰りなさい

  There is no general equivalent for this when returning to the office, although "I'm back" can be said if necessary. The response is usually just "Okay" or something like that. When returning home, some people call out "I'm home," although not always.

使い方が難しい日本語のフレーズ

- お先に失礼します ／ お疲れさまでした

退社する際は、たいてい単に「おやすみなさい」か「また明日」と声をかけます。言われた人はこれに対して同じように「おやすみなさい」か「また明日」と応えます。仕事を終えた後の「お疲れさまでした」というフレーズは、「よくできました」とか「良い仕事をしましたね」とたいてい表現されます。

- いただきます ／ ごちそうさまでした

食後に「ありがとうございました、おいしかったです」というようなことが言われますが、これには決まったフレーズはありません。プレゼントなどをもらう際の「いただきます」というフレーズは単に「ありがとうございます」で応じられます。

- 行ってきます ／ 行ってらっしゃい

このフレーズはたいてい「今外出します」や「後で戻ってきます」で表され、「わかりました」や「またあとで／明日／来週」で返答されます。

44

- ただいま ／ お帰りなさい

必要であれば「戻りました」と言われますが、会社に戻ってきた際のこれにあたる一般的な同義語はありません。この返事はたいてい、ただ「わかりました」のようなものになります。帰宅した際、いつもではありませんが「ただいま」と呼びかける人もいます。

クイックQ&A

Q > **What phrase is used to praise somebody after they have finished a task?**
（仕事をやり終えた人をほめるのに使われるフレーズは何ですか）

POINT

英語に訳しにくい日本語のもう1つの例が「よろしく（お願いします）」です。多くの日本語の決まり文句と同じように、これも英語では多くの場合ただthank youが代わりに使われますが、状況によっていくつか言葉を付け加えたりもします。例えば、誰かが駅まで車で送ろうかと提案してくれたら、Thank you, that's very helpful.（ありがとうございます、とても助かります）と言うことができます。また、誰かに手伝ってくれないか尋ねて相手が了承してくれたら、Thank you, I really appreciate it.（ありがとうございます、ぜひお願いします）と言うことができます。その他の言い方には、Thank you for your help.（手伝ってくれてありがとう）、That's very nice of you.（ありがたいです）、You are very kind.（優しいですね）などがあります。

A > "Well done" or "Good job".（「よくできました」や「良い仕事をしましたね」）

pleasant evening out with Mr. Yonezawa ► CD 1-27

実際の会話を聞いて話してみよう!

SETTING:

Nitobe and Mr. Yonezawa are sitting in a wine bar discussing the differences between Japanese and English.

Yonezawa: So, how are you enjoying London?

Nitobe: Very much. Everybody has been very friendly.

Yonezawa: Do you think the experience has improved your English?

Nitobe: Yes, definitely. I've picked up many new words. I've also learned a lot about the words and phrases that are not used. I was listening out to discover what people said when they left the office at night, but nobody says anything like [お先に失礼します] and nobody replies with [お疲れさまでした]. All they say is "good night."

Yonezawa: I'm glad you noticed that. Language is based on culture, and different languages place the emphasis on different things. Japanese culture tends to place the emphasis on other people and social status, which is obvious by the large number of pronouns we use depending on the other person's social position in relation to one's own. English, on the other hand, is more self-centered, which is displayed in the fact that the pronoun "you" is sufficient in all situations, no matter whether you are speaking to a two-year-old child or the prime minister. What other differences have you noticed?

Nitobe: Well, nobody says [いただきます] or [ごちそうさまでした] when dining. From what I can gather, there is no fixed way of saying anything like this. People just start eating. The only thing close to it that I heard was after one of the managers took a few of us out for a meal and paid for it. After he had paid, everybody just said "thank you," which I guess is as close to [ごちそうさまでした] as it gets.

Yonezawa: I suggest you keep a list of all the terms that cannot be translated effectively. Listen carefully to what is going on around you, and see if you can discover how phrases such as [行ってきます], [行ってらっしゃい], [ただいま] and [お帰りなさい], etc., are said in English.

Nitobe: A list?

Yonezawa: Yes, a list. After you have listed the rote phrases, maybe you could add other words that are used differently in Japanese and English. [うるさい] and [こだわる], for example. Good luck!

pleasant evening out with Mr. Yonezawa

場面:

> 新渡戸と米澤支社長代理がワインバーで座って、日本語と英語の違いについて話している。

Y： どうだい、ロンドンは楽しんでいるかね。

N： ええ、とても。皆さん、すごく親切にしてくれます。

Y： ここでの体験で英語が上達したと感じるかい？

N： はい、確実に。新しい言葉をたくさん覚えました。それから、使われない単語やフレーズについても多く学びました。夜オフィスを出るときに皆さんが何と言うか気をつけて聞いていたのですが、誰も「お先に失礼します」のようなことは言いませんし、「お疲れさまでした」という返答もありません。みんなgood nightとだけ言っているんです。

Y： それに気づいてくれてうれしいよ。言語は文化に基づいているから、異なる言語は違う物事に重点を置くんだ。日本文化は、自分と比べた相手の社会的地位に応じて使い分ける代名詞の多さから明らかなように、他人や社会的な立場を重視する傾向がある。一方で英語は、youという代名詞を、相手が2歳児でも首相でも関係なく、あらゆる場面で使えるという事実が示しているように、もっと個人を中心としている。他にはどんな違いに気づいたかな？

44

N： そうですね、誰も食事の際に「いただきます」や「ごちそうさまでした」と言いません。僕が見聞きしたことから判断すると、そのようなことを伝える決まった形はないようです。みんな、ただ食べ始めるだけです。1回だけそれに近いことを聞いたのは、部長の1人が僕たち社員の何人かを食事に連れて行ってくれて、そのお代を払ってくれたときです。彼が支払いをした後、皆thank youとだけ言っていたのですが、たぶんこれが最大限「ごちそうさまでした」に近い形だと思います。

Y： そういううまく訳すことのできない言葉すべてのリストを作ることを勧めるよ。周りの会話によく耳を傾けて、「行ってきます」「行ってらっしゃい」「ただいま」「お帰りなさい」などのフレーズが英語でどのように言われているか調べてみるといい。

N： リストですか。

Y： そう、リストだ。決まり文句のリストができたら、日本語と英語で違うように使われている他の言葉を加えてみてもいい。例えば、「うるさい」や「こだわる」とかね。頑張れよ！

キーワードやフレーズをチェック!

☐ **gets to *one*** 　（〜の）気に障る、（〜に）影響を与える

His constant complaining always **gets to me**.
彼の絶え間ない愚痴はいつも私をイライラさせる。

The air-conditioning in the office is set too low in the summer,
and the cold **gets to me** after a while.
夏場はオフィスの空調の設定温度が低すぎるので、しばらくいると寒さが苦痛になってくる。

☐ **run by 〜** 　〜によって経営されて

The company is **run by** a young man with exceptional talent.
その会社は優れた才能を持つ若い男性によって経営されている。

The shop was originally **run by** a private family, but has now been
overtaken by a franchise.
その店はもともと個人経営だったが、今はフランチャイズに取って代わられている。

☐ **divide into 〜** 　〜に分ける

My office is **divided into** five sections with the use of partitions.
私の事務所は仕切りを使って5つのセクションに分けられている。

The report is **divided into** seven chapters, each concentrating on
one main point.
その報告書は7章に分かれていて、1章がそれぞれ1つの論点に焦点を当てている。

☐ **common sense** 　常識

He is a hard worker, but he lacks **common sense**.
彼は努力家だが、常識が欠けている。

Understanding the state of the market is **common sense** for a
day trader.
市場の状況を把握することはデイトレーダーの常識だ。

by rote　　機械的に、そらで

She was obliged to learn the company anthem **by rote**.
彼女は社歌を暗記することを義務付けられた。

Learning the job **by rote** instead of by experience is not recommended.
仕事を経験によってではなく機械的に覚えることはお勧めできない。

level of frequency　　頻度

The system is backed up at a high **level of frequency**.
そのシステムはかなり頻繁にバックアップされている。

The **level of frequency** at which orders are cancelled is increasing.
注文が取り消される頻度が増している。

44

マナーのヒント

　英語で食事の直前に言う決まったフレーズはありませんが、誰かの家に食事に招かれたときに食べ物をほめることはよくあります。その場合、以下のようなフレーズがよく使われます。
・That looks really good.（すごくおいしそうですね）
・That looks absolutely delicious.（本当においしそうです）

食事が終わった後に使うとよいフレーズには以下のようなものがあります。
・Thank you very much. That was delicious.（ありがとうございました。おいしかったです）
・Thank you. You are a very talented cook.（ありがとうございました。料理がとてもお上手なんですね）

DECEMBER 21ST (SATURDAY)

I have a hangover today. The first serious hangover I've had in many years. This can be blamed on last night's Christmas party which was held in the banquet room of a London hotel. I drank a little too much during the party, and I then went off with Stephen Jones and a couple of the managers to an all-night bar, where we drank several bottles of wine. I arrived home by taxi at just after four o'clock this morning, and slept through to midday.

We also had some good news this week, however. **Kenneth Lewis e-mailed me (p.158)** on Wednesday to say that he had passed all of his tests with flying colors and will be returning to work on January 6th. To celebrate his return to health, he decided that he wanted to attend the Christmas party dressed as Santa Clause and hand out gifts to all employees. He asked us to keep his attendance a secret so that he could surprise everybody and announce his recovery. But, he wanted Stephen and I to dress up as elves! The theme of the party was elves, so we wouldn't be out of place, but top management dressing up seemed to lack dignity to me. Until, that is, Stephen put me right. My secretary went out and bought elf costumes for both Stephen and I, and he taught me another **lesson about management (p.162)** while we were trying them on in my office. When I complained, he said that we had to be humble as well as dignified, and that instead of acting like a boss, I should act like a member of the team. In the end, he was right. I may have looked foolish, but I had a wonderful time at the party.

I have a lot to thank Stephen for.

I also started arranging the motivation course for employees. I contacted Glenda Harlow at Merryweather PLC and got her to send me a copy of a **popular course itinerary for companies (p.160)** so I can customize it into something that would be suitable for Tomizawa UK. It looks very promising. I estimate that the courses could probably be run in March. I won't be here to see the results, but I'm sure that Kenneth will keep me informed.

Yonezawa

キーワード＆キーフレーズ→p.164

12月21日（土曜日）

　今日は二日酔いだ。これほどひどい二日酔いになったのは数年ぶりだ。原因は昨夜ロンドンのホテルの宴会場で開かれたクリスマスパーティーだろう。パーティーで少々飲みすぎたのだが、その後スティーブン・ジョーンズと管理職2、3人と終夜営業のバーへ行って一緒にワインをボトル数本飲んだのだ。今朝4時過ぎにタクシーで帰宅し、正午まで寝てしまった。

　だが、今週は良い知らせもあった。水曜日にケネス・ルイスがメールで、見事にすべての検査を通過した、1月6日に仕事に復帰する予定、と伝えてきたのだ。彼は回復の祝いとして、クリスマスパーティーにサンタクロースの衣装で参加して社員全員にプレゼントを配りたいと考えた。皆を驚かせて回復を発表したいから自分の参加は秘密にしておいてくれと頼まれた。しかし、彼はスティーブンと私にエルフの格好をしてほしいとも言ってきたのだ！　パーティーのテーマがエルフなので周囲から浮くことはないだろうが、私には最高幹部が仮装をするというのは威厳に欠けるように思えた。ただ、その考えはスティーブンに正された。私の秘書が外に出てスティーブンと私2人分のエルフのコスチュームを買ってきてくれ、私の部屋で一緒にそれを試着していたとき、彼は私にまた1つ経営術に関する教訓を教えてくれた。不満を漏らす私に彼は、我々は威厳を保つとともに謙虚でなければならない、上司のようにふるまうのではなくチームの一員のようにふるまうべきだと言ったのだ。結局、彼の言う通りだった。間抜けな格好ではあったかもしれないが、私はパーティーで素晴らしい時間を過ごしたのだから。

　スティーブンには感謝しなければならないことがたくさんある。

　私は社員のためのモチベーション講座の手配も進めている。メリーウェザー有限会社のグレンダ・ハーロウに連絡を取り、富沢UKに合った形にカスタマイズするため、企業向けに人気がある講座の日程表のコピーを送ってもらった。このコースには期待できそうだ。私の予測だと、講座を行うことができるようになるのはおそらく3月になる。私はここにいなくて成果を見ることはできないが、きっとケネスが逐次報告してくれるだろう。

米澤

Kenneth Lewis e-mailed me ►

近況を伝えるＥメールを書いてみよう！

From: Kenneth Lewis <KenLewis@tomizawauk.com>
Sent: Wednesday, December 18, 04:14 PM
To: Mr. Yonezawa <yonezawa@tomizawauk.com>
Subject: An update…

Dear Osamu,

Thanks for visiting me last Sunday. It was great seeing you.

I have some good news! I mentioned on Sunday that I had some tests
earlier this week. Well, the doctor said that I recovered enough to return
to work from January, so I intend to be back at the office on the 6th. If you
wouldn't mind staying for an additional week to bring me up to speed on
everything that has been happening, you will be free to return to Tokyo on
the following weekend.

Also, I have decided that I'd like to attend the Christmas party this Friday.
I want to arrive as Santa Claus and hand out the gifts. I'll contact Greta
myself to arrange the details. I will announce my return to work then. But,
keep it a secret! I want it to be a surprise. Also, as the theme of the party
is Santa's Little Helpers, I want you and Stephen to dress up as elves so we
can make our grand entrance together. I hope you don't mind… See you
on Friday!

All the best, Kenneth Lewis

差出人: ケネス・ルイス <KenLewis@tomizawauk.com>
送信: 12月18日（水曜日）午後4:14
宛先: 米澤様<yonezawa@tomizawauk.com>
件名: 近況…

修へ

先週の日曜日は訪ねてくれてありがとう。会えてとてもうれしかったよ。

いい知らせがあります！　今週初めに検査があると日曜日に話しましたね。医師が言うには、1月から仕事に戻れるくらいに回復したそうなので、6日にオフィスに戻るつもりです。もしこれまであった色々なことを教えてもらうためにもう1週間滞在してくれるなら、その翌週末に東京に戻ってもらって構いません。

また、今週金曜日のクリスマスパーティーに参加しようと決めました。サンタクロースの格好で向かってプレゼントを配りたいと思っています。詳細を詰めるためにグレタに連絡してみます。そしてパーティーで仕事復帰を発表したいと思います。でも、秘密でお願いするよ！　サプライズにしたいから。それと、パーティーのテーマがサンタの小さなお手伝いたちなので、一緒に堂々と入っていくためにも修とスティーブンにエルフの格好をしてもらいたいのですが。そうしてくれるとありがたいです…。では金曜日に！

ごきげんよう。
ケネス・ルイス

45

クイックQ&A

Q ＞ **When will Yonezawa be able to return to Tokyo, in January or in February?**
（米澤が東京に戻ることができるのは1月ですか、2月ですか）

POINT

第2段落にあるbring *one* up to speedというフレーズは、「人にある状況について自分と同じくらい理解できるだけの情報を与える」という意味です。ほぼ同じ意味をbriefという動詞1語でも表すことができますが（例:He briefed me on the situation.―彼はその状況についてかいつまんで説明してくれた）、最近はbring *one* up to speedのほうがよく使われます。以下はその用例です。
・The chairman of the board brought the stockholders up to speed at the general meeting. （取締役会議長は株主総会で株主たちに必要な最新情報を伝えました）
・I didn't know about the scandal until Peter brought me up to speed. （ピーターが事情を説明してくれるまで私はそのスキャンダルについて知りませんでした）

A ＞ January（1月）

popular course itinerary for companies ►
ビジネス講座日程表を読んでみよう!

Dear Mr. Yonezawa,

A popular course for companies of your size and nature is listed below.
Each class consists of a maximum of eight participants, and we are able to
either provide several instructors so that all employees can take the course
simultaneously in different classes, or dispatch a single instructor so that the
course can be taken in rotation over the course of a couple of weeks.

Day 01
  AM: Lecture on the importance of communications in teamwork, involving
  several examples of good and bad communications.
  PM: Skits in which participants act out different roles in solving corporate
  problems by issuing instructions to their staff.

Day 02
  FD: Class given an intricate code to decipher. The instructions are written
  in French, hints that require a knowledge of history, geography and politics
  are provided, and mathematical calculations are needed to reach the final
  answer. This will enable each team member to contribute their own expertise.

Day 03
  FD: Debate. Class divided into two teams (pro and con) and given a topic to
  debate. Each team spends the morning discussing the stance they intend to
  take, and the actual debate is held in the afternoon.

Sincerely yours, Glenda Harlow

クイックQ&A

Q 〉 **How many employees can take part in the course if it is held
three times?**
(この講座が3回行われる場合、参加できる社員は何人ですか)

米澤様

御社の規模と性質に合った企業向けの人気講座は下記の通りです。どのクラスも最大8人の参加者から成り、全社員が様々なクラスで同時に講座を受けられるように何人かの講師を準備すること、または2, 3週間の予定で順番に講座が取れるように1人の講師を派遣することが可能です。

1日目

午前：良いコミュニケーションと悪いコミュニケーションのいくつかの事例とともに、チームワークでのコミュニケーションの大切さについて講義。

午後：社員に指示を出すことで社内の問題を解決するという、参加者が様々な役割を演じるスキット。

2日目

終日：解読すべき複雑なコードが与えられる授業。指示はフランス語で書かれており、歴史、地理、政治の知識が必要となるヒントが与えられ、最終的な答えにたどり着くには数学的計算が必要になります。これによって、チームの各人がその専門知識を発揮することを可能にします。

3日目

終日：ディベート。2つのチーム（賛成と反対）に分かれて、ディベートすべきトピックが与えられます。午前中に各チームは自分たちが取ろうとする立場について話し合い、午後に実際のディベートが行われます。

よろしくお願い申し上げます。
グレンダ・ハーロウ

45

POINT

Day 03にあるproとconは「賛成」と「反対」という意味のラテン語です。ここでは参加者が「賛成」と「反対」の2つのチームに分けられていますが、proとconは、以下のように物事の「利点」と「欠点」という意味でもよく使われます。

・My manager explained the pros and cons of the system to me.（私の上司は私にそのシステムの長所と短所を説明してくれました）

・Allowing employees to work from home has more pros than cons.（社員が家で仕事をできるようにすることは害より利益が大きいです）

（24A）24 〉A

実際の会話を聞いて話してみよう!

SETTING:

> Yonezawa and Jones are trying on elf costumes in Yonezawa's office.

Yonezawa: I can't believe that we're doing this. Green tights and floppy red hats? We're going to look really foolish.

Jones: I shouldn't worry about that, Osamu. It's a costume party! Everybody will be looking foolish.

Yonezawa: But, isn't this a little beneath us? Surely it's important for management figures to maintain their dignity in front of the staff.

Jones: Dignity isn't the only thing that is important for management. We must also show humility. Remember that we are not kings or emperors. We are simply members of a team of company employees. I agree that we must maintain our dignity in business situations, but this is a once-in-a-year event where everybody is allowed to let off steam. I can assure you, dressing up and making a fool of yourself together with the rest of the team will earn you more respect than if you arrive in your business suit and look down on everyone as if you were watching children at play.

Yonezawa: Looking foolish to earn respect? That's a strange concept.

Jones: You are concentrating too much on your own pride. When the rest of the staff sees you dressed up like that, they will not see a man being foolish, they will see a member of the team joining in the fun. They'll think you're cool! I promise!

Yonezawa: Cool? In green tights?

Jones: Yes, in green tights. Think back to when you were young. If there was an office party, would you prefer to see your boss standing proudly in his business suit while you were acting like a fool? Or, would you rather he joined in and placed himself on the same level as everybody else?

Yonezawa: Well, yes, okay. I suppose you have a point.

Jones: Throw away your pride, Osamu. Forget you are the boss for one night. Just be a normal human being and have fun with the rest of the team.

Yonezawa: You're right! I will. Anyway, how do I look in my new costume?

Jones: Absolutely ridiculous!

lesson about management

場面:

> 米澤とジョーンズが米澤の部屋でエルフのコスチュームを試着している。

Y： こんなことをやるなんて信じられないよ！　緑のタイツに赤いへなへなした帽子だぞ。ひどく間抜けに見えるに決まっている。

J： 気にすることはないさ、修。これは仮装パーティーなんだ！　皆が間抜けな格好をするんだから。

Y： だが、これは私たちがやるようなことではないんじゃないか。経営陣の人間が社員の前で威厳を保つことは重要だろう。

J： 経営者にとって重要なのは何も威厳だけじゃない。謙虚さも見せなければいけないんだ。私たちは王様でも皇帝でもないことを忘れちゃいけない。単に会社の従業員というチームのメンバーだ。ビジネスの場では威厳を保たなければならないことには同意するが、これは皆が羽を伸ばすことができる年に1度のイベントだよ。保証しよう、仮装してチームのみんなと一緒にばかをやるほうが、スーツで行って子どもの遊びを眺めるように皆を見下ろすより尊敬を得られる。

45

Y： 間抜けな格好をして尊敬を得る？　変わった発想だね。

J： 修は自分のプライドを重視しすぎているんだよ。他の社員がその格好を見たら、ばかげたことをやっているとは思わず、チームの一員が楽しみに加わりに来たととらえるはずさ。皆、修のことをかっこいいと思うよ！　保証する！

Y： かっこいい？　緑のタイツをはいて？

J： ああ、緑のタイツをはいて、だ。自分の若い頃のことを考えてみてほしい。会社でパーティーが開かれたとして、自分がばかをやっている間上司はスーツを着て堂々と立っているのと、彼が他の皆の仲間に入って同じレベルのことをやっているのと、どちらのほうがいい？

Y： ふむ、ああ、わかったよ。君の言うことも一理あるかもしれない。

J： プライドなんて投げ捨ててしまえ、修。一晩だけ自分が上司だということを忘れるんだ。ただの人間になってチームの他のみんなと楽しめばいい。

Y： そうだな！　そうするよ。ところで、新しい衣装は似合っているかい？

J： ああ、最高におかしな格好だ！

KEY WORDS & PHRASES

CD
1-30

キーワードやフレーズをチェック!

☐ **can be blamed on ～**　　～に責任がある（といえる）

The current recession **can be blamed on** a lack of growth in global markets.
現在の不況は世界市場の低成長に一因がある。

The company's financial troubles **can be blamed on** bad sales in the summer.
その会社の経営難は夏の販売不振に原因がある。

☐ **with flying colors**　　意気揚々と

She passed the examination **with flying colors**.
彼女は試験に楽勝で合格した。

He reached his sales target **with flying colors**.
彼は売上目標を見事に達成した。

☐ **hand out ～**　　～を配る

The company regularly **hands out** packs of tissues containing ads at the station.
その会社はしょっちゅう駅で広告が入ったポケットティッシュを配っている。

The seminar program was **handed out** at the door.
そのセミナーのカリキュラムがドアの前で配られた。

☐ **put _one_ right**　　（人を）正す

Judy mistakenly thought the meeting was to start at 11 a.m., so I **put her right**.
ジュディーは会議が午前11時に始まる予定だと間違えていたので、私が訂正した。

I was convinced that the advertising campaign would be ineffective until soaring sales **put me right**.
私はその広告キャンペーンに効果はないと思い込んでいたが、売上がうなぎ上りになったため考えを改めることとなった。

look promising 　期待できそうだ、有望と思われる

Sales for the new lineup **look promising**.
新しいラインナップの売上は期待できそうだ。

The new employee in the marketing department **looks promising**.
マーケティング部のあの新入社員は将来有望だ。

keep *one* informed 　（人に）逐次報告する

I would appreciate it if you would **keep me informed** of the situation.
その状況について逐次報告してくださるとありがたいです。

I asked her secretary to **keep me informed** of any changes to the schedule.
私は彼女の秘書にスケジュールの変更を逐次伝えてほしいと頼んだ。

45

マナーのヒント

　キリスト教圏の多くの国のクリスマスパーティーは日本の忘年会と同じように行われます。家族や友人で行うプライベートなものの他に、多くの会社も社員のためにパーティーを開きます。これは会社の規模によって、全社員が参加する大きなパーティーであったり、部、課、グループで開かれる小規模なパーティーであったりします。クリスマスプレゼントを交換することもありますが、たいていは計画的に行うイベントなので、事前に予算はいくらかなどが伝えられます。それを基に各参加者が決まった金額内でちょっとしたプレゼントを買うのですが、これには実用的な品物よりも、笑えるジョークの書いてあるマグカップや派手なソックスのような面白グッズを買うのが一般的です。クリスマス柄の包装紙でプレゼントを包むのも忘れずに。

DECEMBER 25TH (WEDNESDAY)

It's Christmas day and I am writing this on the airplane back to Tokyo. I can't believe that my time in London is over already. Three weeks passed far too quickly. I had a very emotional farewell when I left the office for the last time yesterday evening. I made many friends in just a few weeks, so I felt very sad when saying goodbye to them all. My flight left London on time, and we have been in the air for nearly one hour. Surprisingly, I was able to understand nearly all of the **inflight announcements (p.170)** without any trouble. I guess that means that my English has really improved over the past eight months.

The office Christmas party last Friday was amazing fun. It had a buffet-style meal, a free bar, party games, a DJ and dancing. Most people were dressed up as elves, which was sort of crazy. I bought a cheap elf costume from a novelty shop, but it made me look silly (luckily, everybody else looked silly, too ☺). The highlight of the evening was when the president, Mr. Lewis, arrived unexpectedly wearing a Santa Claus outfit and started handing out gifts to everyone. He was helped by Mr. Yonezawa and Mr. Jones, the managing director, who were both dressed up as elves. Mr. Lewis also gave a short speech and announced that he would be returning to work in January, so I suppose that means Mr. Yonezawa will be returning to Tokyo.

I have been trying to write a **thank-you e-mail (p.168)** to everybody in London on my laptop, but I keep getting **interrupted by the man sitting next to me (p.172)**. He is a young British guy, probably in his late teens or early twenties, who is going to Japan for the first time. Apparently, he has a Japanese pen-friend who he has been in contact with for several years, and they are going to spend a few weeks together traveling around Japan. He will be staying with his pen-friend's family over the New Year period, and he is a little nervous about what to expect.

Speaking of the New Year period, I will be spending the holiday with my parents eating, drinking and watching the TV. I'm looking forward to it.

Nitobe

キーワード＆キーフレーズ→p.174

１２月２５日（水曜日）

　今日はクリスマスで、僕は東京へ帰る飛行機の中でこれを書いている。ロンドン滞在がもう終ったなんて、信じられない。3週間はあっという間に過ぎてしまった。昨日の夕方、最後にオフィスを出るときに、皆と感極まりながら別れの挨拶をした。ほんの数週間でたくさんの友達ができたので、全員にお別れを言うのはすごくさみしかった。僕の搭乗便は時間通りにロンドンを出発し、もう1時間近く飛行している。驚いたことに、ほとんどすべての機内アナウンスを苦もなく理解できた。僕の英語力はこの8か月でずいぶん上がったということなんだろうな。

　金曜日の社内クリスマスパーティーはものすごく楽しかった。ビュッフェ形式の食事や無料のバー、パーティーゲームがあり、DJがいてダンスも行われた。ほとんどの人がエルフに仮装していて、少しおかしかった。ノベルティショップで安いエルフのコスチュームを買ったのだけど、それを着た僕は変な格好だった（幸い、他のみんなも変な格好だったけどね ☺）。その夜の山場はルイス支社長がサンタクロースの衣装を着てサプライズで登場して、みんなにプレゼントを配り始めたときだった。彼のことを米澤支社長代理とジョーンズ取締役が手伝っていて、彼らは2人ともエルフに扮していた。また、ルイス支社長が短いスピーチをして1月に仕事に復帰すると発表したので、そのときに米澤支社長代理は東京に戻ってくるということなのだろう。

　僕はさっきからノートパソコンでロンドンのみんなにお礼メールを書こうとしているのだけど、隣に座っている男性にちょくちょく邪魔をされている。彼は若いイギリス人で、たぶん10代後半か20代前半だと思うが、初めて日本へ行くという。どうやら数年間やり取りしている日本人のペンフレンドがいるらしく、一緒に何週間か日本のあちこちを旅行する予定なのだそうだ。彼はそのペンフレンドの家族のところで年末年始を過ごす予定で、どうするものなのかわからなくて少し不安がっている。

　年末年始と言えば、僕は休みを両親と食べたり飲んだりテレビを見たりしながら過ごすつもりだ。楽しみだなー。

新渡戸

167

thank-you e-mail ►

感謝を伝えるEメールを書いてみよう!

From: Shinnosuke Nitobe <snitobe@tomizawais.co.jp>
Sent: Wednesday, December 25, 09:03 PM
To: Clifford Connolly <CConnolly@tomizawauk.com>
Subject: Thanks for everything…!

Hi Cliff,

I'm writing this on my flight back to Tokyo. It's a message for everyone, so would you mind passing it around the office for me? Thanks…!

I would like to thank you all for everything you did for me during my brief stay in London. I had a wonderful time, and I learned much while I was there. The warm friendship you showed me was especially moving, and I will never forget any of you. I would also like to say thank you for inviting me to your Christmas party. I had a great time, and even received a gift. I hope you have all recovered from your hangovers by now (although I doubt it for some of you… :-).

I am using my Tokyo e-mail address here, so please keep in touch if you have time. Happy New Year to you all…!

Thanks again, Shinnosuke "Shin-chan" Nitobe

POINT

感謝の気持ちを伝える定型表現 (I would like to thank you (all) for everything you did for me など) を覚えましょう。

差出人：新渡戸慎之助 <snitobe@tomizawais.co.jp>
送信：12月25日（水曜日）午後9:03
宛先：クリフォード・コノリー<CConnolly@tomizawauk.com>
件名：いろいろありがとうございました…！

クリフさん

東京へ帰る飛行機の中でこれを書いています。皆さまへのメッセージですので、オフィスでこれを回覧していただいてもかまいませんか。よろしくです…！

ロンドンでの短い滞在中に皆さまがしてくださったことすべてに感謝申し上げたいと思います。素晴らしい時間を過ごし、そちらではたくさんのことを学びました。皆さまの温かい友情には特に感動し、僕は皆さまのことを決して忘れることはないでしょう。またクリスマスパーティーにご招待いただいたことも感謝しています。とても楽しく過ごし、プレゼントまでいただいてしまいました。皆さんが今頃には二日酔いから回復していることを祈っています（何人かは怪しいと思いますが…^^）。

こちらでは東京のEメールアドレスを使いますので、お時間があれば連絡を取り合いましょう。皆さま、どうぞ良いお年を…！

本当にありがとうございました。
慎ちゃんこと新渡戸慎之助

46

クイックQ＆A

Q At what function did Nitobe receive a gift?
（新渡戸は何の会でプレゼントをもらいましたか）

POINT

第3段落にあるkeep in touchは、自分と接触を持ち続けてほしいと言うとき、その接触が口頭と文章の両方の場合に使われますが、文章によるコミュニケーションのみに使われる同じ意味の慣用句が他に2つあります。1つはdrop me a lineで、もう1つはput pen to paperです。以下はその例です。
・Drop me a line when you have time.（お時間のあるときに連絡ください）
・If you ever need anything, drop me a line.（何かあったら連絡してください）
・Don't forget to put pen to paper.（忘れずにお手紙くださいね）
・I'll put pen to paper when I have more news.（もっと知らせたいことができたら手紙を書きます）

A The Christmas party（クリスマスパーティー）

機内アナウンスを読んでみよう！

Inflight Announcement

Ladies and gentlemen, the Captain has turned off the seat belt sign, and you may now move around the cabin. However, we recommend that you keep your seat belt fastened while seated.

In a few moments, the flight attendants will be passing around the cabin to offer you hot or cold drinks. Alcoholic drinks are also available with our compliments. Dinner will be served in about one hour. A selection of music and video entertainment is available on the entertainment consoles built into your seats. See page 14 of the *Sky Cruising* magazine located in the pocket of the seat in front of you for instructions on operating the console. Also, we have a selection of duty-free items that you may purchase at your seat. The items available are listed from page 52 of the *Sky Cruising* magazine. Please contact a flight attendant if you wish to make a purchase.

In the meantime, please sit back, relax, and enjoy the flight. Thank you.

POINT

相手に向けた丁寧さを出す助動詞mayの使い方に注目。「〜することをお願いします」の意味合いで、we recommend that 〜を使うことにも注目しましょう。

機内アナウンス

皆さま、機長がシートベルトサインを消しましたので、機内を移動していただいてもかまいません。しかしながら、ご着席の間はシートベルトを締めていただくようお願いしております。

間もなく乗務員が機内を回り、温かいお飲物か冷たいお飲物をお出しいたします。アルコール飲料も無料で提供しております。夕食はおよそ1時間後にお出しいたします。音楽やビデオの数々は、お座席に内蔵された機内エンターテイメント画面でお楽しみいただけます。画面の操作方法については、前座席のポケットにある雑誌『スカイ・クルージング』の14ページをご覧ください。また、お座席で購入できる免税品のセレクションもございます。購入可能な商品は、雑誌『スカイ・クルージング』の52ページに記載されております。購入ご希望の方は乗務員までお知らせください。

ではごゆっくり、おくつろぎになってフライトをお楽しみください。ありがとうございました。

クイックQ&A

46

Q > **Who must be contacted if a passenger wishes to buy duty-free perfume?**
（乗客が免税の香水を購入したいときに声をかけなければならないのは誰ですか）

POINT

最終文にあるin the meantimeは、別のことが起こっているときに「待っている間」と伝える便利なフレーズです。meantimeの長さに時間制限はないので、その場の状況にも長い期間にも使えます。以下はその例です。

その場の状況：
- I'll be with you in about ten minutes. In the meantime, help yourself to coffee.（10分ほどでそっちに着くよ。それまでコーヒーでも飲んで待っていてくれ）
- He's still on the phone, so I'll go outside for a cigarette in the meantime.（彼はまだ電話中なので、私はその間外に出て一服しよう）

長い期間：
- His ambition is to study medicine, but in the meantime, he is working hard to save up for college.（彼の夢は医学を学ぶことだが、当面は頑張って働いて大学のためにお金を貯めている）
- I hope to see flying cars in the future, but I'll just keep driving on the road in the meantime.（将来空を飛ぶ車が登場することを期待しているが、そうなるまでは普通に道路を運転することにしよう）

A > A flight attendant（客室乗務員）

171

interrupted by the man sitting next to me　►

実際の会話を聞いて話してみよう!

SETTING:

> Nitobe is sitting next to a young Englishman named Gary Sanders who will be visiting Japan for the first time. The two start up a conversation.

Sanders: Have you been in England on holiday?

Nitobe: No, business. A study course, actually. I arrived at the beginning of December.

Sanders: Was it your first visit to London?

Nitobe: Yes. I really enjoyed it. What about you?

Sanders: I'll be staying in Japan for a few weeks traveling around with a friend. My name's Gary, by the way. Gary Sanders.

Nitobe: Nice to meet you. My name is Shinnosuke Nitobe. Why are you traveling on Christmas day? You're missing all the fun.

Sanders: I left it too late to book a ticket. Today was the only flight I could get. My friend said that New Year is a big holiday in Japan, so I'll enjoy that instead.

Nitobe: Where will you be staying?

Sanders: I'll spend New Year at my friend's house in Nagano, but after that we'll be backpacking around for about a week. I'm a bit worried about New Year, though. I've never actually met my friend. We've been pen-friends for a couple of years, but this will be the first time we've ever met up. He lives with his parents, and I don't really know the customs. I hope I don't offend anyone.

Nitobe: I don't think you need to worry. As long as you take your shoes off at the door and eat whatever is served, you'll be fine.

Sanders: How is New Year celebrated? Do you exchange gifts like we do at Christmas?

Nitobe: No, nothing like that. Usually we visit a shrine at midnight on the 31st to ring in the New Year. People mostly just sit around eating, drinking and watching TV on New Year's Day.

Sanders: Really? Well, I can do that with no problem. Thanks. You've set my mind at rest.

interrupted by the man sitting next to me

場面:

> 新渡戸がゲイリー・サンダースという、これから日本を初めて訪れる若いイギリス人男性の隣に座っている。2人は会話を始める。

S： 休暇でイギリスに来ていたんですか。

N： いえ、仕事で。正確には研修です。12月上旬から来ていました。

S： ロンドンへは初めての訪問だったんですか。

N： はい。とても楽しかったですよ。そちらはどうなんですか。

S： 僕は何週間か日本に滞在して友達とあちこち旅行する計画なんです。ところで、僕はゲイリー、ゲイリー・サンダースです。

N： 初めまして。僕は新渡戸慎之助といいます。なぜクリスマスの日にこうして移動しているんですか。せっかくの楽しみを逃してしまうのでは。

S： チケットの予約を後回しにしすぎたんです。乗れる便が今日しかなくって。友達が日本の正月は盛大に祝われる祝日だと言っていたので、代わりにそっちを楽しむことにしますよ。

N： どこに泊まる予定なんですか。

S： 正月は長野にある友達の家で過ごすつもりですが、そのあとは一緒に1週間くらいバックパック1つであちこち回ります。ただ、正月のことが少し心配なんです。友達に実際に会ったことはないんですよ。2年ほどペンフレンドを続けていたんですが、顔を合わせるのはこれが初めてになります。彼は両親と一緒に住んでいるんですが、僕は日本の習慣をよく知らないので、誰にも失礼なことをしないといいのですが。

N： 心配する必要はないと思いますよ。玄関で靴を脱いで、あとは出されたものを何でも食べれば、大丈夫でしょう。

S： 正月はどうやって祝われるのですか。イギリスでクリスマスにやるようにプレゼントの交換をしたりするんでしょうか。

N： いえ、そういうことは何も。普通は、31日の真夜中に神社にお参りして新年を迎えます。元日にはみんな主にただ食べたり飲んだりテレビを見ていますよ。

S： そうなんですか。うん、それなら簡単にできます。ありがとうございます。おかげで安心できました。

46

CD 2-02

キーワードやフレーズをチェック！

☐ far too　あまりに

I was asked to help a colleague with his work, but I am **far too** busy.
私は同僚の仕事を手伝ってやるように頼まれたが、忙しすぎて無理だ。

She needed to move the copy machine, but it was **far too** heavy for her to move alone.
彼女はコピー機を動かさなければならなかったが、それは彼女が1人で動かすには重すぎた。

☐ in the air　飛行機に乗って

This time next week, he will be **in the air** on his way to a meeting in Brussels.
来週の今頃、彼はブリュッセルでの会議に向かうため飛行機に乗っているだろう。

We were **in the air** for only thirty minutes, but they still served drinks.
私たちの乗る飛行機が飛んでいたのはほんの30分だったが、それでも機内で飲み物が出された。

☐ dress up　盛装する

The president **dressed up** in his best suit for the TV interview.
社長はテレビインタビューのために自分の一番上等なスーツを着込んだ。

Most employees **dress up** in the company uniform after arriving at the office.
ほとんどの社員はオフィスに着いてから会社の制服に着替える。

☐ sort of　多少、やや

The meeting was informative, but it was also **sort of** boring.
その会議は有益なものだったが、やや退屈でもあった。

We have warm-up exercises before we start work, which is **sort of** old-fashioned nowadays.
うちの会社では仕事を始める前に体操をするが、これは今どき少し時代遅れだ。

arrive unexpectedly   思いがけずに来る

The client **arrived unexpectedly** at the office to deliver his complaint in person.
その顧客は直接苦情を言うためにいきなりオフィスに来た。

The president **arrived unexpectedly** halfway through the meeting.
思いがけず社長が会議の途中で入ってきた。

keep getting   [動詞の過去分詞を伴って]〜され続ける

I've been trying to contact Mr. Peters, but I **keep getting** directed to an answering machine.
先ほどからピータース氏と連絡を取ろうとしているが、留守番電話にばかりつながる。

We have introduced many new sales strategies, but we **keep getting** beaten by rival companies.
我々は多くの新しい販売戦略を導入してきたが、ライバル会社に負け続けている。

マナーのヒント

46

日本の伝統的な風習を説明するときは、日本語の呼び名に簡潔な説明を添えるのが便利す。新年の風習を使って、その例のいくつかを紹介します。

- *Toshikoshi-soba* is a bowl of buckwheat noodles eaten on New Year's Eve. The long, thin noodles are said to represent a long and healthy life.（「年越しそば」とは、大晦日に食べる一杯のそばのことです。その細長い麺は長く健康な一生を表すと言われています）
- *Hatsumode* is the first visit to a shrine or temple during the New Year period to pray for health and good fortune for the coming year.（「初詣」とは、正月に神社や寺にその年最初のお参りをし、一年の健康と幸運を祈ることです）
- *Osechi ryori* are a series of traditional Japanese foods that are eaten at the beginning of the New Year. Each item of food represents a specific wish for the coming year.（「おせち料理」とは、新年に食べる日本の伝統料理のセットのことです。料理の一品一品が新たな年への特定の願いを表しています）
- *Otoshidama* is a tradition in which children are given cash by their parents, grandparents, close relatives and sometimes adult friends in small envelopes.（「お年玉」とは、子どもが両親、祖父母、近い親戚や、時には大人の友達から小さな封筒に入ったお金をもらう慣習のことです）

DECEMBER 31ST (TUESDAY)

It's getting close to midnight on the final day of the year, and here am I sitting all alone in my flat enjoying a bottle of wine after having just eaten a bowl of soba noodles that I purchased from one of the Japanese shops in London. **I spoke to my wife (p.182)** on a conference call from my laptop a little while ago. My daughter and her family are staying at my home over the New Year period, so I got a chance to see my granddaughter, Hikari, for the first time in half a year. She reached her first birthday at the end of November and is now walking, and it was delightful to see her.

I'll soon be seeing her in the flesh, however. Pauline Foster in the General Affairs Department has already made all of the **arrangements for my return (p.178)** to Japan. My flight is booked for January 10th, and I'll arrive the following day, which is a Saturday. My daughter promised to visit with her daughter on my day of return. I must say, I am looking forward to that very much.

But, in the meantime, I am celebrating the New Year alone, and I am ashamed to say I feel rather lonely. I didn't really expect to feel lonely, but I guess it is a touch of homesickness after seeing my family enjoying the year-end shows on TV. I switched on the TV here a little while ago, but all I could find were dramas, B-movies and documentaries, so I switched it off and put on some classical music instead. The New Year is celebrated in England, but mostly by going out to parties, and it is not a family affair. I suppose that is understandable, considering how soon it comes after Christmas, which is the big family affair of the year. I heard, however, that it is celebrated in Scotland. The Japanese word *omisoka* is **Hogmanay (p.180)** in Scottish, and the revelries start on New Year's Eve and continue for several days.

I suppose the past year was a good one for me. I learned a lot, and met many interesting people. I also got the chance to experience life in the United Kingdom, which was very rewarding. Hopefully next year will also be a good one, not only for me, but also my family and all employees of Tomizawa Integrated Solutions.

Yonezawa

キーワード＆キーフレーズ→p.184

１２月３１日（火曜日）

　今は今年最後の日の真夜中近くだ。私はこうして自分のアパートで1人きり、ロンドンにある日本食の店の1つで買ったそばを1杯食べてからボトルのワインを楽しんでいる。つい先ほど、ノートパソコンからビデオ通話で妻と話した。娘とその家族が年末年始を私の家で過ごしているので、半年ぶりに孫の光の顔を見ることができた。光は11月の末に1歳の誕生日を迎えて今は歩き始めており、あの子の姿を見られたのはうれしかった。

　しかし、まもなく孫に直接会えるだろう。総務部のポーリーン・フォスターがすでに私の日本への帰国のための手配をすべて済ませてくれた。私のフライトは1月10日に予約されていて、翌日の土曜日に到着することになっている。娘が私の帰ってくる日に子どもと一緒に家を訪ねると約束してくれた。これは本当に楽しみだ。

　だが、今のところ、私は1人で新年を祝っており、恥ずかしい話だが少しさびしさを感じている。さびしいと思うなんて少々予想外だったが、家族がテレビで年末の番組を楽しんでいるのを見て軽いホームシックになったのだろう。さっきここでもテレビをつけてみたが、ドラマやB級映画、ドキュメンタリー番組しかやっていなかったので、スイッチを切って代わりにクラシック音楽を流している。イギリスでも新年は祝うが、たいていはパーティーに出かけたりするもので、家庭で何かするということはない。1年のうちで大きな家族のイベントであるクリスマスのすぐ後であることを考えると、それも当然だろう。ただ、スコットランドでは新年が祝われていると聞いたことがある。日本語の「大晦日」はスコットランドの言葉ではホグマネイで、そのお祭り騒ぎは大晦日に始まり数日続く。

47

　今年は私にとって良い年であったと思う。たくさんのことを学んだし、面白い人物にも多く出会った。イギリスでの生活を体験する機会も得られ、その価値は非常に大きかった。来年も、私だけではなく、私の家族や富沢インテグレーテッド・ソリューションズの全社員にとって良い年となることを願う。

米澤

帰国手配を報告する文書を書いてみよう!

ATTN: Mr. Yonezawa
From: Pauline Foster (GA Dept.)
Date: December 27

Re: Arrangements for your return to Tokyo

Dear. Mr. Yonezawa,

I have arranged the following schedule for your return to Tokyo. I'll let you
have the air ticket at the beginning of next year. Please contact me if you have
any questions.

- A van from the shipping company will arrive at your flat at 2 p.m. on January
  9th to collect the items you wish to send to Japan by air cargo (these will be
  delivered directly to your home address).
- A limousine will pick you up at your flat at 05:30 on January 10th and take
  you to Heathrow Airport (don't bother cleaning the flat. I'll arrange for that
  after you have left).
- You are booked onto flight XX4608 departing London Heathrow at 09:35 on
  January 10th to Haneda Airport, arriving at 05:25 on January 11th (business
  class).

Thank you, Pauline Foster

POINT

出発までの流れを時系列に、箇条書きにして、わかりやすく伝えましょう。

宛先: 米澤様
差出人: ポーリーン・フォスター（総務部）
日付: 12月27日

Re: 東京へのご帰国の手配

米澤様

東京へお戻りになる下記のスケジュールを調整しました。来年初めに航空券をお渡しします。ご質問があればご連絡ください。

- 運送会社からのバンが1月9日午後2時に米澤さんのアパートに到着し、航空貨物で日本にご送付希望のお荷物を集配します（こちらは直接ご自宅の住所までお届けします）。
- リムジンが1月10日5時30分に米澤さんのアパートにお迎えに行き、ヒースロー空港までお送りします（アパートの掃除はしていただく必要はありません。ご出発後に私が手配いたします）。
- 1月10日9時35分にロンドン・ヒースロー空港発、1月11日5時25分に羽田空港着のXX4608便（ビジネスクラス）を予約いたしました。

よろしくお願いいたします。
ポーリーン・フォスター

47

クイックQ＆A

Q Who will arrange for Yonezawa's flat to be cleaned?
（米澤のアパートの掃除を手配するのは誰ですか）

POINT

第2段落にあるdon't botherは2つの異なる状況で使うことができます。1つは「気にしないでいい」という意味で、「わざわざ〜しなくてもいいですよ」と伝える丁寧な言い方です。ここではこの意味で使われています。以下はその他の用例です。
・Don't bother replacing the ink in the printer. I'll do that later. （わざわざプリンターのインクを交換しなくていいよ。私が後でやっておくから）
・Don't bother calling Mary. She is out all day. （メアリーを呼んでも無駄だ。彼女は終日外出だよ）

don't botherのもう1つの意味は「〜の邪魔をしない」あるいは「〜に面倒をかけない」です。こちらは以下のように使われます。
・Your father is busy, so don't bother him. （お父さんは忙しいんだから、邪魔をしてはダメ）
・Don't bother the teacher with stupid questions! （くだらない質問で先生に面倒をかけるな!）

A Pauline Foster（ポーリーン・フォスター）

Hogmanay ►

ホグマネイの紹介文を読んでみよう！

Hogmanay

Hogmanay is the Scottish word for the last day of the year, but it is a celebration that continues up until January 2nd. Traditionally, Hogmanay is the largest holiday of the year in Scotland, but one of the reasons for this is that the Protestant Church banned Christmas in the nation for 400 years from the end of the 17th century through to the 1950s owing to it being considered a symbol of Catholic extravagance. If the same ban had been enforced in England, there is a possibility that the Hogmanay celebrations would be more popular than Christmas there as well.

It is thought that the origins of Hogmanay were introduced into Scotland by the Vikings in the 8th or 9th centuries, although details on this are few and far between. Hogmanay involves several traditions. The most important among these are that house cleaning, including taking the ashes from the fireplace outside, must be completed before midnight on December 31st, and that all debts must be cleared before the church bells ring in the New Year. Once the clock ticks past midnight and the New Year arrives, it is then important that a male visitor is the first person to step over the threshold into the house. Traditionally, this first visitor must bring a gift of coal, shortbread, salt, black buns or whisky.

Nowadays, however, Hogmanay is mostly about drinking and having fun with family and friends. It is an enormous party that often spills out into the streets to be shared with neighbors, and it is an integral part of Scottish culture.

ホグマネイ

ホグマネイはその年の最後の日を表すスコットランドの言葉ですが、それは1月2日まで続くお祝いです。伝統的にホグマネイはスコットランドで1年のうちの最大の祝日ですが、この理由の1つはプロテスタント教会が17世紀末から1950年代までの400年間、クリスマスがカトリックのぜいたくの象徴と思われたために、同国でのクリスマスを禁じていたことです。同様の禁止がイングランドで施行されていたら、ホグマネイのお祝いはそこでもクリスマスより人気になっていたかもしれません。

ホグマネイの起源は8世紀か9世紀にバイキングによってスコットランドにもたらされたと考えられていますが、これについての詳しいことはほとんどわかっていません。ホグマネイにはいくつかの伝統があります。中でも最も重要な伝統は、暖炉の灰を取り除くなどの家の掃除が12月31日の真夜中までに完了していなければならないことと、新年に教会の鐘が鳴る前にすべての借金が清算されていなければならないということです。時計が真夜中過ぎを刻み、新年になったら、家の敷居をまたぐ最初の人は男性客であることが大切です。伝統的に、この最初の訪問客は石炭、ショートブレッド、塩、黒パンまたはウィスキーのプレゼントを持ってこなければなりません。

しかし今日、ホグマネイとは主に家族や友達と飲んで楽しむことになっています。隣近所の人々でしばしば通りがあふれかえるほど大きなパーティーで、スコットランド文化になくてはなりません。

47

クイックQ&A

Q Who must be invited into the house on January 1st?
（1月1日に家に招かれなければならないのは誰ですか）

POINT

第2段落にあるfew and far betweenは「とても少ない、とても珍しい」という意味の慣用句です。以下はその用例です。
・Sunny days are few and far between this year. (今年は晴れの日がたまにしかない)
・Happy endings are few and far between in real life. (現実にハッピーエンドはとてもまれだ)
・She lives in a district where cheap rents are few and far between. (彼女は安い賃貸物件がとても少ない地区に住んでいる)
・The current labor shortage means that experienced workers are few and far between. (現在の労働力不足は経験豊かな人材が希少なことを意味している)

A A male visitor (男性の訪問人)

I spoke to my wife ►

実際の会話を聞いて話してみよう!

SETTING:

> Yonezawa is speaking to his wife via a video conference call on his laptop
> computer.

Yonezawa: Hikari has grown so much. She was still a baby the last time I saw her, but now she is a little girl. I can't wait to see her in the flesh.

Wife: Yes, she is growing up fast. She is a good girl, though. She has a good temperament, and sleeps through the night without waking up.

Yonezawa: I bet you are enjoying having her stay. What are you all doing now?

Wife: It's eight-thirty in the morning here, so everybody is waiting for breakfast and watching TV.

Yonezawa: Did you visit the shrine at midnight last night?

Wife: No, not this year. Hikari is still too young. We'll probably go this afternoon instead. What will you do to celebrate?

Yonezawa: Just listen to music and drink a glass or two of wine.

Wife: You do that every night.

Yonezawa: Ha, ha, ha… Yes, I suppose I do. There's very little New Year atmosphere here. Tomorrow is a national holiday, but everybody will be back to work on the 2nd. One of the Japanese managers invited me to spend New Year at his place, but I didn't want to intrude on his family on a special occasion, so refused. I think he was relieved.

Wife: Well, just another two weeks to go. You'll be back on the 11th, right?

Yonezawa: Yes, I should be home by about 8 a.m. I'll call you from the airport.

Wife: Aiko said she'll bring Hikari over on that day, so you'll see her then.

Yonezawa: That's great news! I'll make sure I get her a nice gift from London.

Wife: Don't forget my gift!

Yonezawa: What do you want?

Wife: Anything, as long as it's expensive.

Yonezawa: Hah! I'll see what I can do. Anyway, I'll call you again tomorrow. Have a good New Year!

Wife: You too!

I spoke to my wife

場面：

> 米澤が自分のノートパソコンでビデオ通話を通して妻と話している。

Ｙ：光はずいぶん大きくなったなあ。前に会ったときにはまだ赤ん坊だったのに、今では小さな女の子だ。直接会うのが待ちきれないよ。

Ｗ：ええ、あの子はすくすくと成長しているわ。それにすごくいい子なのよ。穏やかな性格だし、夜は途中で起きずにぐっすり眠っているわ。

Ｙ：あの子が泊まりに来て楽しそうだな。みんな今は何をしているんだ？

Ｗ：今こっちは朝の8時30分だから、みんな朝ごはんを待ちながらテレビを見ているわ。

Ｙ：昨日の真夜中は神社にお参りしたのかな？

Ｗ：いいえ、今年は行かなかったわ。光がまだ小さすぎるから。たぶん今日の午後に行くことになるわ。あなたは何をしてお祝いするの？

Ｙ：音楽を聴きながらワインをグラスに1、2杯飲むくらいだね。

Ｗ：あなたそれ毎晩やっていることじゃない。

Ｙ：はは…。ああ、そうかもな。こっちに正月らしい雰囲気はほとんどないよ。明日は祝日だけど、皆2日には仕事に戻ってしまうしね。日本人の管理職の1人が新年を彼の家で過ごさないかと誘ってくれたんだが、特別な日に家族団らんの邪魔をしたくなかったから断った。彼もほっとしたんじゃないかな。

Ｗ：まあ、あと2週間だしね。11日に帰ってくるんでしょう？

Ｙ：ああ、午前8時頃には家に着くはずだ。空港から電話するよ。

Ｗ：愛子がその日に光を連れてくるって言っていたから、そのとき会えるわよ。

Ｙ：それはうれしいな！　ロンドンであの子にいい土産を買っておかなくてはな。

Ｗ：わたしのお土産も忘れないでよ！

Ｙ：何が欲しいんだい？

Ｗ：高いものなら何でもいいわ。

Ｙ：はは！　善処するよ。じゃあ、明日また連絡する。良い新年を！

Ｗ：あなたもね！

47

キーワードやフレーズをチェック!

here am I　（私は）この通り

I had intended to leave the office early today, but **here am I** still working at 10 p.m.

私は今日早めに会社を出るつもりだったが、この通り午後10時になっても働いている。

I was hoping to be a manager in my mid-30s, but **here am I** still an office clerk at 40 years old.

私は30代半ばには部長になりたいと思っていたが、この通り40歳でまだ平社員だ。

conference call　ビデオ［テレビ］通話

I have arranged a **conference call** with our client at 3 o'clock this afternoon.

私は顧客と今日の午後3時にテレビ会議の予定を取っている。

I have known him for many years, but I saw his face for the first time in yesterday's **conference call**.

私はもう何年も彼を知っているが、昨日のビデオ通話で初めて彼の顔を見た。

in the flesh　直接に

I have worked at this company for eight years, but I've never seen the president **in the flesh**.

私はこの会社に8年間勤めているが、直接社長本人を見たことはない。

I was invited to give an interview on TV, and I met several celebrities **in the flesh**.

私はテレビでインタビューを受けるよう招待され、何人かの有名人に直接会った。

I must say　本当に、まったく

I must say, the work is much harder than I expected.

まったく、この仕事は思っていたよりずっと大変だ。

I didn't expect him to succeed, but **I must say**, he did a wonderful job.

私は彼が成功するとは思っていなかったが、本当に彼は素晴らしい仕事をした。

in the meantime　その間に、一方では

I have a meeting soon, but **in the meantime**, I'm going to lunch.
私はこの後すぐに会議だが、それまでの間に昼食をとってしまおう。

My office is being refurbished, and **in the meantime**, I am working from a meeting room.
私のオフィスは今改装中で、当面は会議室で働いている。

I am ashamed to say　恥ずかしながら

I am ashamed to say that I was fired from my job today.
恥ずかしい話だが、私は今日仕事をクビになった。

I am ashamed to say that I failed to meet the deadline.
恥ずかしながら、私は締め切りに間に合わなかった。

47

マナーのヒント

　キリスト教圏での元日の祝われ方は日本よりも小規模な傾向があります。イギリスでは1974年から1月1日（1日が日曜日の場合は1月2日）が祝日になったばかりで、アメリカでは、正式な祝日である12月31日の遊び疲れから社員が回復できるよう、多くの企業が1月1日を休みにしているものの、いまだに正式な祝日ではありません。いずれにしても、たいてい両方の年にまたがる深夜のパーティーが行われ、家族よりも友人と一緒に祝うのが一般的です。ニューヨークはタイムズスクエアで行われる「ボールドロップ」が有名で、いくつかの大きな都市では花火やその他の野外イベントが楽しめます。年賀状を送ったり新年のあいさつのために人を訪ねたりするような風習はありませんが、仕事に復帰した際 Happy New Year.（新年おめでとう）とあいさつを交わすことはよくあります。

JANUARY 6TH (MONDAY)

Back to work after the New Year holiday. I spent most of the holiday with my parents in Yokohama, and then went hiking in Hakone for a couple of days. The weather was fine, but a cold wind was blowing the whole time, which was exhausting. Still, the hiking helped me lose the extra weight I had gained from my mother's cooking over New Year.

Today was my first day in the **Legal Affairs Section (p.188)**. I was given an outline of the section's duties, and the work looks really difficult. Most of it involves contracts, agreements and patents, and from what I can see, a basic understanding of legal affairs is necessary to do the job properly. The **people in the section (p.190)** are very nice, though, and none of them seem too stressed out from the work, so maybe I'll get used to it. I also **had a meeting with Ms. Uchiyama (p.192)**, the manager, this morning. She was very encouraging, and suggested that I ask Misaki-san about his experiences in the section, where he was stationed before he went on his overseas study course.

I still haven't managed to find the time to talk to Misaki about the Legal Affairs Section, but both he and I gave our reports about our overseas trips to Mr. Winston in this afternoon's English lesson. It was the first lesson we have had since November, and Mr. Winston seemed genuinely pleased to welcome us back. Misaki had a wonderful time in America, and he said he'd love to be transferred over to the New York office sometime in the future. I know exactly how he feels. It has been two weeks since I returned from my trip to London, and the experience now seems like just a pleasant dream. I'd love to go back there for a longer period of time, although I doubt if that is possible for the foreseeable future.

Mr. Yonezawa is due back in the Tokyo office from next Monday. I wonder if he will end up feeling like Misaki and I do after he has been back here for a few weeks. Maybe he'll ask for a permanent position in London (although I doubt that...).

Nitobe

キーワード&キーフレーズ→p.194

1月6日（月曜日）

　年末年始の休暇から仕事に復帰したところだ。僕は休みのほとんどを横浜の両親のところで過ごし、それから箱根に2日ほどハイキングに行った。天気は良かったのだけど、ずっと冷たい風が吹いていたので疲れてしまった。でもこのハイキングのおかげで、正月の間に母の料理を食べて増えてしまった分の体重を減らすことができた。

　今日は僕の法務課での最初の日だった。課の業務の概要を説明されたけど、ここの仕事はとても難しそうだ。そのほとんどが契約書や同意書、特許に関わるもので、僕が見た限りでは、仕事をちゃんとこなすには法律に関する基礎知識が必要だ。でも課内の人は皆とても親切だし、誰も仕事でそんなにストレスをためている様子はないので、僕もやっているうちに慣れるかもしれない。それと、今朝は内山課長と打ち合わせをした。彼女は僕を勇気づけてくれて、岬さんは海外研修に行く前にこの課に配属されていたから、ここでの経験について聞いてみたらどうかと提案してくれた。

　まだ岬と法務課について話す時間は取れていないけど、岬と僕は2人とも今日の午後の英語の授業でウィンストン先生に僕たちの海外研修に関するレポートを提出した。これは11月以来初めての授業で、ウィンストン先生は僕たちが帰ってきて心からうれしそうだった。岬はアメリカで素晴らしい時間を過ごしてきて、将来いつかニューヨーク支社に移れたらいいなと言っていた。彼の気持ちはよくわかる。僕はロンドンへの旅から帰ってきて2週間になるが、今ではあの体験はまるで楽しい夢だったかのように思える。また向こうに行ってもっと長い期間滞在できたら素敵だと思うけど、当分の間は無理だろうな。

48

　米澤部長は来週の月曜日から東京本社に戻ってくる予定だ。彼もこっちに帰ってきて数週間したら岬や僕と同じことを思うようになったりするのかな。ロンドンでずっと働きたいと言い出したりして（それはないだろうけどね…）。

新渡戸

Legal Affairs Section ►

課の業務内容を書いてみよう!

Legal Affairs Section		
Duties	**Details**	**Staff Members**
Contracts and Agreements	Preparing all memorandums of intent, contracts, agreements and other legal documents in Japanese (which are sent to the Documentation Section to be translated into the target languages)	Kyoko Uchiyama (Mgr.) Norika Hirai Hiromi Inoue Yasushi Kimura Tomomi Fukuda
Patents	Preparing the prior art and all other documentation for patent applications, and the documents for licensing out existing patents	Akira Sasaki Sumika Yokoyama
Compliance	Ensuring that all company policies and activities are in compliance with laws and regulations	
Overseas Attorney Liaison	Maintaining contact with overseas attorneys with regard to legal affairs and licensing, and monitoring any amendments made to overseas laws and regulations	

法務課

業　務	詳　細	社　員
契約書と同意書	すべての覚書、契約書、同意書、その他の日本語の法的書類の準備(ドキュメンテーション課へ目的の言語に翻訳されるよう送られる)	内山京子(課長) 平井紀香 井上博美 木村靖 福田知美 佐々木明 横山澄香
特許	先行技術と特許出願のための他のすべての書類、および既存特許のライセンスを供与するための書類の準備	
コンプライアンス	あらゆる企業方針と活動が法律と規制に沿っているかを確認する	
海外の弁護士との連携	法律全般とライセンスに関して海外の弁護士との連絡を維持し、海外の法律や規制になされたあらゆる修正を監督する	

クイックQ&A

Q 〉 **What happens to the documents prepared in Japanese?**
（日本語で作成された書類はどうなりますか）

48

POINT

Dutiesの欄の一番下にあるliaisonという語は「情報を伝達する人」、あるいは「他の人や団体に情報を伝達する行為」という意味です。動詞形はliaiseです。多くの場合、liaisonは日本語の「窓口」と同義として使えますが、liaiseは一般的にただ「連絡を取る」という意味で使われます。以下はその用例です。
・She works as a liaison for the French Embassy.（彼女はフランス大使館の受付として働いています）
・Visit the liaison counter in the town hall for more information on taxes.（税金に関する詳細は町役場の窓口までお問い合わせください）
・I suggest you liaise with the maintenance department.（営繕部に連絡するべきでしょう）

A 〉 **Sent to the Documentation Section for translation**
（翻訳のためドキュメンテーション課へ送られる）

課の社員の印象を読んでみよう!

Impressions of Legal Affairs Section Staff Members

Kyoko Uchiyama	Mid-fifties. A motherly type, who takes good care of her staff. Uses a wheelchair.
Norika Hirai	Around fifty. Married with two grown-up children. Quiet and dedicated to her job.
Hiromi Inoue	Early-forties. Single, but has several cats. Desk covered in cat photographs.
Yasushi Kimura	Mid-forties. Studied corporate law at university, and is very knowledgeable about law in general.
Tomomi Fukuda	Mid-thirties. Recently married, but claims to have no plans for children. Very friendly.
Akira Sasaki	Mid-thirties. Returnee (USA). The joker of the section (particularly fond of American-style jokes and Japanese *oyaji* gags).
Sumika Yokoyama	Late-twenties. Single. Very fond of fashion.

法務課の社員の印象

内山京子	50代半ば。お母さんタイプで課の良い世話役。車椅子を使っている。
平井紀香	50歳前後。2人の成人した子どもがいる既婚者。静かで仕事に集中している。
井上博美	40代前半。独身だが何匹か猫を飼っている。机が猫の写真でいっぱい。
木村靖	40代半ば。大学で企業法を学び、法律全般にとても知識がある。
福田知美	30代半ば。最近結婚したが、子どもを持つ予定はないという。とてもフレンドリー。
佐々木明	30代半ば。帰国子女（アメリカ）。課のひょうきん者（特にアメリカンジョークと日本のおやじギャグが好き）。
横山澄香	20代後半。独身。大のファッション好き。

クイックQ&A

48

Q ＞ **Who does not want to become a mother?**
（母親になりたくないのは誰ですか）

POINT

日本語の「おやじギャグ」は以前まで英語でcorny jokeと呼ばれていましたが、最近になって日本語そのものをより忠実に訳すようになり、今では一般的にdad jokeと呼ばれています。以下はdad jokeの例です。

・How many apples grow on a tree? ―All of them. （木に実るリンゴはいくつ？ ―すべてのリンゴ）

・What side of a sheep does the wool grow? ―The outside. （ウールは羊のどちら側からとれる？ ―外側）

・What is the best time for a dentist appointment? ―Tooth hurt-y (two thirty). （歯医者の予約にベストな時間は？ ―歯が痛い[トゥース・ハーティーという英語の発音から2時30分]）

A ＞ Tomomi Fukuda（福田知美）

had a meeting with Ms. Uchiyama　►　CD 2-05

実際の会話を聞いて話してみよう!

SETTING:

> Ms. Uchiyama and Nitobe are sitting in a meeting room discussing the work he
> will be doing in the Legal Affairs Section.

Uchiyama: First of all, let me say welcome back from London. We haven't had a chance to speak since you returned. Did you enjoy yourself?

Nitobe: Yes, very much, thank you. I learned a lot.

Uchiyama: That's good. Well, you will now begin working in the Legal Affairs Section for three months. It's rather a specialized job, so you may find it a little confusing at the beginning. But don't worry about that. Your main work will be assisting other people.

Nitobe: I understand. I don't know much about the law, so I'm not sure how much help I will be.

Uchiyama: Don't worry, we won't be asking you to fight any legal battles in a court of law. A lot of the work we do is routine. Checking details, updating documents, communicating with people overseas, and things like that. You'll be helping out there. Your colleague Misaki managed to get through three months without any problems, so you may want to ask him about his experiences in the section.

Nitobe: That's a good idea. Thank you. I'll check with Misaki as soon as I see him.

Uchiyama: I have assigned Akira Sasaki to take care of you at the beginning, so you will be working with him. He grew up in America and speaks fluent English, so he is mostly in charge of communicating with lawyers and customers overseas.

Nitobe: The section deals with customers directly? I thought only the Customer Support Section was in direct contact with overseas clients.

Uchiyama: No, we also keep in close contact with them with regard to legal matters that affect their contracts or licensing agreements due to revisions to laws and regulations. Any other questions?

Nitobe: No, I think I understand now. Thank you. I look forward to starting work.

had a meeting with Ms. Uchiyama

場面:

> 内山課長と新渡戸が会議室に座って、法務課で新渡戸がこれから行う仕事について話している。

U：まずは、ロンドンでの研修お疲れさま。あなたが戻ってきてから話す機会がなかったわね。向こうでは楽しく過ごせた？

N：はい、とても。ありがとうございます。たくさんのことを学びました。

U：それはよかったわ。さて、あなたはこれから3か月間、法務課で働くことになります。やや専門的な仕事だから、最初は少し戸惑うかもしれないわね。でも心配しないで。あなたの主な仕事は他の社員のアシストだから。

N：わかりました。法律のことはあまり知らないので、どれだけお手伝いできるかわかりませんけど。

U：安心して、何も裁判所で法廷闘争をしてもらおうというわけじゃないんだから。うちの仕事の多くはルーティンよ。詳細を精査したり、書類を更新したり、海外と連絡を取ったり、そんな感じね。あなたはその手伝いをするの。同僚の岬さんは問題なくここでの3か月をこなしたから、彼にうちの課での経験について聞いてみたらいいかもしれないわ。

N：それはいい考えですね。ありがとうございます。岬に会ったらすぐに話してみます。

U：初めのうちだけ面倒を見てくれるように佐々木明さんを指名したから、あなたは彼と働くことになるわ。彼はアメリカ育ちで英語がペラペラだから、主に海外の弁護士や顧客とのコミュニケーションを担当しているの。

N：この課は直接顧客に対応するのですか。海外の顧客と直接連絡を取るのは顧客サポート課だけかと思っていました。

U：ええ、うちも法律や規制の改正に対応するために、顧客との契約書や特許同意書に影響する法的な問題に関して顧客と緊密な連絡を取り続けているわ。他に質問はあるかしら。

N：いえ、もう理解できたと思います。ありがとうございました。仕事が始まるのを楽しみにしています。

48

キーワードやフレーズをチェック!

☐ the whole time　その間ずっと、終始

I attended the keynote speech at the seminar, but I slept **the whole time**.

私はそのセミナーの基調講演に出席したが、その間ずっと居眠りしていた。

He spends **the whole time** checking the stock market on his smartphone.

彼は始終スマートフォンで株式市場をチェックしている。

☐ from what I can see　私が見る限り

From what I can see, the production plant will not be able to keep up with orders.

私が見る限り、その生産工場は受注についていくことができないだろう。

The company will begin to experience cashflow problems **from what I can see**.

私が見たところでは、その会社は資金難になり始めるだろう。

☐ stressed out　ストレスがたまって、疲労して

I feel completely **stressed out** after working overtime every day this week.

今週は毎日残業をしていたので、もうすっかりくたくただ。

He listens to classical music during lunchtime to avoid getting **stressed out**.

彼はストレスがたまるのを防ぐためランチタイムにクラシック音楽を聴く。

☐ suggest that ～　～することを提案する、示す

The auditor **suggested that** the company establishes firmer compliance rules.

会計監査人はその会社に、より堅固な遵守事項を確立することを勧めた。

194

The rapid drop in sales **suggests that** we are doing something wrong.

売上の急激な低下は我々が間違ったやり方をしていることを示している。

find the time 時間を取る

I can't help you now, but I should be able to **find the time** on Wednesday.

今は手伝うことができないけど、水曜日には時間を作れる。

She is having trouble **finding the time** to complete the report.

彼女は報告書を書き終えるための時間を取れないでいる。

end up 〜 結局〜になる

He will **end up** with a warning if he continues to arrive late every day.

毎日遅刻し続けていれば彼は注意されることになるだろう。

We **ended up** canceling the project after it overran the budget.

我々はそのプロジェクトが予算オーバーになったため、結局それを中止した。

マナーのヒント

人の性格、特徴、外見などを表す形容詞はとても数多くあります。代表的なものを以下に紹介します。

性格: calm「落ち着いた」／serene「穏やかな」／tranquil「静かな」／charismatic「カリスマ的な」／modest「慎み深い」／loyal「誠実な」／humble「謙虚な」／courageous「勇気がある」／eccentric「風変わりな」／emotional「感情的な」／impatient「せっかちな」／arrogant「傲慢な」／cowardly「臆病な」／cynical「ひねくれた」／egoistical「自己中心的な」

特徴: clever「頭がいい」／smart「賢い」／wise「賢明な」／creative「創造力豊かな」／generous「気前がいい」／cheerful「明るい」／mysterious「神秘的な」／fussy「小うるさい」／bad-tempered「怒りっぽい」／immature「子どもっぽい」／irritable「短気な」／provocative「挑発的な」

外見: beautiful「きれいな」／handsome「ハンサムな」／attractive「魅力的な」／tall「背の高い」／short「背の低い」／lanky「ひょろっとした」／skinny「痩せた」／squat「ずんぐりした」／athletic「運動神経がいい」／muscular「筋骨たくましい」／plump「ぽっちゃりした」／fashionable「おしゃれな」／chic「上品な」／old-fashioned「古風な」

48

JANUARY 14TH (TUESDAY)

This is my first journal entry since arriving back in Japan. My flight was delayed by about an hour, but I still managed to get home in time for breakfast on Saturday morning. My daughter, her husband and my granddaughter visited later in the day, so I finally got the chance to hug little Hikari after six months. She's a sweet little girl, and smiled at me whenever I spoke to her. Although I enjoyed my sojourn in London, it is very nice to be back at home.

My final week in London was very busy. In addition to packing and preparing for my return home, I also spent a lot of time briefing Kenneth and visiting as many of the clients I had got to know during my stay as I could. I also had several farewell dinners, and was nearly exhausted by the time I arrived at the airport. Kenneth and his wife gave me a beautiful Baccarat whisky glass as a farewell gift. I also received a **charming letter from Kenneth** (p.200), in which he said he would "welcome me with open arms" if I ever decided that I wanted a permanent position in London.

I also received a **charming farewell card** (p.198) from my secretary, Greta Hayworth. I had given her a set of three nicely-framed prints by Katsushika Hokusai (from his Thirty-Six Views of Mt. Fuji series) as a token of my appreciation, and she gave me a fountain pen as a farewell gift.

Coming so soon after Kenneth's job offer, I experienced a strange coincidence this afternoon. One of our clients **offered me a job** (p.202)! I have spent the past two days visiting some of our major clients to let them know I am back in Japan, and the president suggested that I visit Toru Sano, the managing director of SJF Engineering. SJF is a major IT company that has subcontracted work out to us since the early days. We still handle most of their mobile application development, and I have built up a good relationship with Sano over the years. During our chat, he suddenly offered me a very attractive job with a high salary and stock options. I declined, naturally, but it was very flattering.

Yonezawa

１月１４日（火曜日）

　これは私が日本に帰国してから最初の日誌記入になる。私のフライトは1時間ほど遅れたが、土曜日の朝、朝食に間に合う時間にはなんとか帰宅することができた。その日のうちに娘夫婦と孫が訪ねてきたので、6か月ぶりにようやく小さな光を抱きしめられた。光は優しくてかわいい女の子で、私が話しかけるたびにニコニコと笑ってくれた。ロンドン滞在は楽しかったが、やはり家に帰ってくるとほっとする。

　ロンドンでの最後の1週間はとても忙しかった。荷造りや帰国の準備に加え、ケネスに私が代理をしていた間のことをかいつまんで説明したり、滞在中に知り合った顧客をできる限り多く訪問したりして多くの時間を過ごした。何回か送別会にも参加したので、空港に着いた頃にはかなりへとへとだった。ケネスと彼の妻は餞別としてきれいなバカラのウイスキーグラスをくれた。ケネスからは素敵な手紙ももらって、そこにはもし私がロンドンで正式に職が欲しいと思うことがあれば「心から歓迎する」と書いてあった。

　私の秘書をしていたグレタ・ヘイワースからも素敵な送別カードをもらった。私は彼女への感謝のしるしとしてセンスのいい額に入った葛飾北斎の版画3枚セット（富嶽三十六景からのものだ）を贈り、彼女は餞別として万年筆をくれた。

　ケネスからの仕事のオファーに続き、今日の午後は不思議な偶然を体験した。我が社の顧客の1人が私に仕事のオファーをくれたのだ！　この2日間は重要な顧客のいくつかを訪問して私が日本に戻ってきたことを知らせていたのだが、社長にSJFエンジニアリングの代表取締役の佐野徹氏を訪問するよう勧められた。SJFは大手のIT企業で、我が社の創業間もない頃からこちらに仕事を委託してくれている。現在でも我が社はSJFの携帯アプリの開発のほとんどを請け負っており、私も長年にわたって佐野氏とは良い関係を築いてきた。2人で雑談をしていると、彼はいきなり高収入でストックオプションまで付いた魅力的な仕事をオファーしてきた。当然ながら辞退したが、そこまで私のことを高く買ってくれているのは非常にうれしかった。

米澤

49

Charming farewell Card ▶

送別メッセージカードを書いてみよう!

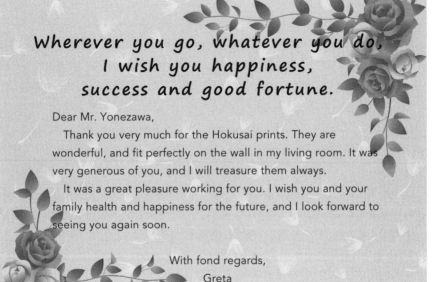

Wherever you go, whatever you do,
I wish you happiness,
success and good fortune.

Dear Mr. Yonezawa,

Thank you very much for the Hokusai prints. They are wonderful, and fit perfectly on the wall in my living room. It was very generous of you, and I will treasure them always.

It was a great pleasure working for you. I wish you and your family health and happiness for the future, and I look forward to seeing you again soon.

With fond regards,
Greta
xxx

POINT

冒頭に、目立つように、最も伝えたいことを一言で表す文言を入れましょう。(できれば心を打つような、印象的でしゃれた表現で)

どこへ行こうと、何をしようと、
あなたの幸せと成功、幸運を祈っています。

米澤様

　北斎の版画をどうもありがとうございました。それは素晴らしく、私のリビングの壁にぴったりです。なんて優しい方なのでしょう。ずっと宝物にします。

　米澤さんと働けたことをとてもうれしく思います。米澤さんとご家族の今後の健康と幸せをお祈りし、またじきにお会いできることを楽しみにしています。

敬意をこめて、
グレタ
xxx

クイックQ＆A

Q ＞ **What will Greta treasure?**
（グレタは何を宝物にするでしょうか）

49

POINT

英語圏では様々な出来事を対象にしたメッセージカードが用意されていて、普通のバースデーカードやクリスマスカードをはじめ、出産祝い、退職祝い、退院祝い、離婚祝いなんていうのまであります。すべてのカードに共通している点は、内側に簡単なメッセージが印刷してあって、それが送り手の伝えたいことをまとめてくれ、他に個人的な短いメッセージを書けるようになっていることです。個人的なメッセージはほんの１文だけでも、必要ならもっと長くても構いません。

ちなみに、このグレタのカードで送り手の名前の下にあるxxxは、キスを表しています。当然ながら、これを使うかどうかは自分と受け手との関係を考慮に入れて慎重に判断しなければなりません。

A ＞ The Hokusai prints（北斎の版画）

charming letter from Kenneth ►

感謝の送別レターを読んでみよう!

From the Desk of Kenneth Lewis

January 9th

Dear Osamu,

Thank you very much for the hard work you have put in over the course of the past six months. It truly was an honour and a pleasure to have you in London. Everybody I have spoken to, both inside and outside of the company, tells me how pleasant it was working with you, and I am jealous over the amount of respect you managed to earn in so short a period of time.

If you ever decide that you would like to live in the UK and seek a permanent position over here, then I can assure you that everyone in the company will welcome you with open arms.

Thank you once again for everything. Tomizawa is a better company for having a man with so much integrity, dignity and compassion working for it.

Sincerely yours
Kenneth Lewis

POINT

若干のユーモアを加えることで(ここでは、I am jealous over the amount of 〜)、感謝の気持ちや相手のすばらしさを素直に伝えることに効果があります。

ケネス・ルイスのデスクより

1月9日

修へ

ここ6か月にわたり一生懸命働いてきてくれて本当にどうもありがとう。ロンドンに修がいてくれたことは実に名誉で喜ばしいことでした。私が話した人たちは皆、社内の人も社外の人も修と働けてどれだけ楽しかったかと語っていて、私はこれほどの短期間で君が得た尊敬の数々に嫉妬してしまいます。

もしイギリスに住んでこちらで正式な職を探したいと思ったならば、そのときは社の全員が心から修を歓迎することを請け合います。

改めていろいろとありがとう。こんなにも誠実で威厳があり、また思いやりのある社員が働いていてくれて、富沢はなおさら良い会社ですね。

敬具
ケネス・ルイス

クイックQ&A

Q 〉 **What is Kenneth Lewis envious of?**
（ケネス・ルイスが羨んでいるものは何ですか）

49

POINT

英語の手紙を書くときは、個人的な手紙でもビジネスレターでも、基本的に同じ形式に従います。敬辞（頭語：Dear〜, など）は受取人との関係によって異なり、その後にくる、手紙の3つの主な要素は以下のようになります。

・導入：最初の段落は手紙の主な目的を述べます。ここでは、手紙の主な目的は感謝を伝えることなので、すぐにそれがなされています。
・本文：手紙の真ん中の（いくつかの）段落は、導入で述べた情報の詳細を伝えるか、他の内容を付け加えます。
・結び：手紙の最後の段落はそれより前の段落の内容をまとめます。

A 〉 The respect that Yonezawa earned（※米沢が得た尊敬）

実際の会話を聞いて話してみよう!

SETTING:

> Yonezawa is in the office of Toru Sano on a courtesy visit. Having given a brief report about his visit to the UK, the conversation turns to his job in Tokyo.

Sano: I'm sure Tomizawa is glad to have you back in the office. Are you back as the director of the Global Logistics Department, or have you been assigned elsewhere?

Yonezawa: No, I'm still in the Global Logistics Department.

Sano: You've been in that department for years. Isn't it about time you did something different?

Yonezawa: Being assigned to London was something different. In fact, it's a pleasure being back at my old job.

Sano: Listen, Osamu. We've been friends for many years, right?

Yonezawa: Yes.

Sano: How would you feel about working with me?

Yonezawa: With you? I'm not quite sure what you mean.

Sano: I'm offering you a position at SJF Engineering. A directorship with a seat on the board. Interested?

Yonezawa: Well, I'm flattered that you ask, but no. I'm afraid I'm not interested.

Sano: Whatever they are paying you at Tomizawa, I'll double it.

Yonezawa: I'm sorry, Toru, I'm just not interested. It's nothing to do with money. Tomizawa is my life, and the Global Logistics Department is my life's work. I could never leave it.

Sano: We can offer you attractive stock options. You'd never regret it.

Yonezawa: There's where you are wrong. I'd regret it immediately, and would never be able to forgive myself. I've worked hard for many years to build the company up to what it is today. Thank you for your offer, Toru, but I'm afraid I must respectfully decline.

Sano: Why don't you think about it for a while? Get back to me when you've made your decision.

Yonezawa: I've already made my decision. Thank you, but no thank you.

offered me a job

場面：

> 米澤が表敬訪問で佐野徹氏の会社に来ている。米澤がイギリスに行ったときのことをかいつまんで伝えた後、話題は彼の東京での仕事のことに移る。

S： 君が本社に戻ってきて富沢はうれしく思っているだろうな。それで、海外事業部長に戻ったのかい、それとも何か他の役職についたのかい？

Y： いや、海外事業部のままだよ。

S： もう長年その部署にいるじゃないか。そろそろ何か違うことをしてもいい頃じゃないかな。

Y： ロンドンに配属されたことは「違うこと」だろう。それに、私は元の仕事に戻れてうれしいと感じているよ。

S： なあ、修。私たちはもう何年も前からの友達だ、そうだろう？

Y： ああ。

S： 私と一緒に働くことになったとしたらどう思う？

Y： 君と？　どういう意味かよくわからないんだが。

S： SJFエンジニアリングでの仕事をオファーしたいんだ。役員の1人としての職務だ。興味はあるかい？

Y： いや、誘ってくれるのはうれしいが、断るよ。すまないが興味はない。

S： 富沢ISが払っている給料がいくらかはわからないが、こちらはその2倍払おう。

Y： 徹、申し訳ないんだが、本当にただ興味がないんだ。金の問題じゃない。富沢ISは私の人生そのもので、海外事業部はライフワークなんだよ。あそこを去ることはできない。

S： 良いストックオプションも付けるぞ。絶対に後悔はさせない。

Y： そこが違うんだよ。仮にそのオファーを受けたら私は即座に後悔する、一生自分を許せないだろう。私は今のあの会社を築き上げるために何年も身を粉にして働いてきたんだ。徹、申し出はありがたいのだが、丁重に断らせてもらうよ。

S： 少し考えてみてはくれないか。決断ができたら連絡してほしい。

Y： もうとっくに決断はできているさ。気持ちはありがたく受け取るが、辞退させてもらうよ。

49

キーワードやフレーズをチェック!

delayed by 〜　　〜だけ遅れて

The launch of the new product was **delayed by** three months because of the strike at the factory.
新商品の発売は工場でのストライキのせいで3か月先延ばしになった。

He was due to arrive before midday, but he was **delayed by** twenty minutes because of heavy traffic.
彼は正午には到着する予定だったが、渋滞のせいで20分遅れた。

in time for 〜　　〜に間に合って

The reference material I ask my staff to prepare was not ready **in time for** the meeting.
私が部下に用意を頼んだ参考資料は会議の時間に間に合わなかった。

I arrived late for the seminar, but I was **in time for** the presentation.
私はセミナーに遅れて到着したが、プレゼンテーションには間に合った。

welcome with open arms　　歓迎する

Every worker in the country **welcomed** the tax rebate **with open arms**.
国内のすべての労働者が税金の還付を大いに歓迎した。

She was **welcomed** back to the office **with open arms** after clinching the contract.
彼女はその契約を獲得した後、オフィスに帰り喜んで迎え入れられた。

token of appreciation　　感謝のしるし

He received a large sum when he retired as a **token of appreciation** for many years' hard work.
彼は退職したとき、長年よく働いてくれたことに対する感謝のしるしとして高額な退職金を受け取った。

She was promoted as a **token of** the company's **appreciation**.
彼女は会社からの感謝のしるしとして昇進した。

coming so soon after 〜　〜の直後に起こる

A recession **coming so soon after** the tax increase was disastrous for the company.
増税の直後に景気後退が来たことは会社にとって大変な災難だった。

His resignation **coming so soon after** the scandal suggests that the company had had enough.
そのスキャンダルのすぐ後に彼が辞職したことは、会社がもううんざりしていたということを示唆している。

stock option　ストックオプション（自社株購入権）

It is the company's policy to give **stock options** to all executives.
重役全員にストックオプションを与えるのがその会社の方針だ。

He received **stock options** in lieu of a pay rise.
彼は昇給に代えてストックオプションをもらった。

マナーのヒント

49

　ビジネスの現場では、上司や顧客からの要求を断らなければならないこともあります。こういう場合の伝え方は友達や家族に対して断るときと基本的に同じですが、以下のようにsorryの前にveryやterriblyなどを添えて謝罪を強調するとよいでしょう。

・I am very sorry, but I have an appointment tonight, so I won't be able to work overtime.（大変申し訳ありませんが、今夜は予定があるので残業はできません）

・I am terribly sorry, but I'm afraid we don't provide an installation service.（誠に申し訳ありませんが、弊社では設置サービスは提供しておりません）

・I am extremely sorry, but owing to other work, I won't be able to complete the report until next week.（大変申し訳ありませんが、他の仕事もあるので、来週まで報告書を書き上げることができません）

50

DAY

JANUARY 25TH (SATURDAY)

January is flying past very quickly. It only seems like only the other day that I returned from England, but it has already been one month. January and February are the months of the year I dislike the most. I like winter up until the end of the year, but I spend the first two months of the year yearning for the spring. January and February are cold, windy and the humidity is very low, which I find uncomfortable. This year, however, seems to be slipping by at top speed.

Mr. Winston is keeping us busy with our English lessons. We still go out into the streets sometimes, but the lessons start at 4 p.m., so it is nearly dark by the time we leave the office and we don't go very far (mostly to coffee bars). Our homework still involves a lot of lists. The assignment we completed this week was a list of **international people we would like to meet** (p.208). Both living and historical people were acceptable, so I chose two living and two deceased people.

Mr. Yonezawa is back in the office, by the way. He returned on the 13th, and I see him around the office quite regularly. Apart from thanking him for all his help when I was in London and a brief greeting when we bump into each other around the office, I haven't had the chance to speak to him yet.

My work in the Legal Affairs Section also keeps me busy. Akira Sasaki, the section joker, is **teaching me the job** (p.212), and one of the tasks I have been assigned is checking for revisions to laws and regulations in the countries where we have contracted clients. Mostly we are contacted by local attorneys advising us of amendments and revisions, but sometimes this is forgotten or delayed, so we have to check regularly on our own to make sure nothing is overlooked. When a revision is found, I have to **write out a memo** (p.210) with a summary of the amendment, and then make a list of the contracts that may be affected.

To be truthful, it is a very boring job, but it is extremely important to make sure our clients, and even Tomizawa, are not in violation of any laws.

Nitobe

キーワード＆キーフレーズ→p.214

1月25日（土曜日）

　1月は飛ぶように過ぎていっている。僕がイギリスから帰ってきたのはついこの間のことのように思えるけれど、あれからもう1か月たった。1月と2月は1年のうちで一番嫌いな月だ。いつも年末までの間は冬を楽しめるのだが、1年の最初の2か月間は春が待ち遠しい。1月と2月は寒くて風が強く、湿度がとても低いので、それが僕には過ごしにくいのだ。でも、今年は知らないうちにフルスピードで過ぎ去っていくようだ。

　ウィンストン先生の英語の授業で僕たちはずっと忙しい。僕たちは今でも時々街へ出かけたりするけど、何しろ授業は午後4時から始まるので、オフィスを出る頃には日が暮れかかっていて、そんなに遠くへは行けない（たいてい行き先はコーヒーバーだ）。僕たちへの宿題は相変わらずリスト作りが多い。今週僕たちがやった課題は会ってみたい世界の人々のリストだった。現在生きている人物と歴史上の人物のどちらでもよかったので、僕は現在生きている人を2人、もう亡くなっている人を2人選んだ。

　さて、米澤部長が本社に戻ってきた。彼が帰ってきたのは13日で、社内でちょくちょく彼を見かける。僕がロンドンに滞在していた間にいろいろ助けてくれたことへのお礼を言ったときと、たまたま社内で顔を合わせたときに軽く挨拶する以外では、まだ部長と話す機会を得ていない。

　ずっと忙しいのは法務課での仕事もそうだ。課内きってのひょうきん者の佐々木明さんが僕に仕事を教えてくれていて、僕に与えられた仕事の1つは、我が社が契約している顧客のいる国の法律や規制の改正をチェックすることだ。たいていは向こうの国の弁護士がこちらに修正や改正を報告してくれるのだけど、たまにこれが忘れられていたり遅れたりすることもあるので、定期的に自分たちで何も見落としがないかチェックする必要がある。僕は法改正を見つけたら、その改正を要約した連絡書を書いて、影響を受ける可能性のある契約書のリストを作らなければならない。

50

　正直に言うとすごく退屈な仕事だけど、我が社の顧客、ひいては富沢ISがいかなる法律にも違反していないようにすることは極めて重要だ。

新渡戸

international people we would like to meet ►

会ってみたい人々のリストを書いてみよう!

International People I Would Like to Meet
—Shinnosuke Nitobe

1. Steve Jobs

Steve Jobs has probably inspired more young people than anybody else. He was truly the Thomas Edison of the modern era. Not only was he innovative in the field of computers and communications, he was also instrumental in making Pixar the world's greatest animation producer.

2. Lionel Messi

I don't think anybody can doubt that Messi is the world's greatest ever soccer player. His skills on the field have entranced me since I was in junior high school, and I'd love to chat to him about soccer in general over a beer (or two).

3. Stephen Hawking

I am still amazed at the level of intelligence Stephen Hawking was gifted with. He brought physics and astronomy closer to the average person in an easy-to-understand way. I read his book *A Brief History of Time* in high school, and was surprised to find that I understood it.

4. Barack Obama

Barack Obama is a hero to me. Not only am I inspired by his political savvy, but also his integrity, compassion, dignity and humility. I still run Internet searches on him, despite it being quite a long time since he was US president, and he has the ability to impress me even now.

POINT

not only... (but) also ～などの構文を使って、その人の業績の数々を強調すると効果的です。

僕が会ってみたい世界の人々
──新渡戸慎之助

1. スティーブ・ジョブズ

スティーブ・ジョブズは、おそらく他の誰よりも多くの若者を刺激しました。彼はまさに現代のトーマス・エジソンでした。コンピュータや通信の世界で革新的であっただけでなく、ピクサーを世界で最も素晴らしいアニメ会社にすることにも貢献しました。

2. リオネル・メッシ

メッシが世界で最も素晴らしいサッカー選手であることを疑う人は誰もいないと思います。僕は中学生のときから、メッシのフィールド上での技術にはうっとりさせられていて、ビールを1杯（か2杯）飲みながらサッカー全般について彼と是非とも話をしてみたいです。

3. スティーブン・ホーキング

僕はスティーブン・ホーキング氏が持っていた知的レベルにいまだに驚いています。彼は物理学と天文学をわかりやすい方法で一般の人々の身近なものにしました。僕は彼の著書『ホーキング、宇宙を語る』を高校時代に読んで、それが理解できたことに驚きました。

4. バラク・オバマ

バラク・オバマは僕にとってヒーローです。彼の政治能力だけでなく、誠実さや思いやり、威厳、謙虚さに励まされています。アメリカ大統領になって以来ずいぶん経つにもかかわらず、僕はいまだに彼についてネット検索しており、彼には今でも僕を感動させる力があります。

クイックQ&A

Q > **Which of the above four people is a sportsman?**
（上記の4人の人物のうち、スポーツ選手は誰ですか）

50

POINT

instrumentという名詞は大まかに言えば道具や装置のことですが、楽器や医療機器のような精密な器具を示すのに最もよく使われます。しかし、スティーブ・ジョブズの紹介文で出てきたように、形容詞instrumentalとして使われるときは、「大きな役割を持つ」あるいは「目的を果たす助けになる」という意味にもなります。以下はその用例です。

・She was instrumental in the company's success.（彼女はその会社の成功に大きく貢献した）
・The hot weather was instrumental in increasing beer sales.（この暑さはビールの売上の上昇を助けた）
・He introduced them to each other, and was therefore instrumental in their marriage.（2人を引き合わせたのは彼なので、彼は2人の結婚の大きな要因だった）

A > Lionel Messi（リオネル・メッシ）

write out a memo ►

法改正の連絡書を読んでみよう!

Internal Law Revision Memo

To :　All section members
From : S. Nitobe (A. Sasaki)
Date : January 25
Re :　Potential Revision to Australia's National Privacy Act

Country	Status	Enactment
Australia	Under parliamentary debate	June if passed

Australia's parliament is currently debating changes to data breach regulations in the National Privacy Act. If the revisions are passed, they are expected to be enforced from around June this year.

Outline:
- Companies with an annual turnover of AUS$3 million or more will be required to comply with the Notifiable Data Breaches regulations.
- A data breach is defined as personal information being illegally accessed or intentionally or accidentally released.
- The revisions will obligate the company to notify the individual concerned and the Office of Australian Information Commissioner (OAIC) of the breach.

Comments:
- Only applies to Tomizawa for systems that are being operated from Japan on behalf of clients.
- Does not concern systems that are being operated in-house by Australian clients.
- Further details and a list of projects that are potentially affected are attached.

社内法改正連絡書

宛先: 全課員
差出人: 新渡戸（佐々木）
日付: 1月25日
Re: オーストラリアの個人情報保護法に行われる可能性のある改正

国	状況	制定
オーストラリア	議会で審議中	通過すれば6月

オーストラリア議会は現在、個人情報保護法のデータ漏洩規制の変更について議論している。改正案が通過すれば、本年6月頃から施行される見通し。

概要:
- 年商300万豪ドル以上の企業はデータ漏洩通知規制に従うよう求められる。
- データ漏洩は個人情報が違法アクセスされること、または意図的、事故的に漏洩されることと定義される。
- 改正によって、企業は関係者とオーストラリア情報委員会(OAIC)に漏洩の通知をする義務を負う。

コメント:
- 富沢には顧客の代わりに日本から運用されているシステムにのみ適用される。
- オーストラリアの顧客によって企業内で運用されているシステムには関係しない。
- さらなる詳細と影響を受ける可能性のあるプロジェクトのリストは添付の通り。

クイックQ&A

Q > **The revisions only apply to companies operating Tomizawa systems themselves. True or false?**
（この法改正は富沢ISのシステムを自ら運用している企業にのみ適用されます。正しいですか、誤りですか）

50

POINT

Outlineの1行目にあるannual turnoverとは、売上や役務収益などの収入からくる会社の歳入から税金などが差し引かれる前の総額のことです。これはgross incomeと同義ですが、annual turnoverが「会社の1年間の粗収入」を指すのに対し、gross incomeは期間が限定されておらず、個人に対しても使うことができます。一方、net incomeとは税金その他が差し引かれた後に残る総額のことで、会社と個人どちらにも使えます。例えば、ある社員が1か月に5000ドル稼いで、税金その他で600ドル支払うとすると、当人のgross incomeは5000ドルでnet incomeは4400ドルです。

A > False（誤り）

teaching me the job ►

実際の会話を聞いて話してみよう!

SETTING:

Akira Sasaki is explaining the job to Nitobe at his desk.

Sasaki: First of all, we have to check through all of the e-mail that comes in from overseas attorneys to see if any of them concern revisions to laws or regulations. Not all e-mail comes directly to us, so anybody who receives something that looks like a revision will forward the message to us. Okay?

Nitobe: Okay.

Sasaki: Right, here is an e-mail we received from an attorney in Australia. He has outlined potential changes to a law covering data leaks, as you can see here. We must therefore fill out an Internal Law Revision Memo containing all of the details and send it to all members of the section. Here is the form, so you can fill this one out.

Nitobe: Okay, first of all I'll fill in the header. Can I use the same title as the attorney has used?

Sasaki: No, that's a bit long-winded. Something that can be understood at a glance is better. Something like, "Potential Revision to Australia's National Privacy Act."

Nitobe: What do I write for "Status?"

Sasaki: That just means present situation. Whether revisions have simply been proposed, whether they are being debated in parliament, whether they have passed parliament, or whether they are already in effect.

Nitobe: Okay, I've got that. So, this one will be "Under parliamentary debate," right?

Sasaki: That's right. Now briefly summarize the details the attorney sent us, add any comments that you think are relevant, and then run a search on the projects that may be affected. Then take copies of the original details received from the attorney, attach them to the memo together with your list of projects and hand them out.

Nitobe: Well, that's not as difficult as I expected. Thanks for explaining it.

Sasaki: Don't let your guard down. You still have another seven forms to fill out, then you have to check to see if there are any others we haven't been informed of.

teaching me the job

場面：

> 佐々木明が新渡戸のデスクで彼に仕事の説明をしている。

S： まずは、海外の弁護士から来るメールを全部調べて、法律や規制の改正に関するものかどうか確認しなければならない。すべてのメールが直接うちに来るわけではないから、改正に関するものっぽいメールを受信した社員はこちらにそれを転送してくる。わかったかな？

N： はい。

S： よし、それじゃあここにオーストラリアの弁護士から送られてきたメールがある。そこに書いてある通り、彼は情報漏洩に関する法律に行われる可能性のある改正の概要を説明している。だから、社内法改正連絡書にその詳細をすべて記入して、全課員に送らなければならない。これがその用紙だから、君が書き込んでごらん。

N： わかりました、まずは件名を書きますよね。弁護士が使ったのと同じタイトルを使えばいいんでしょうか。

S： いや、それはちょっと長すぎるな。一目で理解できるようなもののほうがいいよ。例えば「オーストラリアの個人情報保護法に行われる可能性のある改正」とか。

N： 「状況」には何を書けばいいですか。

S： それは単純に現在の状況という意味だよ。改正が提案されただけなのか、議会で審議されているところなのか、議会を通過したのか、それとももう施行されているのかということさ。

N： なるほど、わかりました。それでしたら、この場合は「議会で審議中」ですね。

50

S： その通り。次は弁護士が送ってきた詳細情報を簡潔に整理して、必要だと思ったらそれに関するコメントを加えて、それから影響を受ける可能性のあるプロジェクトを検索して。そうしたら、弁護士から送られてきた元の詳細説明のコピーを取って、君が作ったプロジェクトのリストと一緒に連絡書に添付してからみんなに配るんだ。

N： なるほど、思っていたよりも難しくありませんね。説明してくれてありがとうございます。

S： 気は緩めないようにね。まだ君が書き込まなければならない用紙が7枚残っているし、その後はまだ知らされていない改正かないかどうかチェックしなければいけないんだから。

キーワードやフレーズをチェック!

☐ only the other day　つい先日

My manager discussed the matter with me **only the other day**.
つい先日、うちの部長はその件について私と話していた。

She took a data backup **only the other day**.
彼女がデータのバックアップを取ったのはついこの間だ。

☐ yearn for ～　～を待ち望む、なつかしむ

He **yearns for** the days when it was not unusual to receive five-months' bonus every year.
彼は毎年5か月分のボーナスをもらえることが珍しくなかった頃を恋しく思っている。

She hates her new boss, and is **yearning for** him to be replaced.
彼女は新しい上司が嫌いで、彼が交代することを待ち望んでいる。

☐ slip by　過ぎ去る

The time **slips by** quickly when I am busy.
忙しいと時間があっという間に過ぎていく。

The meeting was boring, but the time **slipped by** quicker than I expected.
その会議は退屈だったが、時間は思ったよりも早く過ぎていった。

☐ bump into ～　～に偶然会う

I **bumped into** an old work colleague at the library today.
私は今日、図書館で昔の仕事仲間にばったり会った。

He didn't mention that he was planning on quitting when I **bumped into** him in the cafeteria.
私がカフェで彼に偶然会ったときには、彼は辞めることを考えているとは言わなかった。

☐ advise *one* of ～   （人に）～のことを知らせる

He **advised me of** next week's meeting on Monday.
彼は私に来週の月曜日の会議のことを知らせてくれた。

Her co-worker **advised her of** the new overtime rules by phone when she was off sick.
彼女が病気で休んでいたとき、仕事仲間が電話で新しい残業のルールについて報告してくれた。

☐ nothing is overlooked   何も見落としがない

I want you to create a spreadsheet, and make sure **nothing is overlooked**.
集計表を作ってほしいのだけど、何も見落としがないようにしてほしい。

He checked through the report to make sure **nothing had been overlooked**.
彼は何も見落としがないように報告書を一通り調べた。

マナーのヒント

　社内通知の書き方や使われる形式は、当然会社によって異なりますが、共通点の1つは情報が簡潔にわかりやすく書かれていることです。長々とした説明では全部読まれない可能性が高いので、できれば内容を1)「結論」、2)「詳細」、3)「補足」の3点に分けるのがベストです。以下はその例です。

1) The lavatories on the third floor will not be available for use between July 6th and July 14th. （3階のトイレは7月6日から7月14日の間ご利用できません）

2) The lavatories will be renovated during this period to allow wheelchair access. （この期間にトイレは車椅子で利用できるよう改装されます）

3) You are requested to use the lavatories on the second or fourth floor during this period. （この期間中は2階か4階のトイレをご利用ください）

50

UNIT

未来への
ステップ

51

FEBRUARY 5TH (WEDNESDAY)

I made an unforgivable mistake in front of Mr. Yonezawa today. I feel so angry with myself. I really should have known better.

It all started when Mr. Yonezawa invited me into his office to discuss my Kaizen proposal. Apparently, he was quite impressed with it and wanted to see how far I had researched the subject so that he could check my figures. At first, I thought that meant that he is seriously considering adopting it, although after my gaffe today, I very much doubt it. Anyway, while we were discussing it, I foolishly made a derogatory remark about Mr. Takeda, the manager of the Documentation Section, and **Mr. Yonezawa went ballistic (p.224)**.

The general impression of Mr. Takeda around the office is of somebody rather ineffectual. One of the biggest reasons for this is that he is one of the three original founding members, but he is still a manager. The other two founding members are Mr. Tomizawa, the president, and Mr. Kobayashi, the managing director. He also doesn't seem interested in getting involved in daily work. He mostly just checks everybody's work and then tells them to redo it. Because of this, I guessed that the management shared the same opinion of him. When I badmouthed him, Mr. Yonezawa told me that I did not have the right to form opinions of people without knowing all the details. He said that Mr. Takeda was the reason that I had a job in Tomizawa now. Apparently, it was Mr. Takeda who came up with the idea that the **millennium bug (p.222)** could be used to generate more business. It was an enormous success that more than doubled the number of employees almost immediately, and set the company on the path to expansion. He even showed me the **ad that was placed in various newspapers (p.224)**, which was written by Mr. Takeda.

It was also Mr. Takeda's idea to establish companies in America, Europe and India so that code could be programmed on a 24-hour basis because of the time zones, thereby offering shorter development periods than rival companies.

I feel so stupid now. Mr. Winston taught us the saying "never judge a book by its cover," but that is exactly what I did. Unforgivable!

Nitobe

キーワード＆キーフレーズ→p.226

２月５日（水曜日）

　今日は米澤部長の前で許しがたい間違いを犯してしまった。自分で自分がすごく腹立たしい。なんてバカなことをしたんだろう。

　きっかけは米澤部長が僕を部長室に呼んで僕の改善案について話し始めたことだ。どうやら部長はその案にとても感心したらしく、僕の出した数字が合っているか確認するため、そのテーマについて僕がどこまで調べたのか知りたがっていた。最初は部長が案の採用を真剣に考えてくれているのかもと思ったが、今日の僕の失態の後では、それも極めて怪しい。それはともかく、2人で改善案について話し合っているとき、僕はよく考えずにドキュメンテーション課の武田課長の悪口を言ってしまい、それに米澤部長が激怒したのだ。

　社内での武田課長の一般的なイメージは、どちらかというと能力の低い人というものだ。その最大の理由の1つが、彼はこの会社の3人の創業者の1人にもかかわらず、いまだに課長だということだ。他の2人の創業者は富沢社長と小林取締役なのに。課長は日常的な仕事にもあまり関わろうとしない。主にただみんなの仕事をチェックしてやり直すように言ったりするだけだ。だから、僕は経営側も彼について同じ意見だろうと思ったのだ。課長の悪口を言ったとき、米澤部長からは事情を全部知らない者に人を評価する権利はないと言われた。部長は僕が今富沢で働くことができているのは武田課長のおかげだと言った。2000年問題を利用して会社の利益を上げることができるというアイデアを思いついたのは武田課長だという。その案は大成功を収めてすぐに社員の数を2倍以上にし、会社を発展への道に導いた。部長は、武田課長が作って数々の新聞に載せられたという広告も見せてくれた。

　アメリカやヨーロッパ、インドに支社を設立し、時差を利用して24時間体制でコードを書くことを可能にし、ライバル企業より開発期間を短くできたのも武田課長のアイデアだった。

　今は本当に自分が恥ずかしい。ウィンストン先生が僕たちに「本を表紙で判断するな」ということわざを教えてくれたことがあったのに、僕がやったのはまさにそれだ。言い訳のしようもない！

新渡戸

ad that was placed in various newspapers ►

新聞広告を書いてみよう!

Are You Sure Your System is Reliable? Can You Survive Y2K?

If you cannot answer "yes" to the above two questions, you are advised to get your system checked.

Our team of experts will run a full diagnostic analysis of your system to determine your level of security against the Y2K bug. All potential problems will be repaired swiftly and inexpensively.
Call us for a quotation!

Free Quotations

You will be visited by one of our engineers, who will gauge the scale of your system and provide a FREE quotation within three working days.

Call Tomizawa & Co., Ltd.　03-0450-XXXX
PIC: H. Takeda

御社のシステムは本当に信用できますか？
Y2Kを生き延びることができますか？

もし上の2つの質問に「はい」と答えられなければ、
システムを確認することをお勧めします。

当社の専門家チームが、御社のシステムの完全な診断分析を行い、2000年問題に対する
セキュリティレベルを判断いたします。可能性のある問題すべてを迅速かつ安価で修正いた
します。

お見積りのお電話をください！

無料お見積り

当社のエンジニアの1人がおうかがいして御社のシステムの規模を評価し、
3営業日以内に無料でお見積りをご提供いたします。

（株）富沢にお電話ください

03-0450-XXXX
責任者: 武田

クイックQ&A

Q Diagnosing the level of system security is provided as a free service. True or false?
（システムのセキュリティレベルの診断は無料サービスとして提供されます。正しいですか、誤りですか）

POINT

you are advised to ～というフレーズはit is recommended that you ～の別の言い方ですが、
recommendを使うと、相手は最適なことが何かわかっていないというニュアンスが含まれるため、前者
のほうがやや丁寧な言い回しです。そのため、前者のほうが顧客とのやり取りではよく使われます。以下
はその用例です。

・You are advised to contact our sales representative if you have any questions.
（ご不明な点がございましたら、営業担当者にご連絡ください）
・You are advised to replace the batteries when performance deteriorates. （パフォー
マンスが低下した場合はバッテリーの交換をお勧めします）
・You are advised to report all unsolicited e-mail to the administrator. （迷惑メールは
すべて管理者に報告することをお勧めします）

A False（誤り）

2000年問題の説明を読んでみよう!

Millennium Bug

The millennium bug, which was also known as the year 2000 problem and the Y2K problem, arose through the custom in the 20th century of storing calendar data in computers using only the last two digits of the year instead of four. This made the year 2000 indistinguishable from the year 1900 at "00," and chaos on a global scale was predicted.

The problem was triggered by the fact that storage on both mainframe and personal computers was both limited and expensive at the end of the last century. There was consequently much pressure for programmers to reduce the amount of data generated, and one of the techniques for doing this was to store calendar data as six digits, with two digits each for the month, day and year. The date "July 22nd 1995" was therefore stored as 072295.

A rush to correct potential malfunctions started throughout the world. The companies that could afford it expanded their storage space and had all programs modified to accept and store four-digit years, which was time-consuming and very expensive. The least expensive method was known as windowing and involved adding a small patch directing the computer to treat all two-digit years larger than a specific value (year) as 20th century dates and all two-digit years smaller than that value as 21st century dates.

There were a few problems reported during the roll-over to 2000, such as cellphones deleting new messages instead of old messages, but in general there was none of the chaos or disruption that everybody had expected.

2000年問題

ミレニアム・バグは、西暦2000年問題、Y2K問題としても知られていましたが、4桁の代わりにその年の下2桁だけを使ってコンピュータの日付表示の保存をしていた20世紀の習慣によって起こりました。これによって「00」では2000年が1900年と見分けがつかなくなり、地球規模での大混乱が予測されました。

問題はメインフレームとパソコンの両方のメモリが前世紀の終わりには限りがあり高価だったという事実が引き金となりました。その結果、プログラマーたちには生み出されるデータの総量を少しでも減らすという重圧がかかり、それをする技術の1つは年月日をそれぞれ2桁で、計6桁の表示で日付を保存することでした。従って1995年7月22日は072295と保存されました。

世界中で潜在的な誤作動を修正することが大急ぎで始まりました。余裕のある企業はストレージを増やしたり、4桁の年を受け入れて保存するようにすべてのプログラムを修正したりしましたが、これには時間と費用がとてもかかりました。最も安価な方法はウィンドウイングとして知られ、それは特定の値（年）よりも大きい2桁の年すべてを20世紀の日付として、その値よりも小さい2桁の年を21世紀の日付として扱うようにコンピュータに指示する小さな修正を加えるといったものでした。

2000年になるまでの間、携帯が古いメッセージの代わりに新しいメッセージを消去してしまうなどの、いくつかの問題は報告されましたが、全体としては誰もが思っていたような混乱や崩壊は何もありませんでした。

クイックQ&A

Q ＞ **Why would computers potentially confuse 1910 with 2010?**
（コンピュータが1910年と2010年を混同する可能性があったのはなぜですか）

POINT

第2段落にあるtriggerはオランダ語で「引く」という意味を表すtrekkerに由来しており、「ある出来事や一連の反応のきっかけになる」という意味を持ちます。以下はその例です。
- The earthquake triggered widespread landslides. （その地震は広範囲の土砂崩れを引き起こした）
- The controversial TV documentary triggered a deluge of complaints from viewers. （物議を醸しているそのドキュメンタリー番組は視聴者からの苦情を殺到させた）
- Her anger was triggered by his insensitive remarks. （彼女の怒りのきっかけは彼の無神経な言葉だった）

A ＞ Because the last two digits are the same. （下2桁が同じだからです）

223

CD
2-11

実際の会話を聞いて話してみよう!

S e t t i n g :

> Mr. Yonezawa and Nitobe have just finished discussing the Kaizen competition.

Yonezawa: So, do you think the Documentation Section can save as much money as you forecast?

Nitobe: That depends on whether we can manage to keep Mr. Takeda awake.

Yonezawa: Enough! Don't comment on things you know nothing about! It's because of Mr. Takeda that you have a job here. I demand that you give him the respect he deserves!

Nitobe: I... I'm sorry. I didn't mean to...

Yonezawa: I've heard the rumors about why Mr. Takeda is still a manager. Well, let me put you straight. He is a manager because he wants to be a manager. He has no interest in administration, and specifically requested that he is not promoted. But that man is a savior, and he is welcome to stay in the company until he is 100 years old if that is what he wants. Do you understand?

Nitobe: Yes, sir. I'm sorry...

Yonezawa: Have you ever heard of the millennium bug?

Nitobe: I've heard of it, but I don't know much about it.

Yonezawa: The millennium bug was a computer glitch that gave rise to concerns of all computer systems failing on January 1st, 2000. At that time, Tomizawa had only fourteen employees. Mr. Takeda came up with the idea of offering a service that would check customer's systems for the bug and make all repairs necessary to survive the switch across to the new millennium. The service was incredibly popular and led to the employment of another twenty people, but we still had to subcontract out about 40% of the work. It is this simple idea that helped Tomizawa grow into the company it is. Without it, we probably would not be here today.

Nitobe: I'm sorry, sir. I had no idea...

Yonezawa: It was also Mr. Takeda who suggested that we open offices abroad and develop systems in modules so that we can speed up development periods. He is an idea man, not an administrator, but he is probably the most important man in the company. Respect him!

Mr. Yonezawa went ballistic

場面：

> 米澤部長と新渡戸がちょうど今、改善コンペについて話し終わった。

Y： それで、ドキュメンテーション課は君の計画と同じだけの金額を節約できると思うかい？

N： 武田課長が居眠りさえしなければですが。

Y： 黙りなさい！　知りもしないことについてとやかく言うんじゃない！　君がここで働くことができているのは武田課長のおかげだ。それなりの敬意を示しなさい！

N： す、すみません。そんなつもりは…。

Y： 武田さんがなぜいまだに課長なのかについてのうわさ話は私も聞いている。だがここではっきりさせておこう。あの人が課長なのは課長のままでいたいからだ。経営に興味はないから昇進はしたくないとわざわざ要望したのだよ。だがあの人は我が社の恩人で、それが彼の願いなら100歳まで会社にいてくださってもいいくらいだ。わかったかね。

N： はい、部長。申し訳ありません…。

Y： 2000年問題のことは知っているかい？

N： 聞いたことはありますが、よく知りません。

Y： 2000年問題は、2000年1月1日にすべてのコンピュータシステムが誤作動を起こすという懸念を生じさせたコンピュータの欠陥だった。当時、富沢ISの社員は14人しかいなかった。武田課長は、顧客のシステムにそのバグがないか検査して新千年紀への移り変わりを無事に乗り切るのに必要なすべての修復を行うサービスを提供するというアイデアを考えたんだ。そのサービスは非常に人気になって、さらに20人の社員を雇用することになったんだが、それでも仕事の約40％は下請けに出さなければならなかったくらいだ。このシンプルなアイデアが、富沢ISが現在のような会社に発展する助けになったんだ。それがなければ、私たちは今日ここにはいないだろう。

N： 申し訳ありません、部長。全く知りませんでした…。

Y： 海外に支社を設立してシステムをモジュール単位で開発し、開発期間を短縮することを提案したのも武田課長だ。あの人はアイデアマンで経営者ではないが、おそらく社内で最も重要な人物だ。敬意を払いなさい！

キーワードやフレーズをチェック!

☐ make a mistake　　間違いを犯す

Make sure that you don't **make a mistake** with the figures.
数字にミスがないよう確認してください。

She **made the mistake** of overestimating her own capabilities.
彼女は自分の能力を高く見積もりすぎるという失敗をした。

☐ should have known better　　うかつだった、愚かだった

He **should have known better** than to arrive at work without a necktie.
ネクタイをしないで会社に来るなんて彼はうかつだな。

He criticized the manager's decision, but he **should have known better**.
彼は部長の決定を批判するなんてバカなことをした。

☐ derogatory remark　　悪口

The director was forced to resign after he made a **derogatory remark** at the General Meeting.
その役員は株主総会で軽蔑的な発言をしてから辞職に追い込まれた。

I was shocked when he used a **derogatory remark** as his system ID.
彼が自分のシステムIDに悪口を使ったのにはギョッとした。

☐ go ballistic　　激怒する

The auditor **went ballistic** when wrongly accused of embezzlement.
監査役は無実の横領で告発され激怒した。

He is usually fairly temperate, but he tends to **go ballistic** when insulted.
彼は普段はかなり穏やかだが、侮辱されるとすごく怒る傾向がある。

have the right　権利がある

She **has the right** to access confidential information on the company's system.
彼女は会社のシステムの機密情報にアクセスする権利を持っている。

The company does not **have the right** to make us work on Sundays.
会社には私たちを日曜日に働かせる権利はない。

on a 24-hour basis　24時間体制で

The Customer Support Section operates **on a 24-hour basis**.
顧客サポート課は24時間体制で営業している。

The company expects me to be available **on a 24-hour basis**.
会社は私に24時間仕事ができることを求めている。

マナーのヒント

　ことわざは、ある状況を極めて少ない言葉でまとめるのにとても役立つことがあり、そのため日常的な仕事の場でよく使われています。以下は最も頻繁に使われることわざの例です。

- A bad workman always blames his tools.（下手な職人は自分の道具にケチをつけるものだ）
- A chain is only as strong as its weakest link.（鎖の強さはその最も弱い環で決まる）
- Action speaks louder than words.（行動は言葉よりも雄弁に語る）
- All that glitters is not gold.（光るものがすべて金とは限らない）
- A stitch in time saves nine.（時を得た一針は九針を省く）
- Barking dogs seldom bite.（吠える犬はめったに噛まない）
- Don't bite off more than you can chew.（噛めないほどの量をほおばるな）
- Don't blow your own trumpet.（自分のためにラッパを吹くな>自画自賛するな）
- Fortune favors the brave.（幸運は勇者に味方する）

FEBRUARY 9TH (SUNDAY)

I had the shock of my life on Friday, and I still haven't fully recovered. It all started on Thursday when the president called an irregular meeting of the board for the following afternoon. Nobody knew what the meeting was about, but irregular meetings are not that uncommon, so nobody thought much about it. Then, on Friday morning, I **received an e-mail from the president** (p.232) informing me of the reason for the meeting.

He intends to resign, effective from the last day of March.

I was astounded to hear this, although I can understand his reasons. He will be 72 years old this year, and he wants to enjoy the remaining time he has without having to attend the office every day. He is also satisfied with the way that the company is steadily growing, and he feels the time has come to step aside and let somebody else take control. He basically said the same thing **during the afternoon meeting** (p.234).

There are **eight members of the board** (p.230) in total, seven of whom have voting rights. The president, who is the chairman of the board, only casts his vote if there is a 3-3 tie, giving him the deciding vote. The next president will be selected from among the board members, and we have been given until February 21st to either put up our names as candidates or drop out. The president instructed me to stand as a candidate.

I had to read my protégé, Nitobe, the riot act last week for disrespecting Hiroshi Takeda, the manager of the Documentation Section, although all in all, I think everything worked out well. In the eyes of the people who have been with the company since the beginning, Takeda is an unsung hero. It is because of him that the company grew to the size it is today. However, the people who don't know of his contributions to the company tend to look down on him because of his lack of interest in administrative matters. He is a manager through choice. If he wanted to be a director, all he has to do is say so. Now that I have explained things to Nitobe, however, I believe that he will stick up for Takeda and spread the word of his importance to the company.

Yonezawa

キーワード＆キーフレーズ→p.236

２月９日（日曜日）

　金曜日に心底ショックな出来事があり、いまだに完全には立ち直ることができていない。事の始まりは、木曜日に社長が、翌日の午後に臨時の役員会議を開催すると通知してきたことだ。誰も何に関する会議かわからなかったが、会議の臨時開催はそれほど珍しいことではなかったため、皆深くは考えなかった。だがその後、金曜日の朝、私は会議の理由を伝えるメールを社長から受け取った。

52

　社長は３月末をもって辞任するつもりだという。

　私はこれを知って衝撃を受けたが、彼がそう言う理由は理解できる。彼は今年で７２歳になるので、毎日会社に通うことなく余生を楽しみたいのだ。社長は我が社が着実に成長していっている今の状態にも満足していて、自分は身を引いて誰か他の者に主導権を渡すときが来たと感じているらしい。その午後の役員会議でも彼は大体同じことを言っていた。

　役員会のメンバーは全部で８人おり、そのうち７人が議決権を持っている。議長を務める社長は３対３で票が同数だった場合のみ投票し、決定権を有する。次期社長は役員会のメンバーから選ばれるのだが、私たちは２月２１日までに候補者として名乗り出るか辞退するかしなければならない。社長は私に立候補するように言った。

　部下の新渡戸が先週、ドキュメンテーション課長の武田宏さんをばかにしたときは強く叱責しなければならなかったが、全体としてみれば結果的にこれでうまくいったのだろうと思っている。創業当時から我が社にいる者たちの目から見れば、武田さんは陰の英雄だ。この会社が今日の大きさまで成長したのはあの人のおかげなのだ。しかし、彼の我が社への貢献を知らない人間は、彼の経営マターへの関心のなさのために彼を見下しがちだ。彼は自ら望んで課長のままなのだ。仮に役員になりたいのなら、彼はそう言うだけでいい。だが、私が新渡戸に事情を説明したので、新渡戸もこれからは武田さんを支持し、彼の我が社にとっての重要性を広めてくれるだろう。

米澤

役員メンバーの紹介を書いてみよう!

Tomizawa Integrated Solutions, Inc.

Members of the Board of Directors

The Tomizawa Board of Directors presides over all decisions relating to the company's strategic, corporate, financial and technological policies, and monitors the implementation of these policies.

Hideyuki Tomizawa:
　President and Chairman of the Board. Holds deciding vote.
Seiji Kobayashi:
　Managing Director. Voting rights.
Osamu Yonezawa:
　Director of the Global Logistics Department. Voting rights.
Jiro Okada:
　Director of the Sales Department. Voting rights.
Masami Fujiwara:
　Director of the General Affairs Department. Voting rights.
Mami Uchida:
　Director of the Accounting Department. Voting rights.
Yuji Sugimoto:
　Director of the Systems Development Department. Voting rights.
Kosuke Kaneko:
　Auditor. No voting rights.

（株）富沢インテグレーテッド・ソリューションズ

役員会人員

富沢の役員は企業戦略および企業、財務、技術的な方針に関するすべての決定を統括し、これらの方針の遂行を監督する。

富沢秀幸：
　社長兼役員会議長。決定票を有する。

小林誠司：
　専務取締役。議決権。

米澤修：
　海外事業部部長。議決権。

岡田次郎：
　営業部部長。議決権。

藤原正美：
　総務部部長。議決権。

内田真美：
　経理部部長。議決権。

杉本雄二：
　システム開発部部長。議決権。

金子幸助：
　会計監査役。議決権なし。

52

クイックQ&A

Q) **The Board of Directors is in charge of making sure that the company's policies are correctly carried out. True or false?**
（役員会は会社の方針が正しく遂行されるようにするという責任を負っています。正しいですか、誤りですか）

POINT

1文目にあるpresideはラテン語で「守る、防御する」という意味のpraesidereに由来しています。presidentという語もそのラテン語から来ています。presideはたいていoverと組み合わせて使われますが、The meeting started with the chairman presiding.（その会議は議長が取り仕切る形で始まった）のように現在分詞で、あるいはThe presiding judge pronounced him not guilty.（裁判長は彼に無罪の判決を言い渡した）のように形容詞的に、単独で使うこともできます。
なお、preside overの類義語にはadminister、supervise、govern、oversee、manageなどがあります。

A) True（正しい）

社長から役員へのEメールを読んでみよう!

From:	H. Tomizawa <htomizawa@tomizawais.co.jp>
Sent:	Friday, February 07, 10:41 AM
To:	O. Yonezawa <oyonezawa@tomizawais.co.jp>
Subject:	Today's Board Meeting

Osamu,

I have some news that may surprise you. The reason why I have called this afternoon's board meeting is because I have decided to retire. If we can elect the next president within a reasonable time, I intend my resignation to be effective from the last day of March.

The only other person who knows about this is Seiji Kobayashi, so please don't discuss it with anyone else until after the meeting.

My main reason for this is my age. I'll be 72 this year, and I'd like to relax a little after working hard for fifty straight years. The company is running smoothly and enjoying steady growth, so I think the time is ripe for me to step aside. I want you to put your name up as a candidate for the next president. I think you are the perfect choice. Don't let me down.

See you at this afternoon's meeting.

Tomizawa

POINT

まず初めに最も大切な要件（ここでは、自身の退職）を伝えてから、その理由や詳細、相手への希望などが続けられています。また、相手が受けるであろうショックを和らげるような配慮もされています。

差出人: 富沢 <htomizawa@tomizawais.co.jp>
送信: 2月7日（金曜日）午前10:41
宛先: 米澤様 <oyonezawa@tomizawais.co.jp>
件名: 本日の役員会議

修へ

驚くかもしれない知らせがあります。今日の午後の役員会議を招集した理由は、退職することを決めたからです。相応の期間内に次期社長を選任できれば、3月末日をもって私は辞職するつもりです。

このことを知っている他の者は小林誠司だけなので、会議が終わるまでは他の誰にも話さないでいただきたい。

退職の主な理由は年齢です。私も今年で72歳になるし、50年間ずっと働きづめだったので少しゆっくりしたいと思います。会社は順調に回って、着実に成長しているので身を引くにはちょうどよい頃合いだと思います。次期社長候補としては君に名乗り出てもらいたいのだが。君は完璧な候補だと思います。私を失望させないでくれたまえ。

では午後の会議で。

富沢

52

クイックQ&A

Q 〉 **How many people within the company have knowledge of Tomizawa's resignation?**
（社内で富沢の辞任のことを知っている人は何人ですか）

POINT

英語では、人間だけでなく無生物を主語にしても何かをenjoyしていると表すことができますが、その場合のニュアンスはexperience「～を経験している」になります。以下はその例です。
・Japan is enjoying a period of high employment. （日本は近頃高い雇用率を経験している）
・Contrary to last year, ski resorts are enjoying sufficient snowfall this year. （昨年とは対照的に、今年スキー場は十分な積雪量を得ている）
・Hawaii enjoys clement weather throughout the year. （ハワイは1年を通して温暖な気候だ）

A 〉 Three(3人)

実際の会話を聞いて話してみよう!

SETTING:

> After exchanging pleasantries with the directors, Tomizawa starts the meeting
> in his role as Chairman of the Board.

Tomizawa: Thank you all for gathering at such short notice. There is only one item
on today's agenda, so I won't keep you long. I called today's meeting to
announce my retirement.

Directors: (Gasps and muttering)

Tomizawa: It may seem like a sudden decision, but I have been thinking about this
for more than a year. I will be 72 years old soon, and I no longer have
the stamina to work at the same level as I always have. I have therefore
decided that staying at the helm will be detrimental to the company, and
intend to step aside to allow fresh blood to take over.

Fujiwara: Are you sure that this is the best thing for the company? You look strong
enough and healthy enough to me. You could continue to lead us for
many years yet.

Tomizawa: Thank you for that diagnosis, doctor.

Directors: (Laughs)

Tomizawa: But that will only be delaying the inevitable. At some time, I will have to
leave. I'd rather do that in a well-orchestrated manner while I am still of
sound mind than to suddenly be forced to leave due to illness, dementia
or even death. I won't live forever, but, in the right hands, maybe the
company can.

Sugimoto: Who will take over from you? Are you thinking of appointing a new
president from outside the company?

Tomizawa: Nobody knows more or cares more about Tomizawa Integrated Solutions
than the people in this room. The company has grown into a large family,
and I will not accept somebody from outside of this family. I therefore
want one of you to take my place.

Directors: (Applause and cheers)

Tomizawa: You will decide the next president from among yourselves. You have
up until the 21st of this month to decide whether you wish to put your
name forward as the next president or stand down. A vote will then be
taken on whom the next president will be.

during the afternoon meeting

場面：

役員たちと挨拶を交わした後、富沢が役員会議長として会議を始める。

T： みんな、突然の招集だったが集まってくれてありがとう。今日の議題は1つ
しかないので、長い時間は取らせない。私が今日の会議を開いたのは自
身の辞任を発表するためだ。

D： （息をのむ音やざわめき）

T： 唐突な決断に思えるかもしれないが、このことはもう1年以上考えていた。
私はもうすぐ72歳になるし、以前と同じだけの仕事を続ける気力がもはや
ない。よって、私がこれ以上主導権を握っていることは会社にとって害にな
ると判断し、引退して若い人材に役目を引き継がせようと考えている。

52

F： 本当にこれがこの会社にとって最善のことなのですか。私には社長は十分
しっかりとして健康に見えます。まだこの先何年も私たちを率いていくことが
できるでしょう。

T： 診断ありがとうございます、先生。

D： （笑い）

T： しかしそれでは、避けられない問題を先送りにするだけだ。いつかは退か
なければならない。ならば私は病気や認知症、もっと言えば死のせいで
突然会社を去らなければならなくなるより、自分の頭がしっかりしているうち
にきちんと計画した形で辞職したい。私は永久には生きられないが、ふさ
わしい人間の手にあれば、会社は永遠に残ることができるかもしれないか
らな。

S： 誰が社長の役割を引き継ぐのですか。社外から新しい社長を任命するお
つもりですか。

T： この部屋にいる人間以上に富沢インテグレーテッド・ソリューションズのこと
をよく知り、また大切に思っている者はいないだろう。この会社は大きな家
族に育っており、私はこの家族外からの人材は受け入れない。なので、こ
の中の誰か1人に後任になってほしい。

D： （拍手と歓声）

T： 自分たちで君たちの中から次の社長を決定してほしい。今月の21日までに
次期社長として名乗り出るか辞退するか決めてくれ。その後に、次期社長
を誰にするかについて投票を行う。

KEY WORDS & PHRASES

CD
2-14

キーワードやフレーズをチェック!

☐ shock of *one's* life　大変な驚き、ショック

We received the **shock of our lives** when Mr. Humphrey was fired.
ハンフリーさんがクビになったとき、私たちは心底ショックを受けた。

She had the **shock of her life** when she was transferred overseas.
彼女は海外転勤になったことにひどく驚いた。

☐ step aside　退く、人にゆずる

He decided to **step aside** to take responsibility for the scandal.
彼はスキャンダルの責任を取って引退することにした。

He ran the department for eighteen years before **stepping aside**.
彼は18年間その部署を運営してから引退した。

☐ take control　統制する、管理する、主導権を握る

She **took control** of the meeting by banging her fist on the table.
彼女はテーブルにこぶしを打ちつけることによって会議の主導権を握った。

The company was nearing liquidation until the new president **took control**.
その会社は破産寸前だったが、新しい社長が対処した。

☐ drop out　脱落する

He played for the company softball team, but **dropped out** after an injury.
彼は会社のソフトボールチームの選手をしていたが、けがをして脱退した。

She was the original leader of the project, but **dropped out** when the responsibility became too heavy.
彼女はそのプロジェクトのもともとのリーダーだったが、責任が重すぎるようになって辞退した。

read *one* the riot act （〜を）強く叱責する

Graham was **read the riot act** for being late every day.
グラハムは毎日遅刻していることで強く注意を受けた。

The manager **read him the riot act** for insulting a customer.
部長は彼が顧客をばかにしたことを強く叱った。

unsung hero 陰の立役者、縁の下の力持ち

The **unsung heroes** of the project were the clerks who documented every step.
このプロジェクトの陰の英雄は、すべての段階を文書化した社員たちだった。

The president's secretary is an **unsung hero** for making sure he has every item of information he needs.
社長の秘書は彼が必要な情報をすべて持っているようにしている縁の下の力持ちだ。

52

マナーのヒント

　社内の階級を表す肩書は、以前はシンプルなものでした。会社におけるトップの立場がpresident「社長」（イギリスではchairman「会長」）、次にmanaging director「取締役」、その次がgeneral manager「本部長」となっていました。一部の会社は現在でもこれに従っていますが、近年はCEO、CFOなどのCレベルと呼ばれる肩書で示される傾向にあります。presidentは現在では名目上の地位というニュアンスを含んでおり、presidentに代わって会社を経営するのがChief Executive Officer (CEO)「最高経営責任者」です。会社のトップであり実際の経営も行う人の正式な肩書がPresident and CEO「社長兼CEO」なのはこのためです。ちなみに、chairmanという語は会社の取締役会の会長や、協会、組合、連合会などのトップの立場を示します。他のCレベルの肩書には以下のようなものがあります。

　CAO: Chief Administrative Officer「最高総務責任者」
　CFO: Chief Financial Officer「最高財務責任者」
　COO: Chief Operations Officer「最高執行責任者」
　CMO: Chief Marketing Officer「最高マーケティング責任者」
　CCO: Chief Communications Officer「最高コミュニケーション責任者」
　CBO: Chief Business Officer「最高業務責任者」
　CSO: Chief Strategy Officer「最高戦略責任者」
　CTO: Chief Technology Officer「最高技術責任者」

DAY 53

FEBRUARY 21ST (FRIDAY)

There's a strange atmosphere in the company the last couple of weeks. Mr. Yonezawa seems preoccupied, and it is not uncommon to see the directors chatting in groups or holding meetings. All of the staff have noticed it, and many are worried that we are heading for some sort of upheaval. Some are even speculating that the company is in financial trouble and that we may be in for a restructure.

I certainly hope not. I would hate to be put in a position where I have to find another job. Personally, I am trying to be optimistic. They are probably just discussing opening a new branch in Japan or overseas. I'm keeping my fingers crossed, anyway.

I went out for dinner with Aya Shibata last night. We've managed to keep a platonic relationship going, and we both enjoy each other's company. We usually meet up and go out for dinner or a drink together or with a few other people about once or twice a month. She always has a bright outlook and amusing sense of humor, and it is great fun being around her. Last night we went to an inexpensive Italian restaurant for pasta and shared a bottle of wine. I really enjoyed it.

Misaki and I had a fun day on Wednesday. We received an **e-mail from Mr. Winston (p.242)** asking us to take part in a market survey for an American ice-cream company. A friend of his, Sandra Baker, works for a Tokyo-based marketing company named Plimsole Marketing, and they are carrying out a survey for the ice-cream company, which is planning on starting up a chain of ice-cream parlors in Asia sometime in the future. Sandra sent us a **questionnaire to fill in and return (p.240)**, and then Mr. Winston took us to the company for an interview on Wednesday afternoon.

Apparently, the ice-cream company is determined to enter the Asian market, but has still not decided where to start. They are therefore carrying out market surveys in Japan, China, South Korea and Taiwan. Sandra came across as very efficient at her job, and I **enjoyed the interview very much (p.244)**. Mr. Winston has so many interesting friends.

Nitobe

キーワード＆キーフレーズ→p.246

２月２１日（金曜日）

　ここ２週間ほど、社内にいつもと違う空気が流れている。米澤部長は何か考え事をしているようだし、重役たちが何人かで話し合っていたり会議を開いたりしているのをよく見かける。社員の皆もそれに気づいていて、多くはこれから何か大きな変動があるのではないかと心配している。会社が財政難に陥っていて、自分たちはリストラされるのでは、と憶測を巡らせている人までいる。

　そうではないことを僕は心底願っている。別の仕事を探さなければならない立場に立たされるのはごめんだ。けれど自分はもっとポジティブでいようと思っている。経営陣は日本国内か海外に新しい支社を設立しようと相談しているだけかもしれない。でもとりあえず、何もないことを祈っておこう。

　昨夜、柴田彩さんと夕食に出かけた。彼女とはプラトニックな交際を続けることができていて、お互い一緒に過ごすことを楽しく感じている。僕たちは大抵１か月に１、２回くらい会って、２人で、もしくは他の何人かと一緒に夕食に行ったり飲みに行ったりする。彼女はいつも明るいものの見方と素晴らしいユーモアのセンスを持っていて、彼女といるのはとても面白い。昨夜は２人でそんなに高くないイタリアンレストランに行ってパスタを食べて、一緒にワインを１本飲んだ。本当に楽しかったな。

　水曜日は岬と僕にとって楽しい１日だった。僕たちはウィンストン先生から、アメリカのアイスクリームの会社の市場調査に協力してくれないかというメールを受け取ったのだ。彼の友達のサンドラ・ベーカーさんが、東京拠点のプリムソール・マーケティングというマーケティング会社で働いていて、この会社で、将来的にアジアでアイスクリームチェーン店をオープンすることを計画しているアイスクリーム会社のための調査を行っているという。サンドラさんから回答を記入して送り返すためのアンケート用紙が送られてきて、水曜日の午後にインタビューを受けるため、ウィンストン先生がサンドラさんの勤める会社に僕たちを連れて行ってくれた。

　聞いたところによると、そのアイスクリーム会社はアジア市場への進出を決意しているけれど何から始めるべきかはまだ決めていないらしい。なので日本、中国、韓国、台湾で市場調査を実施しているそうだ。サンドラさんはとても仕事がうまいという印象だったし、取材を受けるのはとても楽しかった。ウィンストン先生には興味深い友達がたくさんいるなあ。

新渡戸

questionnaire to fill in and return ►

アンケートを書いてみよう!

Ice Cream Marketing Survey

Plimsole Marketing Japan, Inc.

Thank you for taking part in this survey. Kindly fill in the details below, and then answer the questions.

Name: Shinnosuke Nitobe   Gender: Male   Age: 27

1. How often do you eat ice cream? (once a week, once a month, etc.)
Approximately once per week in summer, once per month in winter

2. How do you prefer to eat ice cream? (cones, with a spoon, etc.)
Ice cream cones

3. Where do you usually eat ice cream? (home, restaurants, ice-cream parlors, etc.)
At home, at amusement parks, on the beach, when out shopping, etc.

4. What flavor ice cream do you prefer? (vanilla, chocolate, strawberry, etc.)
Vanilla, caramel, mint, chocolate

5. What ice cream toppings do you prefer? (nuts, fruit, cookies, etc.)
Nuts, sometimes cookies

6. How often to you visit ice-cream parlors? (once a week, once a month, etc.)
Very rarely (unless I'm with someone who suggests it)

7. When did you last visit an ice-cream parlor?
Early summer last year

POINT

回答には主語や動詞は必要なく、要点だけを簡潔に書けばよいです。

プリムソール・マーケティング・ジャパン（株）

アイスクリーム・マーケティング調査

当調査にご協力いただきありがとうございます。下記詳細をご記入いただき、質問にお答えいただきますようお願いいたします。

お名前: 新渡戸慎之助　　　　性別: 男性　　　　　　　　ご年齢: 27

1. どのくらいの頻度でアイスクリームを食べますか (週に1度、月に1度など)。
   夏はだいたい1週間に1度、冬は月に1度

2. どのようにアイスクリームを食べるのが好きですか (コーン、スプーンで、など)。
   コーンで

3. アイスクリームはたいていどこで食べますか (家、レストラン、アイスクリーム店など)
   家で、遊園地で、海辺で、買い物で外出しているときに、など

4. どんな味のアイスクリームが好きですか (バニラ、チョコレート、ストロベリーなど)
   バニラ、キャラメル、ミント、チョコレート

5. どんなアイスクリームのトッピングが好きですか (ナッツ、フルーツ、クッキーなど)
   ナッツ、たまにクッキー

6. アイスクリーム店にはどのくらいの頻度で行きますか (週に1度、月に1度など)
   ほぼめったに行かない (行こうという人と一緒でない限り)

7. アイスクリーム店に最後に行ったのはいつですか。
   昨年の夏の初め

53

クイックQ&A

Q〉 In what situations will Nitobe visit an ice-cream parlor?
（新渡戸がアイスクリーム店を訪れるのはどんなときですか）

POINT

通常、アンケートには2つの形式があります。記述式 (上記で使われているのはこちら) と多肢選択式です。多肢選択式では可能な回答の横にそれぞれ小さなボックスがあり、適切な回答のボックスに☑のように印をつけるようになっています。このマークはtickと呼ばれ (日本語のように「チェック (check)」とはいいません)、この語は動詞としても使うことができます。なので指示文はTick the boxes that best represent your answers. (あなたの答えに最も近い項目にチェックを入れてください) やAdd a tick to the boxes that best represent your answers . (あなたの答えに最も近い項目にチェックを加えてください) のようになります。このマークは採点されたテストや答案用紙でも見られますが、日本では一般に不正解を示すのに対し、英語圏ではこれは正解を意味し、間違った答えには「×」がつけられます。

A〉 If he is with someone who suggests it (そうしようという人と一緒のとき)

e-mail from Mr. Winston ►

ウィンストン先生からのEメールを読んでみよう!

From:	Mr. Winston <paulwinston@wmail.ne.jp>
Sent:	Thursday, February 18, 07:14 PM
To:	Shinnosuke Nitobe <snitobe@tomizawais.co.jp>;
	Ichiro Misaki <imisaki@tomizawais.co.jp>
Subject: Market survey	

Hi guys...!

Do either of you guys like ice cream? I just received an e-mail from a
friend of mine who works for a marketing company. She (Sandra Baker)
is carrying out a market survey for a US ice-cream company that wants to
set up a chain of parlors in Japan, and she is looking for men to interview.
She asked me if I knew anybody, and I immediately thought of you two.

I'll get her to e-mail you both a questionnaire, and then we can visit her
office in Yurakucho on Wednesday afternoon for the interview. Don't
forget to fill in the questionnaire and e-mail it back to her!

You may be asked to taste the ice cream, so don't eat too much for
lunch... :-)

Cheers, Paul Winston

POINT

教え子（友人関係とほぼ一緒）へのメールなので、くだけた調子でOK。いきなり、「アイスクリームは好き？」と聞いて関心をつかみます。

差出人：ウィンストン先生 <paulwinston@wmail.ne.jp>
送信： 2月18日（木曜日）午後7:14
宛先： 新渡戸慎之助 <snitobe@tomizawais.co.jp>;
　　　　岬一郎<imisaki@tomizawais.co.jp>
件名： 市場調査

こんにちは、お2人さん！

君たちのどちらか、アイスクリームは好きですか。マーケティング会社に勤める友達からEメールを受け取りました。彼女（サンドラ・ベイカー）は日本にチェーン店を出したがっているアメリカのアイスクリーム会社の市場調査をしているところで、インタビューできる男性を探しています。誰かいないかと尋ねられて、すぐに2人のことが思い浮かんだというわけ。

彼女から君たちにアンケート用紙をメールさせるようにするので、そうしたら水曜日の午後、有楽町にある彼女のオフィスを訪ねてインタビューを受けることになります。アンケートに記入してメールで送り返すのを忘れないでくださいね！

アイスクリームの試食を頼まれるかもしれないから、ランチは食べ過ぎないように…:-)

それじゃ
ポール・ウィンストン

53

クイックQ&A

Q > **What must Nitobe and Misaki do when they receive the questionnaire?**
（新渡戸と岬はアンケート用紙を受け取ったら何をしなければなりませんか）

POINT

interviewという語は質問をしたり質問に答えたりするどんな場面にも使うことができます。就職の面接の他に、容疑者が警察に尋問されるのも、子どもが教師に質問されるのも、一般人がレポーターにインタビューされるのも、政治家が記者会見で取材を受けるのもinterviewです。もともとの意味では直接顔を合わせたやり取りに限られていましたが、現在ではその他の形の質問・返答も含むようになっています。以下はその例です。

・A journalist for the local newspaper interviewed me by e-mail.（その地方新聞の記者はメールで私への取材をした）
・She received her job interview via video conference.（彼女は就職の面接をテレビ会議で受けた）
・The real estate agent called me and interviewed me over the phone.（その不動産業者は私に電話をかけてきて質問をした）

A > Fill it in and e-mail it back（回答を記入してメールで送り返す）

実際の会話を聞いて話してみよう！

SETTING:

> Nitobe and Misaki are being interviewed by Sandra Baker as part of her market research into ice cream preferences.

Baker: First of all, I'd like to thank you very much for taking part in our survey. Our client operates an ice-cream parlor franchise that is a household name in America and Europe, but it has no presence in Asia. We are in charge of market research in Japan, South Korea, China and Taiwan, and they will decide where to launch their first parlor in Asia based on the results of our survey.

Misaki: Mr. Winston said that you wish to interview men. Is there any reason for that?

Baker: Yes, there is. We have been concentrating our research on women, who typically use ice-cream parlors more frequently than men, but our client hopes to build up a chain of parlors that is popular among couples. It is therefore necessary to make sure that the items preferred by men are also available, so men are the target of the second phase of our survey.

Nitobe: Please go ahead. Ask us anything you want.

Baker: Thank you. I noticed that you both chose savory flavors for your preferred ice cream. Are you not fond of fruit-based flavors?

Misaki: Personally, no. Fruit makes ice cream too sweet. My favorite flavor is matcha.

Nitobe: I agree with Misaki. Ice cream is ice cream, and fruit is fruit. I can't see the reason for mixing them together.

Baker: If you visited an ice-cream parlor serving only fruit-based flavors, what would you order?

Nitobe: If I had no choice, then I'd probably go for mango or orange?

Baker: Not strawberry or cherry?

Nitobe: No, definitely not.

Misaki: If they only had fruit flavors, I'd just order a coffee.

Baker: I see. That's very interesting. So, now let's move onto toppings...

enjoyed the interview very much

場面:

> 新渡戸と岬が、サンドラ・ベーカーにアイスクリームの好みに関する彼女の市場調査の一環としてインタビューを受けている。

B： まずは、調査にご協力いただき誠にありがとうございます。私どもの顧客はアメリカとヨーロッパで有名なアイスクリームのフランチャイズ店を経営しているのですが、アジアにはまだ進出していません。私たちは日本、韓国、中国、台湾における市場調査を請け負っていて、顧客はその調査結果に基づいてアジアのどこに１号店をオープンするかを決めることになっています。

M： ウィンストン先生はあなた方が男性からアンケートを取りたいのだと言っていました。何か理由があるんですか。

B： ええ、ありますよ。今までは一般に男性よりも頻繁にアイスクリーム店に行く女性のほうに調査を絞ってきたのですが、顧客はカップルに人気があるチェーン店をつくりたいと考えています。そのため男性好みの商品も置く必要があるので、調査の第２段階は男性をターゲットにしているのです。

N： どうぞ。必要なことは何でも聞いてください。

B： ありがとうございます。では、お２人とも好みのアイスクリームの味としてフルーツ以外の風味を選んだことに気づいたのですが。フルーツ系の味は好きではないのですか。

M： 個人的には好きではありません。フルーツのアイスクリームは甘すぎるんです。僕の好きな味は抹茶です。

N： 僕も岬と同じです。アイスクリームはアイスクリーム、フルーツはフルーツです。一緒に混ぜたくはありません。

B： フルーツ系の味しか置いていないアイスクリーム店に行ったとしたら、何を注文しますか。

N： それしかない場合は、たぶんマンゴーかオレンジでしょうか。

B： ストロベリーやチェリーは？

N： いえ、それは絶対ないです。

M： フルーツの味しか置いていなかったら、僕はコーヒーだけ頼みます。

B： なるほど。とても興味深いですね。それでは、今度はトッピングについて…。

53

キーワードやフレーズをチェック!

☐ **not uncommon to see ～**　　～を見かけることはよくある

It is **not uncommon to see** Roger complaining to his manager.
ロジャーが上司のことを愚痴っているのを目にするのは珍しいことではない。

It is **not uncommon to see** stock prices fall when a company revises its profit forecast.
企業が利益予測を修正したときに株価が下がるのはよくあることだ。

☐ **head for ～**　　～に向かう

We may be **heading for** a recession if the economy doesn't pick up soon.
経済がすぐに回復しないなら、これから不景気になるかもしれない。

The company is **heading for** disaster if it doesn't change its sales strategies.
この会社は販売戦略を変えない限り大惨事に向かうだろう。

☐ **put in a position**　　立場に置く

She was **put in a position** where she had to defend her decision.
彼女は自分の決断を擁護しなければならない立場に立たされた。

I hate being **put in a position** where I have to work excessive overtime.
私は過度の残業をしなければならない状況に置かれるのは嫌いだ。

☐ **keep *one's* fingers crossed**　　祈る

I'm **keeping my fingers crossed** that we receive a substantial pay rise next year.
来年はそれなりの昇給があることを祈っている。

I doubt if I'll receive the promotion, but I'm **keeping my fingers crossed**.
私が昇進するかどうかは疑わしいが、一応祈っておく。

start up 〜　　〜を操業開始する

She **started up** a small accessory company ten years ago, and it grew into a well-known brand.
彼女は10年前に小さなアクセサリー会社を立ち上げ、それは有名なブランドへと成長した。

He is thinking of **starting up** a restaurant in Shibuya if he can find an investor.
彼は出資者が見つかれば渋谷でレストランを開業しようかと考えている。

come across as 〜　　〜のような印象を与える

He **comes across as** childish when people criticize him.
彼は人に批判されると子どもじみた態度になる印象だ。

53

She **came across as** extremely talented when she gave her first presentation.
彼女は最初のプレゼンテーションで非常に有能に見えた。

マナーのヒント

　面接にも様々なものがありますが、中でも最も重要なのが就職の面接です。従って、想定される質問に対して事前に準備しておく必要があります。会社によって異なりますが、英語圏の就職面接で最もよくある質問の例を紹介します。

- ・Why should we hire you?（当社があなたを採用するべき理由は何ですか）
- ・What is your greatest strength?（あなたの一番の強みは何ですか）
- ・What is your greatest weakness?（あなたの一番の弱みは何ですか）
- ・What can you do better for us than the other applicants?（あなたが他の志望者よりも当社に貢献できることは何ですか）
- ・What are your salary expectations?（給与に希望はありますか）
- ・Why do you want this job?（なぜこの仕事をしたいのですか）
- ・How do you handle stress and pressure?（ストレスやプレッシャーにどのように対処しますか）
- ・What are your goals for the future?（将来の目標は何ですか）
- ・How do you handle success?（成功とはどのように向き合いますか）
- ・How do you handle failure?（失敗とはどのように向き合いますか）
- ・Do you work well with other people?（他の人と協力することは得意ですか）
- ・Why are you the best person for the job?（あなたがこの職にベストな人材なのはなぜですか）

DAY 54

FEBRUARY 23RD (SUNDAY)

I was delighted to hear last week that my young protégé Shinnosuke Nitobe has won this year's Kaizen competition for his idea of reducing translation costs in the Documentation Section. The official announcement will not be released until March 3rd, but the director of the General Affairs Department, Masami Fujiwara, sent a **confidential internal memo** (p.250) to all department heads the other day announcing the decision of the judges.

And while I am on the subject of confidential memos, the Directors of the Board all **received one from the president** (p.252) on Friday stating that only two directors will run as candidates for taking over the position of company president when Mr. Tomizawa retires; Yuji Sugimoto and me. I had expected more, but everyone else dropped out. I was hoping that our managing director, Seiji Kobayashi, would run, but he is nearing retirement age and decided not to. I also thought that Mami Uchida of the Accounting Department would run. She is an excellent administrator and very ambitious, but it appears as if she doesn't have the confidence to run the company.

So, it looks like I am one step closer to a promotion. I must admit, I am experiencing mixed emotions over the possibility. Part of me is convinced that I will make a very good president and be able to navigate the company into the future in the same spirit as our founders, but another part of me is very nervous. It will be an enormous responsibility, and I'm sure there are many parts of the job that I still don't understand. My wife, on the other hand, is delighted at the prospect. Anyway, the final decision is out of my hands, so all I can do at the moment is wait for the result.

The **president called me into his office** (p.254) on Friday afternoon to say that he would vote in my favor in the event of a tie. He also informed me that being headhunted last month by Toru Sano of SJF Engineering was, in fact, a setup to test my loyalty to Tomizawa. I was furious when I first heard this, but with the benefit of hindsight, I can see that it was probably a good idea from the president's point of view.

Yonezawa

キーワード＆キーフレーズ→p.256

2月23日（日曜日）

　先週、私の若い教え子の新渡戸慎之助がドキュメンテーション課での翻訳コストを削減するアイデアで今年の改善コンペで優勝したと知って、とてもうれしく思った。正式な発表は3月3日までないが、先日、総務部長の藤原正美が審査員の決定を知らせる機密の社内通知を部長全員に送ったのだ。

　機密の通知と言えば、富沢社長が辞任する際に社長の座を引き継ぐ候補として立つことになったのは役員のうち2人だけ、杉本雄二と私だと知らせるそれを、金曜日に役員の全員が社長から受け取った。私は候補者がもっと多いことを予測していたが、他の皆は辞退したらしい。取締役の小林誠司が立候補することを期待していたが、彼はもう定年が近いからとそうしなかった。私は経理部長の内田真美も立候補すると思っていた。彼女は優れた管理者で大変な野心家でもあるのだが、どうも会社を経営するだけの自信はないように見受けられる。

　そういうことで、私はまた一歩昇進に近づいたようだ。正直、この可能性については複雑な気持ちだ。私はとても良い社長になれる、創業者の志を引き継いで会社を未来に向けて導いていくことができる、と確信している自分もいるのだが、逆にひどく緊張している自分もいる。社長になれば重大な責任を負うことになるし、その仕事には私がまだ理解していない部分も多いだろう。一方、私の妻はこの可能性に喜んでいる。いずれにせよ、最終決定権は自分にはないので、今私ができることは結果を待つことだけだ。

　金曜日の午後、社長が私を社長室に呼んで、2人の票が同数だったら彼は私に票を入れると言った。また、先月私がSJFエンジニアリングの佐野徹氏にスカウトされたのは、実は私の富沢ISへの忠誠心を試すための芝居だったことを教えられた。それを聞いて最初は腹が立ったが、今改めて考えると、あれは社長の立場から見れば良いやり方だったのだろうとわかる。

米澤

社外秘の社内通知を書いてみよう!

Tomizawa Integrated Solutions, Inc.

Confidential Internal Memo

Confidential

To: All Department Heads (to be delivered by hand)
From: Masami Fujiwara (General Affairs Dept.)
Date: February 21st
Re: Kaizen Competition Winner

For your information, the winner of this year's Kaizen Competition has been decided. The official announcement will be issued on March 3rd. You are therefore requested to keep this information confidential until then.

After careful deliberation, it has been decided that Shinnosuke Nitobe of the Global Logistics Department is the winner for his entry entitled [The Tomizawa Nursery].

[The Tomizawa Nursery] was highly-acclaimed for formulating a proposal that not only advocates establishing a facility within the company for taking care of employees' children, it also provides viable methods for financing it. Whether the proposal is adopted or not is open to future debate, but the audacity of suggesting widespread changes to company business practices in order to finance this ambitious project struck a chord with the judges and resulted in it being selected as the winner.

The prize of ¥100,000 will be presented to Nitobe by the president on March 25th.

Thank you, M. Fujiwara

POINT

for your informationやyou are requested to keep this information confidentialなどの表現を使って、特定の人向けの通知であることを念押しします。

（株）富沢インテグレーテッド・ソリューションズ

社外秘の社内通知

社外秘

宛先：　部長各位（手渡しでお願いします）
差出人：藤原正美（総務部）
日付：　2月21日
Re：　改善コンペ優勝者

今年の改善コンペの優勝者が決まりましたので、お知らせします。公式発表は3月3日に行われますので、それまではこの情報は口外されないよう、お願いいたします。

慎重に審査しました結果、海外事業部の新渡戸慎之助さんが、そのエントリー「富沢託児所」で優勝者と決定いたしました。

「富沢託児所」は従業員の子どもの世話をする社内施設を造るということを提唱するだけでなく、そのための費用を捻出する実行可能な方法も明確に提案していることが高く評価されました。この提案が採用されるかどうかは将来の議論に委ねられますが、このような野心的なプロジェクトの資金調達をするために会社のやり方を広く変えるように提案するという大胆さは審査員に感銘を与え、優勝者として選ばれることとなりました。

賞金10万円は3月25日に社長から新渡戸さんに授与されます。

よろしくお願いいたします。
藤原

54

クイックQ&A

Q From whom will Nitobe receive his prize?
（新渡戸は誰から賞金を受け取りますか）

POINT

第3段落にあるstrike a chordという表現は、何かに対して心から同意したり何らかの感情が動かされたりすることを表す慣用句です。同様の意味を表す他の表現にはresonate、on the same frequency、in harmonyなどがあります。以下はその用例です。
・Her love of music resonates with mine.（彼女の音楽好きに私は共感を覚えた）
・I could tell we were on the same frequency when he spoke of his love for Italian food.（彼は自分がイタリア料理が好きだと話したとき、私たちは気が合うと思った）
・Our thoughts are in harmony with regard to gender issues.（私たちの性差別に対する考えは一致している）

A The president（社長）

社長からの社内通知を読んでみよう!

Tomizawa Integrated Solutions, Inc.

Confidential Internal Memo

To: Members of the Board of Directors (to be delivered by hand)
From: Tomizawa
Date: February 21st
Re: Candidates for next president fixed

Having received notifications of intention from all directors, the candidates running for the position of president of Tomizawa Integrated Solutions have been decided. The two official candidates are: Yuji Sugimoto and Osamu Yonezawa. All other potential candidates have officially dropped out.

Also, I have been requested by several directors to stay on as Chairman of the Board after my retirement, and I have agreed. A vote will be taken on this during the same meeting for voting on the next president. The meeting will be held at 16:00 on March 24th (Mon.) in the main meeting room, and an announcement regarding the changes will be issued to the press and distributed throughout the company on the same day.

Once all details have been determined, the new president will commence his duties from April 1st. I will stay on in an advisory capacity for two months, and my final day in the office will be May 31st. I will, of course, return for board meetings following this.

Tomizawa

（株）富沢インテグレーテッド・ソリューションズ

社外秘の社内通知

宛先：　役員各位（手渡しでお願いします）
差出人：富沢
日付：　2月21日
Re：　次期社長候補の決定

すべての役員からの意思通知を受け取り、富沢インテグレーテッド・ソリューションズの社長に立候補する候補者が決まりました。正式な2人の候補は杉本雄二さんと米澤修さんです。他の候補は全員、正式に辞退されました。

また、私は退任の後も役員会議長に留まるよう何人かの役員に頼まれ、同意しました。これに関する投票は、次期社長の投票のための会議中に一緒に行われます。会議は3月24日（月）16時に大会議室で行われ、変更に関する発表が報道陣に行われ、同日に全社内にも通達されます。

54

すべの詳細が決まった後、新代表取締役社長が4月1日から就任します。私は2か月間は相談役として残り、最終出社日は3月31日になります。もちろん、この後も引き続き役員会へは出席します。

富沢

クイックQ&A

Q > **Why will Tomizawa remain at the company for two months?**
（富沢が2か月間、会社に残るのはなぜですか）

POINT

最終段落にあるcapacityは、大きさや能力を表すのにとてもよく使われます。例えば、工場のcapacityとはその最大の生産量のことですし、劇場のcapacityとは収容人数のことです。しかし、人の義務や立場を表すのにも使うことができ、ここではこの使い方がされています。以下はその他の用例です。
- He worked for the company in a temporary capacity after his retirement. （彼は退職後、嘱託社員として会社で働いた）
- She attended the seminar in her capacity as a representative of the government. （彼女は政府代表としてそのセミナーに出席した）
- He has worked in many capacities throughout his academic career, including as a field researcher, a lecturer, and as a faculty head. （彼はその学問的経歴を通して、野外研究者、講師、学部長など様々な立場で働いてきた）

A > To provide advice to the new president（新しい社長に助言をするため）

253

president called me into his office ▶

実際の会話を聞いて話してみよう!

SETTING:

President Tomizawa and Yonezawa are sitting in the president's office discussing the president's retirement.

Tomizawa: You received the memo, right?

Yonezawa: Yes, I did. So, it's down to two people. Me and Yuji.

Tomizawa: Yes, that's right. But I think you'll get the vote. Yuji is a fine manager and people trust him, but he can be a little vague sometimes. I'm pretty sure the other directors realize that you are more suited to the job.

Yonezawa: That's a little scary. I'm still not sure if I'm ready for this. Part of me wants to win, but another part of me wants Yuji to win.

Tomizawa: Well, you and Yuji will not be able to vote, and I'm sure that Seiji and Masami will vote for you. That at least gives you the two votes you need for me to pass the deciding vote. Jiro will probably vote for Yuji, which leaves Mami as the dark horse, although I think she will go for you, giving you a 3-1 majority. I would therefore say that you will be the next president of this company without a shadow of a doubt.

Yonezawa: Are you sure you really want that? How can you be sure that I will be able to cope with the job?

Tomizawa: Oh, I'm sure. I've known you for many years, and I've seen the effort you have put in to make sure that Tomizawa IS developed into the company it is today. I'm also convinced of your loyalty to the company.

Yonezawa: How can you be convinced? For all you know, I may be on the lookout for another job right now.

Tomizawa: Another job, huh? Like working for Toru Sano of SJF Engineering, maybe?

Yonezawa: Wait! What?

Tomizawa: Sano told me how adamantly you refused his very generous offer.

Yonezawa: You know about that? But that's...

Tomizawa: Just a little test to see if you were the right man for the job. And you passed the test with flying colors! There is not another man in the world that I would feel more comfortable passing the company onto.

president called me into his office

場面：

> 富沢社長と米澤が社長室で座って社長の辞任について話し合っている。

T： 社内通知は受け取ったよな？

Y： ええ、受け取りました。これで私と雄二の2人に絞り込まれましたね。

T： ああ、そうだ。だが、俺は君が票を獲得すると思っている。雄二は良い部長で社員の信頼も厚いが、時々はっきりしないところがあるからな。他の役員たちは君のほうが社長の職に合っているとわかっているだろう。

Y： 少し不安です。まだあまり心の準備ができていなくて。自分が選ばれたい気持ちもあるんですが、雄二が選ばれてほしい気持ちもあります。

T： ふむ、君と雄二は投票できないし、誠司と正美はきっと君に票を入れるだろう。そうすると君は少なくとも俺が決定票を投ずるのに必要な2票は得る。次郎はたぶん雄二に票を入れるだろうから、真美がダークホースとして残るわけだが、俺は彼女も君に票を入れるんじゃないかと思う。すると3対1で君が過半数になるな。だから俺は疑いの余地なく君が我が社の次期社長になると断言できる。

Y： 本当にそれでいいのですか。私がその役割をこなせるとどうして確信できるんですか。

T： おや、俺は確信しているぞ。君のことは長年知っているし、富沢ISを今のような会社に発展させるために君が注ぎ込んできた努力も見てきている。君の会社への忠誠心についても信用しているしな。

Y： なぜ信用できるんです？　私は今まさによその仕事を探しているところかもしれないでしょう。

T： ほう、よその仕事ねえ。例えば、SJFエンジニアリングの佐野徹のところで働く、とか？

Y： ちょっと待ってください！　何ですって？

T： 君がどれほどかたくなに彼の極めて好条件なオファーを断ったか、佐野が教えてくれたぞ。

Y： そのことを知っているんですか。しかしそれは…。

T： 君がこの役目にふさわしい人材かどうかを確かめるちょっとしたテストさ。そして君はテストに見事合格した！　俺がこの会社を安心して託すことができる人間は、君をおいてこの世に1人もいないよ。

54

キーワードやフレーズをチェック!

☐ be delighted to hear 聞いて大喜びする

She **was delighted to hear** that her client is going to renew the contract.
彼女は顧客が契約の更新をするつもりだと聞いて大喜びした。

He **was delighted to hear** from his former manager after so many years.
彼は昔の上司から数年ぶりに連絡が来てとても喜んだ。

☐ on the subject of ～ ～に関して

He spoke for two hours **on the subject of** artificial intelligence.
彼は人工知能について2時間語った。

A meeting **on the subject of** the new long-term strategy was held this afternoon.
今日の午後、新しい長期戦略に関する会議が開かれた。

☐ one step closer 一歩近づいて

Increased sales have put the company **one step closer** to achieving this year's target.
売上の上昇はその会社を今年の目標達成に一歩近づけた。

Passing the examination put him **one step closer** to becoming a certified accountant.
試験に合格して彼は公認会計士への道をまた一歩前進した。

☐ mixed emotions 複雑な気持ち

It was with **mixed emotions** that she learned that the head office would be moving to Sapporo.
本社が札幌に移転すると知って彼女は複雑な心境だった。

He was experiencing **mixed emotions** on his final day in the office.
その会社での最後の日、彼は複雑な気持ちを味わっていた。

---

at the prospect   期待して、見込みで

He was a little nervous **at the prospect** of being promoted.
彼は昇進を期待して少し緊張していた。

She was excited **at the prospect** of being able to work in the field of research.
彼女は研究分野で働けるかもしれないことにワクワクしていた。

with the benefit of hindsight   今となってみれば

With the benefit of hindsight, quitting my job was not a very good idea.
今になって思い返すと、仕事を辞めるのあまり良い考えではなかった。

It is easy to see how the company grew into a major brand **with the benefit of hindsight**.
後から見れば、その会社がどのように大手ブランドにまで成長したかがよくわかる。

54

マナーのヒント

　英語圏でヘッドハンティングは特別よくあることではありませんが、日本においてよりは頻繁に行われます。ただし、スカウトされやすいのは一般の就職希望者層からは得られない特別なスキルや経験を持つ人材です。これには語学スキルも含まれ、例えば日本と取引するニューヨークの企業なら、他の会社から英語と日本語を流暢に話せる社員を引き抜くかもしれません。スカウトされる人は必然的に、その時点のものよりも高い報酬や良い条件を提示されますが、オファーを受けるかどうかの最終的な判断は本人次第です。

DAY

MARCH 3RD (MONDAY)

I won the Kaizen competition! I can't believe it! There were thirty-six entries in total, but the judges chose mine because it was "audacious." At least, that is what Ms. Uchiyama, my section manager told me. It was the first time I have come across this word, and she told me that it means "bold," "cheeky" and "daring." She **called me into one of the meeting rooms (p.264)** after lunchtime this afternoon to tell me that I had won before the **official announcement (p.260)** was issued. At first, I thought I was in trouble for something, but she handed over a copy of the announcement and congratulated me.

I will receive the prize of ¥100,000 from the president in a small ceremony held in the Global Logistics Department on March 25th. Ms. Uchiyama asked me what I intended to spend it on, but I couldn't think of anything specific during our meeting. I've been considering it since, however, and I think I'll use it to buy the equipment I need for overnight hiking trips. Hiking is one of my hobbies, but I usually stay in cheap hotels or inns when I go on trips lasting more than one day. I have been thinking of purchasing a lightweight tent and all of the other gear I would need for camping out for some time, and now it looks as if I can afford it.

And, for my first trip, I think I'll try my hand at walking the Tokai Shizen Hodo, which is known as the **Tokai Nature Trail (p.262)** in English, during the Golden Week holiday. This trail passes through eleven prefectures between Tokyo and Osaka for a total length of more than 1,000km, but it is possible to do it in stages. The first stage is from Mt. Takao to Lake Yamanaka, although I believe that would require at least one week. If I go for a two or three-day trip, I could probably make it through to Hokizawa in Kanagawa Prefecture. That doesn't sound very far, but it includes some rather difficult mountain trails, so I'll probably only manage about 25km to 30km a day.

I think I'll start making a list of the gear I need and planning the trip this weekend.

Nitobe

キーワード＆キーフレーズ→p.266

３月３日（月曜日）

　改善コンペで優勝した！　信じられない！　合計３６件の応募があったのだけど、審査員は僕の案をaudaciousだという理由で選んでくれた。少なくとも、僕のいる課の内山課長が伝えてくれたことによるとそうだ。僕はこの言葉を聞くのは初めてだったけど、課長が「大胆」「生意気」「斬新」という意味だと教えてくれた。今日の午後、昼休みの後に課長に会議室の1つに呼ばれ、僕が優勝したことを正式な発表の前に知らされた。最初は何かで怒られるのかなと思ったけど、課長は僕に発表のコピーを渡しておめでとうと言ってくれた。

　僕は3月25日に海外事業部で行われる小さな式典で社長から10万円の賞金を受け取ることになっている。内山課長に賞金を何に使うつもりか聞かれたけれど、その時は特に何も思いつかなかった。でも、それからずっと考えて、1泊するようなハイキング旅行に必要な装備を買うのに使おうと思った。ハイキングは僕の趣味の1つなのだけど、日帰りより長い旅に行くときは大抵安いホテルか旅館に泊まっている。軽量テントやしばらくキャンプ生活をするのに必要なその他の用具一式を買おうとだいぶ前から考えていたので、これでそうするだけのお金の余裕ができそうだ。

　そこで、最初の旅はゴールデンウィークに腕試しとして、英語ではTokai Nature Trailとして知られる東海自然歩道を歩いてみようと思う。この遊歩道は東京から大阪までの11都府県にまたがっていて、全長は1000キロメートル以上だけど、何回かに分ければクリアできる。最初のステージは高尾山から山中湖までで、最低でも1週間はかかるだろうな。2、3日かけて歩けば、神奈川県の箒沢までたどり着くことができると思う。そう言うとあまり遠い感じがしないけど、かなり険しい山道も入っているので、おそらく1日25キロから30キロくらいしか歩けないだろう。

　今週末、必要な用具のリストを作ったり、旅の計画を立てたりし始めよう。

　　　　　　　　　　　　　　新渡戸

55

社内発表を書いてみよう!

Official Announcement

IC-LP-003761

Attn : All Staff Members
From: General Affairs Department (M. Fujiwara)
Date : March 3rd

Re: Winner of This Year's Tomizawa Kaizen Competition

It is with delight that I announce Shinnosuke Nitobe of the Global Logistics Department the winner of this year's Tomizawa Kaizen Competition for his proposal [The Tomizawa Nursery]. Mr. Nitobe will receive the prize of ¥100,000 from the president on March 25th.

The Tomizawa Nursery proposal was extremely ambitious in that it challenged the way in which translation is handled within the Documentation Section (Global Logistics Department) and sought to reduce translation costs for the purpose of financing a nursery school for the pre-school children of Tomizawa employees. The proposal has been posted on the internal Intranet and can be viewed at: https://internal/kaizen-winner/tomizawais.co.jp.

The judges examined a total of thirty-six Kaizen proposals, and the decision to select The Tomizawa Nursery as the winner was unanimous. Congratulation to Mr. Nitobe.

Thank you
M. Fujiwara (General Affairs)

クイックQ&A

Q How many judges decided that Nitobe's proposal was the winner?
（新渡戸の改善案が優勝だと判断した審査員は何名でしたか）

正式発表

IC-LP-003761

宛先：全社員
差出人: 総務部(藤原)
日付: 3月3日

Re: 本年度富沢改善コンペ優勝者

海外事業部の新渡戸慎之助さんが、提案「富沢託児所」によって本年度の富沢改善コンペの優勝者になられたことを喜びを持ってお知らせいたします。新渡戸さんには3月25日に社長から賞金10万円が授与されます。

富沢託児所の提案は、翻訳作業がドキュメンテーション課(海外事業部)内で行われている方法に異論を唱えたということにおいて極めて野心的であり、富沢の社員の未就学児たちの保育所の資金を捻出する目的で翻訳費用を削減しようと試みています。提案は社内イントラネットに掲載されており、https://internal/kaizen-winner/tomizawais.co.jp.で閲覧できます。

審査員は全36の改善案を検討し、「富沢託児所」を優勝に選ぶことは満場一致で決定されました。新渡戸さん、おめでとうございます。

よろしくお願いいたします。
藤原(総務部)

POINT

何かを公式に発表する言葉は多くの場合It is with ～ that I announceで始まり、「～」に入れる名詞によってその発表内容の全体的なムードが決まります。入れる語はdelight、joy、pride、regret、sadness、sorrow、その他感情を表す名詞なら何でも構いません。以下はその例です。

・It is with joy that I announce the birth of our first child. (私たちの初めての子どもの誕生を、喜びをもってお知らせします)
・It is with pride that I announce my acceptance at the university of my choice. (志望大学に合格したことを、誇りをもってお知らせしたいと思います)
・It is with sadness that I announce the death of my father. (悲しいお知らせですが、私の父が亡くなりました)

A 〉 All of them (全員)

Tokai Nature Trail ►

東海自然歩道の説明文を読んでみよう!

Tokai Nature Trail

The Tokai Nature Trail is a long-distance hiking course that stretches from the Meiji no Mori Takao Quasi-National Park in Tokyo to Meiji no Mori Minō Quasi-National Park in Osaka, and it can be hiked in both directions. The trail runs through eleven prefectures and covers a total distance of 1,697km, including bypass trails offering different routes, although the direct Tokyo to Osaka route is just over 1,000km in length. Hiking the entire trail is considered to require between 40 to 50 days under normal circumstances.

The trail takes hikers up mountains, through valleys and past villages, and it is liberally sprinkled with temples, shrines and historical landmarks. It is a physically demanding trail, with most of the course passing through mountainous terrain requiring peaks in the 1,000m range to be ascended almost every day. The trial also passes through villages and small towns practically on a daily basis, so hikers are able to restock with food and water regularly without having to carry large quantities of supplies.

東海自然歩道

東海自然歩道は東京の明治の森高尾国定公園から大阪の明治の森箕面国定公園まで延びる長距離ハイキングコースで、双方向からハイキングできます。歩道は11の都府県にまたがり、東京・大阪間の直線ルートはちょうど1000キロメートルを超える長さですが、様々なルートがあるバイパス歩道を含めると総距離は1697キロメートルに及びます。全歩道をハイキングするには通常の条件で40から50日かかるとされています。

歩道ではハイカーたちは山を登り、谷を通り、村を過ぎていき、そこには寺や神社、歴史的名所がかなりたくさん点在しています。コースのほとんどがほぼ毎日登る1000メートル級の山頂を誇る山岳地帯を通っているので、体力的にはきつい歩道です。歩道はまた実質的にほぼ毎日、村や小さな町も通っているので、ハイカーたちは大量の必需品を持ち歩くことなく食べ物や水を定期的に補充できます。

55

クイックQ&A

Q〉**The Tokai Nature Trail can be hiked from Osaka to Tokyo. True or false?**
（東海自然歩道は大阪から東京までハイキングできます。正しいですか、誤りですか）

POINT

第2段落にあるdemandingという語は「かなりの努力を要する」という意味で、physically demanding「肉体的にきつい」やmentally demanding「精神的にきつい」のように副詞を前に置いて使うこともできます。以下はその用例です。

・He runs his own restaurant, but it is a physically demanding job requiring long hours of work.（彼は自分のレストランを経営しているが、これは長時間の労働を必要とする大変な仕事だ）

・Rugby is a physically and mentally demanding sport that requires both strength and determination.（ラグビーはパワーと決断力の両方を必要とする、肉体的にも精神的にも過酷なスポーツだ）

・She studied advanced mathematics at university, which is a very mentally demanding course.（彼女は大学で、非常に精神的に厳しい科目である高等数学を学んだ）

A〉True（正しい）

実際の会話を聞いて話してみよう!

SETTING:

> Ms. Uchiyama calls Nitobe into a meeting room and invites him to sit down.

Uchiyama: I thought maybe you should see this before it is distributed around the company.

(She hands him a copy of an internal memo)

Nitobe: What is it?

Uchiyama: Take a look and see.

Nitobe: I won the Kaizen competition? Are you serious? But, that's amazing!

Uchiyama: Congratulations! The judges were very impressed with your proposal. Not only was it ambitious, it was also audacious, which they found very refreshing.

Nitobe: Audacious? I don't think I know that word.

Uchiyama: Bold, cheeky, daring. They were impressed with the fact that you had the courage to question firmly-established operational policy and come up with a suggestion for improving efficiency. But that does not mean that your proposal will automatically be adopted. It will be considered, of course, but there is no guarantee that it will be implemented.

Nitobe: Wow, I don't know what to say. This is a real surprise.

Uchiyama: A small ceremony will be held in the department on March 25th during which the president will hand you the prize. That's ¥100,000! Any ideas what you're going to do with it?

Nitobe: Well, no. Not yet. Maybe buy some new clothes. Or maybe a camera. Or maybe even a new tablet terminal. I'll have to think about it.

Uchiyama: Well, whatever you decide to spend it on, remember that you earned it. I read your proposal, and I was also very impressed. I hope that it eventually gets implemented. Young working parents need all the help that they can get.

Nitobe: Thank you.

Uchiyama: The internal memo will be distributed to everyone in the company at around 4 p.m. I'm sure you will be congratulated by a great many other people. Especially those with young children.

called me into one of the meeting rooms

場面：

> 内山課長が新渡戸を会議室に呼び、座るように促す。

U：社内で配られる前にこれをあなたに見せておいたほうがいいかなと思って。
　　（新渡戸に社内通知を1枚手渡す）

N：これは何ですか。

U：見てごらんなさい。

N：僕が改善コンペで優勝したんですか。本当に？　すごくうれしいです！

U：おめでとう！　審査員はあなたの改善案にすごく感心していたのよ。大がかりなだけでなくaudaciousで、とても新鮮に感じたみたい。

N：audacious？　その単語は知りません。

U：大胆、生意気、斬新という意味ね。審査員はあなたが、しっかり確立されている運営方針に疑問を投げかけて効率を上げるための案を出す勇気があったという点にとても感心したらしいわ。でも、それであなたの案がそのまま採用されるわけではないわよ。もちろん考慮はされるけど、実行に移される保証はないから。

N：わあ、なんと言ったらいいかわかりません。ものすごい驚きです。

U：3月25日に部署で小さな式典が行われて、そこで社長があなたに賞金を手渡すことになっているわ。10万円よ！　何に使うか考えはある？

N：うーん、いいえ。まだないですね。新しい服を買おうかな。それかカメラを。新しいタブレット端末もありかも。考えておかなければいけませんね。

U：まあ、何に使うことにするにしても、あなたが実力で手に入れたお金だということを忘れないで。私もあなたの改善案を読んで、すごく感心したのよ。実践されるという結果を願っているわ。若い共働きの親はできる限りの助けを必要としているもの。

N：ありがとうございます。

U：その社内通知は午後4時頃に社内の全員に配られるわ。私以外にもたくさんの人に祝われること間違いなしね。特に小さな子どものいる社員には。

55

キーワードやフレーズをチェック!

☐ **in total**　　全部で

He had eleven part-time jobs **in total** over the course of four years at university.
彼は大学にいる4年間に全部で11のアルバイトをした。

She was warned six times **in total** before being fired.
彼女は解雇される前に合計6回の警告を受けた。

☐ **at first**　　最初は

I didn't think we would succeed **at first**, but we did in the end.
初めは私たちが成功するとは思わなかったが、最終的には成功した。

She was assigned to the marketing department **at first**, but later moved to sales.
彼女は最初マーケティング部に配属されたが、その後営業部に異動した。

☐ **hand over ～**　　～を手渡す

The auditors asked the company to **hand over** all financial details concerning last year.
監査役はその会社に昨年の財務関係の資料すべてを引き渡すように求めた。

The keys to the new office building were **handed over** after a final inspection.
最終検査の後、新しいオフィスビルの鍵が手渡された。

☐ **try *one's* hand**　　挑戦してみる

He has been a system engineer for ten years, but now he wants to **try his hand** at system design.
彼は10年間システムエンジニアをやっているが、今はシステムデザインに挑戦してみたいと思っている。

The managing director wants to **try his hand** at targeting a new demographic.
部長は新しい購買層を狙ってみたいと考えている。

pass through ～   ～を通る

The train **passes through** Osaka on its way to Hiroshima.
その電車は広島へ向かう途中で大阪を通過する。

We **passed through** Kyoto on our way to the business meeting.
私たちは仕事の会議に向かう途中で京都を通った。

in stages   段階的に

The company was restructured **in stages**, and it took three years to complete the job.
その会社は段階的に改革され、完了まで3年かかった。

The factory was completed in 2004, but new buildings are being added **in stages**.
その工場は2004年に完成したが、少しずつ新しい建物が増やされている。

55

マナーのヒント

　何かの記念日を祝う際はふつう、その記念日の名称の前にhappyを付けて言いますが（Happy birthday「誕生日おめでとう」、Happy wedding anniversary「結婚記念日おめでとう」、Happy Christmas「クリスマスおめでとう」など）、誰かが何かを達成したことを祝うときはcongratulations on ～が一般的に使われます。以下はその用例です。
　・Congratulations on winning the Kaizen competition.（改善コンペ優勝おめでとう）
　・Congratulations on your promotion.（昇進おめでとう）
　・Congratulations on your new assignment.（新しい職務への就任おめでとう）
　ただし、相手が近しい知り合いではない場合は、その功績のことを他のところで聞いたと話してからcongratulationsという祝辞を付け加えるとよいでしょう。
　・I heard you won the Kaizen competition. Congratulations!（改善コンペで優勝したと聞きました。おめでとうございます!）
　・I heard you were promoted. Congratulations!（昇進したと聞きました。おめでとうございます!）
　・I heard you have been given a new assignment. Congratulations!（新しい職務に就任したと聞きました。おめでとうございます!）

MARCH 5TH (WEDNESDAY)

The run for the presidency is still up in the air. As Mr. Tomizawa predicted, Seiji Kobayashi and Masami Fujiwara both approached me and informed me that they would cast their votes for me, but I've heard nothing from Jiro Okada or Mami Uchida, although they can sometimes be seen huddled together. I naturally have no idea what they are discussing, but it seems a safe bet to guess that they are comparing notes on their intentions. I'm beginning to get more used to the idea of being president now that a couple of weeks has passed since the bomb dropped, but I am still a little wary.

Actually, I was discussing this with Harold Baywater last night. Harold is the Japan representative for Beswick Antiques, a British company involved in the import and export of antiques to and from the Far East. Tomizawa developed their operations system some years ago when the company first set up shop in Japan, and we have remained friendly ever since. He is due to return to England next month, and he **e-mailed me** (p.272) so that we could have a final drink together. I **met up with him last night** (p.274), and he noticed that I seemed a little preoccupied. When I explained my predicament, he suggested that my main worry had nothing to do with me becoming president, but achieving the peak of my career too early in life. He said that people need something to aim for. A dream that motivates them to push forward. Once the dream has been removed, the will to move forward disappears with it. I was thinking about this on my way home, and I believe he may be right. Philosophy has never been my strong point, but he definitely gave me food for thought.

Now that Nitobe has been proclaimed the winner of the Kaizen competition, I have decided to examine his proposal in detail to see if it is viable. I am sure that he has been too generous with his figures, so I have **started writing down a few notes** (p.270) and will ask Hiroshi Takeda, the manager of the Documentation Section, to provide me with all of the details once I decide the route I need to take.

Yonezawa

キーワード＆キーフレーズ→p.276

3月5日（水曜日）

　社長への立候補の結果はまだ決まっていない。富沢社長が予想した通り、小林誠司と藤原正美は2人とも私に話しかけてきて、私に票を入れると言ってくれた。岡田次郎と内田真美からは何も聞いていないが、2人で話し合っているところを時々見かける。当然、何の話をしているのかは全くわからないが、自分たちはどうするかについて意見交換をしていると考えて間違いないだろう。衝撃的な知らせから2週間ほど経って、自分が社長になるという考えにもだいぶ慣れてきたが、まだ少し慎重になっている部分もある。

　実は、昨夜このことについてハロルド・ベイウォーターに相談した。ハロルドは極東との間で骨董品の輸入を手掛けるイギリス企業、ベスウィック・アンティークスの日本担当者だ。富沢ISは何年か前、その企業が初めて日本に出店したとき、そのオペレーティングシステムを開発したことがあり、それ以来互いに友好的な関係を築いている。ハロルドは来月イギリスに戻る予定なので、最後に2人で飲みに行こうとメールをよこしてきたのだ。昨夜会ったとき、彼は私が何か考え事をしているようだと気づいた。私が問題を説明すると、彼は私の悩みの主な部分は自分が社長になることではなく、人生の中で仕事の絶頂期に到達するのが早すぎることなのではと指摘した。人には何か目指すものが、前へ進む意欲を起こさせる夢が必要なのだと彼は言った。夢がなくなれば、前へ進む気力もそれとともに消えてしまうと言うのだ。帰り道にそれについて考えてみたが、彼の言う通りかもしれない。昔から哲学は得意ではないけれど、確かに彼は考えるいい材料を与えてくれた。

56

　新渡戸が改善コンペの優勝者として発表されたので、私は彼の提案を実行可能かどうか判断するため細かく調べることにした。彼が予算を多く見積もりすぎていることは確かなので、調べたいことをいくつかメモしておいたから、これから進むべき道を決めたらドキュメンテーション課長の武田宏さんにすべての詳細情報を用意してくれるよう頼むつもりだ。

米澤

started writing down a few notes ►

確 認 事 項 の メ モ を 書 い て み よ う !

The Tomizawa Nursery	
Computer-Assisted Translation	Freelance Translators
● Check the **cost** of CAT software and running costs.	● Check **market prices** for freelance translation.
● Check the **ratio** of English translation vs. other language translation.	● Check the **speed** at which translators work (volume per day).
● Check the **percentage** of translations that can use fixed formats.	● Check the **number of translators** required to handle all translation.
● Check **how many people** will be required to operate the CAT.	● Check the number of people required to **arrange translators**.
● Check **Nitobe's figures!!!**	● Check the number of people required for **checking/editing**.

POINT

するべきことを表す特定の1つの動詞（ここではcheck）ですべての項目を始め、大事な部分を太字にすると見やすいでしょう。

富沢託児所	
コンピュータ支援翻訳（CAT）	**フリーランス翻訳者**
● CATソフトの**費用**と運用費用を確認。	● フリーランス翻訳の**市場価格**を確認。
● 英語翻訳と他の言語の翻訳の**比率**を確認。	● 翻訳者の仕事の**スピード**（1日の仕事量）を確認。
● 決まったフォーマットを使える翻訳の**割合**を確認。	● すべての翻訳を扱うのに必要な**翻訳者の数**を確認。
● CATの操作に必要な**人数**を確認。	● **翻訳者の手配**に必要な人数を確認。
● **新渡戸の見積りを確認！！！**	● 精査・編集に必要な人数を確認。

56

クイックQ&A

Q Which of the following is synonymous with "market price"? :
cost of food, stock prices, or current rates
（「市場価格」の同義語は「食品価格」「株価」「時価」のどれですか）

POINT

メモ中でtranslationという語が単数形と複数形の両方で使われていることに気づいたかもしれません。英語にはwork／works、business／businessesなど、このような使い方ができる単語が多くあり、どちらの形を使うかは以下のように区別されています。
単数形：全体量を指します。例えば、メモのEnglish translationはすべての英訳を指しています。
複数形：全体量の一部を指します。例えば、メモのpercentage of translationsは個別の翻訳の数量を指しています。

A Current rates（時価）

he e-mailed me ►
旧友からのEメールを読んでみよう!

From:　　Harold Baywater <hbaywater@beswickantiques.com>
Sent:　　Friday, February 28, 10:23 AM
To:　　　Mr. O. Yonezawa <oyonezawa@tomizawais.co.jp>
Subject: Returning to the UK

Dear Mr. Yonezawa,

How are you, old friend? Please excuse my unforgivable silence. I have
been spending a lot of time in our new office in Nagoya since last year and
neglected to contact you.

As I mentioned the last time we met up, I will be returning to the UK at the
end of March, and wondered if you would be interested in having a final
drink together for old time's sake. I am free on Monday and Tuesday next
week if you can find the time. I have always considered you to be one of my
first and favorite friends in Japan, and I would never forgive myself if I left
without buying you a final drink before I returned home.

Let me know if you can make it.

Best regards, Harold Baywater

POINT

How are you, old friend?などと呼びかけることで、親しみとなつかしさをアピールしています。相手
を何かに誘うときはI wondered if you would ～などの表現で謙虚さを出します。Let me know
if you can make it.は、こういうメール文の最後に書く決まり文句の1つ。

差出人：ハロルド・ベイウォーター<hbaywater@beswickantiques.com>
送信：　2月28日（金曜日）午前10:23
宛先：　米澤様 <oyonezawa@tomizawais.co.jp>
件名：　イギリスへの帰国

米澤様

お元気ですか。ご無沙汰していて申し訳ない。去年から新しくできた名古屋支社で多くの時間を過ごし、連絡を怠っていました。

最後に会ったときにお話ししたように、私は3月末にイギリスへ戻る予定なので、昔の思い出を語りながら最後に一杯ご一緒できないかなと思いました。もしお時間があれば、私は来週の月曜日と火曜日は空いています。私はいつも君のことを日本で最初の、そして一番の友達の1人だと思っているので、帰国の前に最後のお酒をおごらなかったらきっと自分を許せないことでしょう。

ご都合がつくかどうか教えてください。

ごきげんよう。
ハロルド・ベイウォーター

56

クイックQ&A

Q 〉 **Where has Baywater been recently?**
（ベイウォーターは最近どこにいましたか）

POINT

最終行にあるmake itは、何かのイベントなどに出席もしくは参加できるという意味です。ここでは、その「イベント」は飲みに行くというものですが、make itは他にもちょっとした行動や予定にもよく使われます。また、決められた場所に時間通りに到着することにも使うことができます。以下はその用例です。
・I was unable to make it to the class reunion this year, but I hope to go next year.（今年、私は同窓会に出席することができなかったが、来年は行けるといいなと思う）
・The party is scheduled for March 15th, so let me know if you can make it.（パーティーは3月15日の予定だから、来られそうかどうか知らせてください）
・I overslept and didn't make it to the station in time for the train.（私は寝坊して、電車に間に合うように駅に着けなかった）

A 〉 In Nagoya（名古屋）

273

I met up with him last night　►　

実際の会話を聞いて話してみよう!

SETTING:

Yonezawa and Harold Baywater are sitting in the bar of a hotel near Tokyo
Station when Baywater notices that Yonezawa's mind seems to be elsewhere.

Baywater: What's the matter? You seem preoccupied. Trouble at work?

Yonezawa: No, no, nothing like that. Well, actually, yes, something like that.

Baywater: That was a quick turnaround. Anything I can do to help?

Yonezawa: I doubt it. You see, there is a chance that I may be appointed president of
the company effective from the beginning of April. Although I am slowly
coming to terms with the idea, I can't shake off the feeling that it is not
for me. I'm sure I can do a good job, but something deep inside is telling
me to back off.

Baywater: Ah, a midlife crisis, although one that most people don't get the chance to
experience.

Yonezawa: Excuse me?

Baywater: Your problem is that you have been offered the opportunity of reaching
the peak of your career, and you are subconsciously afraid that it has come
too soon. Tell me, how old are you? Still in your fifties, right?

Yonezawa: Yes. I was fifty-six last birthday.

Baywater: Well, if you manage to avoid illness, there is a possibility that you could
live through to the age of ninety or older. That means that you still have
one third of your life left. More than thirty years with no goals and no
dreams. That's a nightmare for most people.

Yonezawa: My goal will be to ensure that Tomizawa continues growing.

Baywater: That's not a goal, that's your job. Real goals and dreams are personal.
Although your dream up until now has probably been related to doing
well in your job, even reaching the top position, that is still a personal
goal.

Yonezawa: Okay, I think I see what you mean. So, are you suggesting that I refuse
the offer so I can accept it later in life?

Baywater: No, not at all. Accept the job and enjoy it. But, establish a new goal.
Something like writing a novel, or buying a cottage in the country.
Anything is acceptable, as long as you establish a new goal every time you
achieve one.

I met up with him last night

場面：

> 米澤とハロルド・ベイウォーターが東京駅近くのホテルのバーで座っており、ベイウォーターは米澤が心ここにあらずのようだと気づく。

B： どうしたんだい？　考え事をしているようだが。仕事でトラブルでも？

Y： いいや、全然そういうのではないよ。いや、実はそうなんだ、大体そんな感じだね。

B： あっという間に切り替えたな。私に何かできることはあるかい？

Y： どうかな。実は、４月の初めからうちの会社の社長に任命されるかもしれないんだ。そのことを少しずつ受け入れることはできているんだけど、自分には向いていないという気持ちを振り払えないんだよ。うまくやれるとは思っているんだが、私の奥深くにある何かが身を引けと言っているような。

B： ああ、そりゃミッドライフ・クライシスだね、大半の人は経験する機会がないものだが。

Y： どういうことだい？

B： 君の悩みの元は、仕事の絶頂期に到達するチャンスを与えられたけど、それをまだ早すぎると潜在意識で恐れているということさ。教えてくれ、君は何歳だい？　まだ５０代だろう？

56

Y： ああ。この前の誕生日で56になった。

B： それなら、病気にさえならなければ、90歳かそれ以上まで生きられるかもしれないね。つまり君にはまだ人生の3分の1が残っているわけだ。目標も夢もない時間が30年以上。これはたいていの人にとって悪夢だよ。

Y： 富沢ISが発展し続けるようにするという目標ができるだろう。

B： そりゃ目標じゃない、君の仕事だ。本物の目標や夢は個人的なものだよ。これまでの君の夢はたぶん仕事で成功する、もっと言えばトップに立つ、というようなものだったんだろうが、それだって個人的な目標さ。

Y： ああ、君の言いたいことはなんとなくわかったよ。つまり、私はオファーを断って人生のもっと後の段階になってから受けたほうがいいと？

B： いや、そうではないぞ。その仕事は受けて存分にやるといい。だが、新しい目標を作るんだ。小説を書くとか、田舎に別荘を買うとか。目標を達成するたびにまた新しいのを作りさえすれば、何でも構わないさ。

キーワードやフレーズをチェック！

☐ up in the air　未決定で

The arrangements for my trip to Norway are still **up in the air**.
私のノルウェーへの出張の手配はまだ宙に浮いている状態だ。

The final decision on which supplier to use is still **up in the air**.
どの供給元を利用するかの最終決定はまだなされていない。

☐ huddle together　（一所に）集まる

Employees **huddled together** in the canteen and discussed the new policy.
社員たちは社員食堂に集まって新しい規則について話し合った。

Seminar participants **huddled together** to discuss the controversial presentation.
セミナーの参加者は題材になっているプレゼンテーションについて議論するため1か所に固まった。

☐ safe bet　安全策、確実なこと

Investing in startup companies is not a **safe bet** in the current business climate.
現在のビジネス環境で、スタートアップ企業への投資は安全な賭けではない。

It is a **safe bet** to say that the new product lineup will become very popular.
新しい製品のラインナップが非常に人気になることは確実だろう。

☐ set up shop　出店する、開業する

The company is considering **setting up shop** in several European countries.
その企業はヨーロッパのいくつかの国に支社を開設することを考えている。

He **set up shop** in Beijing and was extremely successful.
彼は北京で開業し、大成功を収めた。

achieve the peak　頂点を極める

Everybody aims at **achieving the peak** of their profession, but few manage it.
誰もが自分の職業で頂点を極めることを目指すが、それができる者は少ない。

She **achieved the peak** of her teaching career at the university after twenty-three years of being a lecturer.
彼女は23年間講師を続けてから、大学で教師人生の頂点に立った。

food for thought　思考の材料

The potential of artificial intelligence is providing **food for thought** recently.
人工知能の可能性は近頃、考察の題材になっている。

His speech was long and rambling, but he did provide some **food for thought**.
彼のスピーチは長くてだらだらしていたが、考慮すべき内容はあった。

マナーのヒント

56

悩み事を誰かに相談したいときは、以下のように切り出してみるとよいでしょう。
- I have a problem I'd like to discuss with you. Is that okay?（あなたに相談したい問題があるのですが、よろしいでしょうか）
- Do you mind if I discuss a private problem with you?（個人的な悩みをあなたに相談してもよろしいでしょうか）
- There is something that is bothering me recently. May I discuss it with you?（最近困っていることがあるのですが、相談してもいいですか）

これらに対する典型的な返答は以下のようになります。
- Yes, of course. Go ahead.（ええ、もちろん。どうぞ話してください）
- Not at all. I hope I can be of help.（大丈夫ですよ。お役に立てれば幸いです）
- Of course. What's bothering you?（もちろんです。何に困っているんですか）

また、逆に相談に乗りたいと思ったときは、以下の言い回しが役に立つでしょう。
- You're looking very thoughtful. Is anything the matter?（考え事をしているように見えますが、何か困っていることがあるのですか）
- You're very quiet lately. Is there anything I can help you with?（最近元気がないようですが、私で力になれることはありますか）
- You seem preoccupied. Do you want to discuss it?（何か悩んでいるように見えますが、よければ相談に乗りますよ）

MARCH 14TH (FRIDAY)

Well, there are only two weeks left until the end of this fiscal year, and I'm beginning to feel a little anxious. My year for perfecting English is drawing to a close, but Mr. Yonezawa has still not indicated whether or not I have passed the test. If I fail, I will be sent back to the General Affairs Department. And, even if I have passed, I don't know what section I will be assigned to in the Global Logistics Department.

Mr. Winston told me not to worry. He said my English has improved in leaps and bounds over the course of the year, and that Mr. Yonezawa is sure to feel that I am proficient enough to remain in the GL Department. I hope he is right. I find it very satisfying using a foreign language in everyday work. I have studied hard this year, and I am very pleased with the way I have progressed. I wouldn't say that my English is fluent, but after the intensive practice I have received, I no longer have any problems understanding what people are saying, expressing my own opinions, or reading or writing.

Mr. Winston is a very good teacher. He makes sure that we gain experience in many different forms of English covering all aspects of speaking, listening, reading and writing. This week, for example, our homework was to write six *senryu* poems. Mr. Winston is a big fan of *senryu*, and he always looks forward to reading the winning entries for the Salaryman *Senryu* contest that are announced every year. I **handed him my *senryu* (p.280)** on Wednesday, and he said they were excellent. Personally, I didn't think they were very good, but they gave me a chance to learn about the importance of syllables in English. Mr. Winston also showed us a **poem he wrote in college (p.282)**. It came 4th in a flash fiction competition for writing stories in 55 words.

Misaki is also worried about where he will be assigned. We went out for a drink together last night at a bar under the railway lines in Kanda. We **discussed what sections we hope to be assigned to (p.284)**, and when I said the Documentation Section, he accused me of having an ulterior motive. Aya Shibata! He could be right…

Nitobe

キーワード&キーフレーズ→p.286

３月１４日（金曜日）

　さて、今会計年度末まであと2週間しかなくなり、僕は少し不安になり始めている。英語をマスターするための1年が終わりに近づいているのに、米澤部長はまだ僕が合格かどうか知らせてくれていない。もし不合格なら、僕は総務部に戻されることになる。そして、もし合格したとしても、海外事業部のどの課に配属されるのかはわからないのだ。

　ウィンストン先生は心配するな、君の英語はこの1年間で飛躍的に上達した、米澤部長もきっと海外事業部にとどまるのに十分な実力だと感じているだろう、と言ってくれた。彼の言う通りだといいな。毎日の仕事で外国語を使うのはとても充実感がある。この1年間頑張って勉強したし、自分の上達具合にはとても満足している。ペラペラとまではいかないが、集中訓練のおかげで、人が言っていることを理解したり、自分の言いたいことを表現したり、読み書きしたりするのにはもう苦労しない。

　ウィンストン先生はとてもいい先生だ。話す、聞く、読む、書くのすべての側面を網羅する様々な形の英語の経験を得られるよう考えてくれている。例えば、今週の僕たちの宿題は川柳を6つ書くことだった。ウィンストン先生は川柳の大ファンで、毎年発表されるサラリーマン川柳コンクールの優秀作品を読むのをいつも楽しみにしている。水曜日に僕の川柳を提出したら、彼はよくできていると言ってくれた。僕自身はそんなにうまくないと思ったけど、英語における音節の重要性を学ぶいい機会になった。ウィンストン先生は自分が大学生の頃に書いた詩も見せてくれた。それは55語以内で物語を書くフラッシュ・フィクションのコンテストで4位になったという。

57

　岬も自分がどこに配属になるか気をもんでいる。昨夜、2人で神田のガード下の居酒屋に飲みに行った。どの課に配属されたいかについて話し合っているときに、僕がドキュメンテーション課と言ったら、下心があるだろうと彼に突っ込まれた。柴田彩さんのことだ！

　彼の言う通りかもしれない…。

新渡戸

handed him my *senryu* ►

英語で川柳を書いてみよう!

Senryu (by Shinnosuke Nitobe)

When my work is hard
I know where to find solace
"Another beer, please!"

I have no lover
but I have not given up
Aya Shibata

Documentation
is just another word for
working overtime

The weekend arrives
I have nothing to do but
my English homework

The sign is too small
I cannot see what it says
It says "Optician"

When money is tight
I have a personal bank
The Bank of Parents

川柳（新渡戸慎之助）

仕事が　大変な時は　わかってる
安らぎの場所を　「ビールもう1杯！」

恋人は　いないけど　僕は
諦めない　柴田彩

私には　残業するのと　同じこと
ドキュメンテーション課　書類作成

週末に　すること何も　ないけれど
英語の宿題　だけありました

看板が　小さすぎてて　見えないな
何と書いてる？　「眼鏡屋」だ

きついとき　お金がなくて　困ったら
「両親」という名の　個人銀行

クイックＱ＆Ａ

Q 〉 **What does the term "personal bank" refer to in the last *senryu* on the right?**
（右下の川柳の「個人銀行」とは何のことですか）

57

POINT

英語で俳句や川柳を書く場合、字数や語数ではなく音節の数を数えます。音節とは語の音を区切る単位の1つで、英語のすべての単語は1つかそれ以上の音節でできています。大抵、音節の数は同じ単語をカタカナで書いたときの数よりも少なく、例えば「マクドナルド（McDonald）」という単語は日本語では6音節（もしくは6文字）ですが、英語ではたったの3音節です（Mc-Don-ald）。左上の川柳（When my work...）では1行目の英単語がそれぞれ1音節しかないので、そこに5語使われています。しかし、右上の川柳ではweekendとarrivesが両方とも2音節なので（week-endとar-rives）、1行目に3語しか使われていません。このように、ここでの川柳はすべて5・7・5のルールに忠実に従っています。

（両親からお金をいつでも借りられるという事実のことです）

A 〉 It refers to the fact that money can always be borrowed from parents.

フラッシュ・フィクションポエムを読んでみよう!

55-Word Flash Fiction Poem by Paul Winston

Bill Grant

Stalking the hall on silent feet, Bill Grant sought revenge on his wife
Indiscretions with the lad next door, demanded the end of her life
He opened the door and prepared his aim, then stumbled and fell to the floor
Dazed, he recalled the soup she had served, and the taste of almonds it bore

Explanation of Flash Fiction

Flash fiction is an extremely short story written within a pre-determined number of words. In the same way as a longer story or novel, it is required to contain all of the elements required for the reader to imagine an entire scenario.

In the above case, it is clear that Bill Grant is intending to murder his wife for having an affair with the boy who lives next door. We know that he intends to commit the murder with a gun because he "prepares his aim" in the third line. However, before he can commit the crime he falls ill, and because the "taste of almonds" in the last line refers to the cyanide, we know that his wife has managed to kill him first by poisoning his soup.

55語のフラッシュ・フィクションポエム
ポール・ウィンストン

ビル・グラント

広間に忍び足で近づきながら、ビル・グラントは妻へのリベンジを果たそうとしていた
隣人の男と浮気をした妻の命を奪うのだ
ビルはドアを開け、狙いを定めようとすると、よろけて床に倒れた
もうろうとする意識の中で、彼は妻がさっき出したスープとそこからしていたアーモンド臭を思い出していた

フラッシュ・フィクションの解説

フラッシュ・フィクションとは、あらかじめ決められた語数内で書かれた極めて短い話のことです。長編や小説と同じように、読者が筋書き全体を想像するのに必要な要素すべてを含んでいることが求められます。

上の場合、ビル・グラントが隣人の若者と関係を持った妻を殺そうとしているのは明白です。3行目で彼は「狙いを定めようとする」ので、銃で殺人を犯そうとしていることがわかります。しかし、彼は犯罪を犯す前に気分が悪くなって倒れますが、最終行の「アーモンド臭」とは青酸カリを指しているので、彼の妻がスープに毒を入れることで先手を打って彼をまんまと殺害したことがわかります。

57

クイックQ&A

Q 〉 Why did Bill Grant seek revenge on his wife?
（ビル・グラントが妻に復讐しようとしたのはなぜですか）

POINT

詩には様々なタイプがあり、上記のものはcouplet quatrainと呼ばれます。これは4行で構成されていて、1行目と2行目の最後の単語（wifeとlife）、3行目と4行目の最後の単語（floorとbore）がそれぞれ韻を踏む詩のことです。この詩の形式はAABB押韻構成とも呼ばれ、AAは最初の2行の押韻、BBはその次の2行の押韻を示しています。ABAB押韻構成やABBA押韻構成というものもあり、それぞれalternating quatrain、envelope quatrainと呼ばれています。

（彼が隣人の若者と浮気をしたからです）
A 〉 Because she had an affair with the boy next door.

discussed what sections we hope to be assigned to ▶

CD
2-23

実際の会話を聞いて話してみよう!

SETTING:

> Nitobe and Misaki are sitting in a bar drinking beer and discussing their work.

Nitobe: Have you heard anything from Mr. Yonezawa yet?

Misaki: No, nothing. I suppose that could be good news. If he was going to transfer us back to our old departments, I'm sure we'd get at least one month's warning.

Nitobe: That's a valid point, but I'm still a little anxious. You want to stay in Global Logistics too, right?

Misaki: Yes, very much so. The Sales Department wasn't too bad, but there's a lot of pressure. What section do you want to be assigned to?

Nitobe: The Documentation Section.

Misaki: Yeah, like there's no ulterior motive there, right?

Nitobe: What do you mean?

Misaki: Aya Shibata.

Nitobe: Ah, okay. Actually, no. After working in all three sections, I just enjoyed Documentation the most. Customer Support wasn't too bad either, but you never know what is going to happen. When problems arise, you have to work through the night and over weekends. At least I know what time I can leave the office in the Documentation Section. Of course, being able to work with Aya Shibata wouldn't be so bad, either.

Misaki: Ha, ha, ha. I knew it! I liked the Customer Support Section best. I had lots of chances to speak to people in other countries, which was fun. I wasn't too keen on the Legal Affairs Section. The work is a little boring, and you can't afford to make any mistakes.

Nitobe: I agree with you. It takes a long time to understand the legal writing, too. My vocabulary of legal terms has improved, but the sentences are very long and the structures very complex. I can't wait to get back to regular English.

Misaki: And Aya Shibata, right?

Nitobe: Right! Definitely Aya Shibata…

discussed what sections we hope to be assigned to

場面：

> 新渡戸と岬が居酒屋で座ってビールを飲みながら仕事の話をしている。

N：米澤部長からまだ何も聞いてない？

M：いや、何も。でもこれはいい兆しかもしれないよ。僕たちをもとの部署に戻すつもりなら、少なくともその1か月前には知らされるはずだろ。

N：それは一理あるな、でもまだ少し緊張してるよ。岬も海外事業部に残りたいんだよね。

M：うん、とてもね。営業部も悪くはなかったけど、プレッシャーがすごいから。新渡戸はどの課に配属されたいんだ？

N：ドキュメンテーション課だな。

M：へえ、とか言いつつ下心があるんだろう？

N：どういう意味だよ？

M：柴田彩さんがいるだろ。

N：ああ、はいはい。残念だけど違うよ。3つの課すべてで働いてみて、ドキュメンテーション課が一番楽しかっただけ。顧客サポート課もなかなか良かったんだけど、いつ何が起こるかわからないからさ。問題が起きたら、徹夜してでも週末返上してでも仕事しなきゃならないんだ。ドキュメンテーション課なら少なくとも何時に退社できるかわかるからね。もちろん、柴田彩さんと一緒に働けるのも悪くはないけど。

M：ははは、やっぱり！　僕は顧客サポート課が一番だな。外国の人と話す機会がたくさんあって、楽しかったんだ。法務課はあんまり合わなかった。仕事が少し退屈だし、ミスは許されないしね。

N：確かに。法的な文章を理解するのにも時間がかかるしね。法律用語の知識は増えたけど、文章はやたら長いし構成もすごく複雑だし。普通の英語に戻るのが待ち遠しいよ。

M：柴田彩さんのところに戻るのも、だろ？

N：そう！　もちろん柴田彩さんも含めて…。

キーワードやフレーズをチェック！

☐ fiscal year　会計年度

Focusing on productivity will provide greater benefits during the next **fiscal year**.
生産性を重視することで来年度はさらなる利益が得られるだろう。

The company expects to turn a profit for the **fiscal year** ending next March.
その会社は来年3月までの今会計年度で利益を出すつもりだ。

☐ whether or not　〜かどうか

We will decide **whether or not** to employ more staff during Tuesday's meeting.
私たちは火曜日の会議でもっと多くの社員を雇用するかどうかを決めるつもりだ。

We still don't know **whether or not** the company will accept the revisions to the contract.
私たちはその会社が契約内容の修正を受け入れるかどうかまだわからない。

☐ even if　たとえ〜でも

He is determined to advertise the new product on TV, **even if** it fails to sell.
彼はその新商品を、もし売れなかったとしても、絶対にテレビで宣伝するつもりだ。

The company will retain its production plant in Taiwan, **even if** taxes are raised.
その会社は税金が高くなったとしても台湾の生産工場を維持するようだ。

☐ in leaps and bounds　飛躍的に

Artificial intelligence is advancing **in leaps and bounds**, which is a little worrying.
人工知能は飛躍的に進歩しており、それは少々心配でもある。

Her knowledge of the industry has improved **in leaps and bounds**.

彼女のその業界に関する知識は急速に向上した。

be sure to 〜　　きっと〜する

The new stock system **is sure to** improve traceability throughout all processes.

この新しい在庫管理システムは必ずすべての過程におけるトレーサビリティを向上させるだろう。

I've never known her to be late before, so she **is sure to** be here soon.

今まで彼女が遅刻をすることは私が知る限りなかったので、きっとすぐに来るはずだ。

ulterior motive　　下心

Gerald admitted that he had an **ulterior motive** for visiting the head office.

ジェラルドは本社を訪れたのには下心があったことを認めた。

Everybody in the section is convinced that Mr. Williams had an **ulterior motive** for promoting Susan over Tiffany.

課内の皆が、ウィリアムズ課長がティファニーではなくスーザンを昇進させたのには下心があったと確信している。

57

マナーのヒント

　当然ながらビジネス社会では、性的や人種差別的と解釈されたり、その他のハラスメントと結び付けられるような発言は決して許されません。また、同僚などとの会話でも噂を立てたり広めたりしないようにすることが肝要です。やむをえず他の人に関する確証のない情報を伝える場合は、自分は噂について話しているだけだと断っておくのがよいでしょう。以下はそんな例のいくつかです。

- I don't know if it is true or not, but I heard that Christine is thinking of resigning.（本当かどうか知らないが、クリスティーンが辞めることを考えていると聞いた）
- I heard that Peter is in the middle of a stressful divorce, although it is only a rumor so may not be true.（ピーターが大変な離婚調停の最中だと聞いたけど、ただの噂話だからそうじゃないかもね）
- I doubt if it is true, but people are saying that the manager of the Accounts Department has been caught stealing money.（事実かどうかは疑わしいが、経理部長がお金を盗んで捕まったと皆が噂している）

DAY 58

MARCH 19TH (WEDNESDAY)

I feel as if I am in limbo at the moment. I have no idea what position I will be in from the beginning of next month, but I have to prepare for the eventuality that I will still be the director of the Global Logistics Department. Strangely, it is difficult for me to get into the mindset of department director when there is a chance that I will be doing a completely different job. Conversely, I still don't have the authority to make any presidential decisions right now, so I feel at a loose end.

Having said that, I have already made my decision on who to headhunt for perfecting their English skills next year after Nitobe and Misaki graduate. I have chosen Kimiko Harada of the Accounting Department, and Noritaka Nakamura from our Sendai branch office, both of whom are in their mid-twenties. Nakamura has already agreed to transfer to Tokyo from Miyagi Prefecture, and he will make his appearance in the office during the first week of April.

I spoke to the president, and he has agreed to my suggestion of making Kyoko Uchiyama of the Legal Affairs Section the new department director in my stead if I do become president. Norika Hirai will subsequently be promoted to section manager. Uchiyama is as passionate about English as I am, so she and Paul Winston will make excellent mentors for Harada and Nakamura.

I was very pleased with this year's protégés, and I hope the new ones will do as well next year. Nitobe has done especially well and far exceeded my expectations. Misaki also did extremely well. I have therefore decided to keep both in the Global Logistics Department. Paul Winston sent me his final reports on the progress **Nitobe (p.290)** and **Misaki (p.292)** have made, and it was on these that I based my final decision. I will assign Nitobe to the Documentation Section, but I'm still not sure about Misaki. I therefore **called him into my office (p.294)** yesterday for a chat. He is hoping to be assigned to the Customer Support Section, but I believe that his analytical mind would be more suited to the Legal Affairs Section.

I'll think about it a little longer before deciding.

Yonezawa

３月１９日（水曜日）

　今、私は宙ぶらりんになっているような気分だ。来月の初めから自分がどんな立場に立っているかは全くわからないが、万が一海外事業部長を続けることになった場合の準備もしておかなければならない。不思議なことに、これから全く違う仕事をすることになるかもしれないと思うと、部長としての考えに集中しにくい。一方で、私は現時点では社長としてのいかなる決断をする権限もないため、どうにも心が定まらない。

　そうは言ったが、来年度、新渡戸と岬が卒業した後、誰をスカウトして英語をマスターさせるかはもう決めている。選んだのは経理部の原田貴美子と仙台支社の中村典孝で、２人とも２０代半ばだ。中村はすでに宮城県から東京への転勤に同意しており、４月の第１週にオフィスに顔を出す予定だ。

　社長と話をして、彼は私が社長になった場合、法務課の内山京子を私の代わりに新しい部長にするという私の提案にうなずいてくれた。それに伴い、平井紀香が課長に昇進することになる。内山は私と同じくらい英語に関して熱心なので、彼女とポール・ウィンストンは原田と中村にとって申し分ない指導者になるだろう。

　私は今年の教え子たちにはとても満足しており、来年新しく来る２人も同じように成功してくれることを期待している。新渡戸は特に良い成果を出し、私の予想をはるかに超えてきた。岬も上出来だった。なので、私は２人とも海外事業部に残すことにした。ポール・ウィンストンが新渡戸と岬のこれまでの成長に関する最終報告書を送ってきたので、それに基づいて最終的な決定を行ったのだ。新渡戸はドキュメンテーション課に配属することにしたが、岬はどうするべきかまだ確信が持てていない。そのため、昨日彼を部長室に呼んで軽く話をした。彼は顧客サポート課への配属を望んでいるが、私としては彼の分析的な思考力は法務課により向いていると思う。

58

　この件についてはもう少し考えてから決断しよう。

　　　　　　　　米澤

Nitobe ►

研修報告書を書いてみよう!

Final Report on Intensive One-Year Training Course

Student :　Shinnosuke Nitobe
Instructor : Paul Winston
Date :　　March 17th

Summary:

Nitobe shows excellent aptitude for the English language. He is eager to learn, and repeatedly asks questions until he completely understands complex sentence structures. He has worked diligently on all homework assignments throughout the year, and his reading and writing skills have improved dramatically. If he continues to progress at the same pace from now on, he is likely to achieve fluency within a few years.

Strong Points:

Nitobe's strong points include his tenacity during the learning process. He never gives up until he fully understands everything. He also has a very retentive memory, which has greatly expanded his vocabulary, and he tries to use all new words he learns in everyday usage.

Weak Points:

Nitobe still has a little trouble discerning between articles, and often misuses them. This has improved over the course of the year, but still requires some work.

POINT

まず「概容」を述べ、その中でも最も伝えたいことを最初に書きます。ポジティブなことを書くのが望ましいですが、将来的な予測や希望も添えるとよいでしょう。
「短所」には、その短所の改善方法や改善の見通しなど、前向きなことも入れましょう。

集中年間研修コースの最終報告書

生徒： 新渡戸慎之助
講師： ポール・ウィンストン
日付： 3月17日

概容：

　新渡戸は英語に優れた才能を見せています。熱心に学び、複雑な文構造を完全に理解するまで繰り返し質問をします。年間を通してすべての宿題に熱心に取り組み、リーディングとライティングの技能は劇的に向上しました。これからも同じペースで成長を続ければ、数年以内に完全に流暢になるように思います。

長所：

　新渡戸の長所には学習過程での粘り強さがあります。すべてを十分に理解するまで決して諦めません。非常に優れた記憶力も持っており、そのおかげで大変語彙力が広がりましたし、学んだあらゆる新しい言葉を日常で使う努力をしています。

短所：

　新渡戸は冠詞の見極めにまだ少し問題があり、よく誤用しています。これはこの年間コースの間に改善されましたが、まだ少し訓練が必要です。

クイックQ&A

58

Q 〉 How can Nitobe achieve fluency in English?
（新渡戸はどうすれば英語がペラペラになれますか）

POINT

第2段落に出てくるtenacity「粘り強さ」（形容詞tenacious、副詞tenaciously）と同義と思われている語にpersistence（形容詞persistent、副詞persistently）があります。文脈でそれがポジティブな使い方かネガティブな使い方かが示されていれば、これらの語はどちらが使われていても問題ないのですが、多くの場合、tenacity/tenacious/tenaciouslyはプラスのニュアンス、persistence/persistent/persistentlyはマイナスのニュアンスを持っています。以下はその用例です。
・She is very tenacious, and never leaves a task unfinished. （彼女は非常に粘り強く、作業は必ず終わりまでやる）
・He studied the book tenaciously until he understood it completely. （彼はその本を完全に理解するまで根気強く読み込んだ）
・He was very persistent as a child. （彼は子どもの頃とても頑固だった）
・She persistently refuses to do her homework. （彼女はかたくなに宿題をやろうとしない）

A 〉 By continuing to progress at the same pace（同じペースで成長し続けることによって）

Misaki ►

研修報告書を読んでみよう!

Final Report on Intensive One-Year Training Course

Student :   Ichiro Misaki
Instructor : Paul Winston
Date :   March 17th

Summary:

Misaki is extremely proficient in spoken English, and his written English is improving. The three years he spent in New Zealand as a junior high schoolboy established a firm English foundation within him, although he does have a tendency to rest on his laurels and lacks curiosity over points he does not understand. He has worked hard throughout the year and made significant progress, and I am sure that he will become a valuable asset for the company.

Strong Points:

Misaki has no trouble understanding extremely complex idioms, and he uses them fluently. He has a great memory for obscure words, and is capable of discussing a wide range of subjects that are usually beyond the reach of people who are speaking English in a second language.

Weak Points:

Misaki's spoken proficiency does not extend to his written compositions. Although he is capable of speaking fluently, he is prone to careless mistakes when writing, although this has improved greatly this past year.

POINT

接続詞のalthoughを要所に使い、プラスとマイナスの事柄を効果的に対比させています。

集中年間研修コースの最終報告書

生徒：　岬一郎
講師：　ポール・ウィンストン
日付：　3月17日

概容：

　岬は英語を話すことに非常に堪能で、英語を書くことも上達してきています。今の英語の出来にあぐらをかく傾向があり、自分が理解しないことに好奇心を欠くといったことはありますが、中学生のときにニュージーランドで3年間過ごしたことが彼の中に確かな英語の基礎を築きました。年間を通して一生懸命努力し、著しい成長を遂げたので、彼は会社にとって価値ある財産になると確信しています。

長所：

　岬は極めて複雑なイディオムを問題なく理解し、それらを流暢に使います。あいまいな単語についても優れた記憶力があり、英語を第2言語とする話者が通常は手が届かないような幅広いテーマについて話すことができます。

短所：

　岬の話す堪能さは、彼の英作文までは及んでいません。流暢に話すことはできますが、この1年でかなり改善されたとはいえ、書くときにはケアレスミスを起こしがちです。

58

クイックQ&A

Q 〉 What does "lack curiosity" mean? : shows an interest, has no interest, or is very interested
（「好奇心を欠く」とは「興味を示す」「興味がない」「とても興味がある」のうち、どの意味ですか）

POINT

第1段落に出てくるtendency「傾向」は名詞で、動詞形はtendです。両方の形（例えばshe has a tendency to、she tends toなど）を同じように使っている文をよく見かけますが、使い方には微妙な違いがあります。一般に名詞tendencyは意外な、もしくはたまにしか見ない癖や習慣を表すのに使われ、動詞tendはいつも見られる癖や習慣を表すのに用いられます。以下はその例です。
・He tends to prefer rock music, although he also has a tendency to listen to jazz.
（彼はロックを好む傾向があるが、ジャズを聴くこともよくある）
・She tends to be unpunctual, and her tendency to call in sick is well known. （彼女は時間にルーズになりがちで、たまに病欠の電話をするのはよく知られている）

A 〉 has no interest（興味がない）

called him into my office　►　CD 2-25

実 際 の 会 話 を 聞 い て 話 し て み よ う !

SETTING:

Misaki is sitting in front of Yonezawa's desk.

Yonezawa: I called you in to let you know that I have decided to keep you in the Global Logistics Department.

Misaki: Really? That's wonderful news! Thank you very much. I promise I will do everything I can to make sure you never regret it. How about Nitobe? Did he pass, too?

Yonezawa: Yes, he did. He will also be staying in the department. I will speak to him later. You may be interested to know that Mr. Winston gave both you and Nitobe very high marks, and was extremely pleased with your progress. I am now left with the dilemma of where to assign you. Documentation, Customer Support or Legal Affairs? Do you have any preferences?

Misaki: Yes, sir. I thought the Customer Support Section suited me best. It gave me the chance to use my English by speaking to overseas clients, and I found the work very rewarding.

Yonezawa: I see. When I spoke to Ms. Uchiyama, she said that she thought you would be perfectly suited to the Legal Affairs Section. And, to be frank, I agree with her. I've noticed that you have a very analytical mind, which is essential in Legal Affairs.

Misaki: That's very kind of you, sir. Of course, if that is your decision, then I am quite happy to be assigned there. However, I personally thought that I did my best work in Customer Support.

Yonezawa: Okay, I'll bear that in mind, and let you know my decision before the end of the month. So, tell me, if I asked you to sum up the past year in a single word, what word would you choose?

Misaki: Mmmm, that's difficult. Probably "fruitful."

Yonezawa: Fruitful? That's interesting. In what way was it fruitful?

Misaki: Well, not only did it give me a chance to polish my English, it also gave me a closer look at how the rest of the company works. I think I also gained a lot of confidence in dealing with other people.

Yonezawa: That was a very good answer. Well done. Anyway, congratulations on successfully completing the year, and good luck in the future.

called him into my office

場面：

> 岬が米澤のデスクの前に座っている。

Y：君を呼んだのは、君に海外事業部にとどまってもらうことにしたと伝えるためだ。

M：本当ですか。素晴らしい知らせです！　ありがとうございます。後悔させないよう、精いっぱい働くと約束します。新渡戸はどうだったんですか。彼も合格しましたか。

Y：ああ、合格したよ。彼もこの部署に残ることになる。彼にはあとで話そう。ウィンストン先生は君と新渡戸の両方をとても高く評価し、君たちの成長にとても満足していたと伝えておくよ。そこで私は君をどこに配属するかという選択で悩んでいるんだ。ドキュメンテーション課か顧客サポート課か、それとも法務課か。君の希望はあるかい？

M：はい、部長。僕は顧客サポート課が一番自分に合っていると思いました。海外の顧客と話をすることで英語を使う機会が得られて、とてもやりがいのある仕事だと感じました。

Y：なるほど。私が内山課長と話したとき、彼女は君が法務課にぴったりだと思ったと言っていてね。それで、率直に言うと、私も彼女と同意見なんだ。君はとても分析的な思考ができると感じたし、それは法務課では不可欠だからね。

58

M：ありがとうございます、部長。もちろん、それが部長の判断でしたら、そこに配属されることに不満はありません。ですが、自分が最も力を発揮できるのは顧客サポート課だと個人的に感じたんです。

Y：よし、そのことは心にとどめておこう。今月末までに私の決定を知らせるよ。ところで、聞きたいんだが、この1年を1つの言葉にまとめろと言ったら、どんな言葉を選ぶかね？

M：うーん、これは難しいですね。おそらく「実り多い」でしょうか。

Y：実り多い？　それは興味深い。どのように実り多い年だったと？

M：そうですね、今年度は英語力を磨くチャンスをもらっただけでなく、我が社の他の部分がどのように回っているのかをよりよく見ることができました。人と関わることに大きな自信もついたと思います。

Y：とても良い答えだったよ。素晴らしい。何はともあれ、今年度の成果おめでとう。これからも頑張れよ。

キーワードやフレーズをチェック!

in limbo　宙に浮いた状態で

The negotiations for the new contract are still **in limbo**.
新しい契約の交渉はいまだ宙ぶらりんの状態だ。

He is having trouble securing a visa, so his transfer overseas is still **in limbo**.
彼はビザの取得に手間取っており、海外赴任はまだ宙ぶらりんの状態だ。

prepare for the eventuality　万一の場合に備える

She has to **prepare for the eventuality** of not being offered the job.
彼女は万が一その仕事をオファーされなかった場合に備えなければいけない。

Exporters have to **prepare for the eventuality** of higher tariffs in the current economy.
現在の経済において、輸出企業は関税の引き上げの可能性に備えなければならない。

get into the mindset　心構えを身につける

He was originally a software engineer, but he soon **got into the mindset** of a salesman.
彼はもともとソフトウェアエンジニアだったが、すぐにセールスマンとしての姿勢を身につけた。

It is essential for you to **get into** a positive **mindset** if you want to succeed.
成功したいのなら、ポジティブな心構えを身につけるのが必須だ。

at a loose end　何もすることがなくて

He is **at a loose end** now that the project has finished.
プロジェクトが終わった今、彼は手持ち無沙汰だ。

If you need any help, I am **at a loose end** for the rest of the week.
何か手伝いが必要だったら、私は今週いっぱい何もやることがないから。

having said that そうとは言え

He hated the job at first, but **having said that**, he soon became very proficient.

彼は初めのうちその仕事が嫌だったが、そうは言いつつも、すぐにうまくこなせるようになった。

The product is inferior, but **having said that**, it is quite inexpensive and is sure to sell well.

この製品は劣化版だが、そうとは言え、かなり安価でよく売れること間違いなしだ。

exceed *one's* expectations 予想 [期待] を上回る

Monthly turnover recently is **exceeding everyone's expectations**.

最近の月間売上高は皆の予想を上回っている。

The positive way in which her presentation was received **exceeded her own expectations**.

彼女のプレゼンテーションへの好評価は彼女自身の期待以上だった。

58

マナーのヒント

　欧米企業における海外転勤は通常、事前に従業員の同意を必要としますが、企業内の差別から従業員を保護する厳しい法律により、そのような転勤を拒否しても将来のキャリアに影響はありません。社員が個人的な理由で違う部署や支社への転属を望む場合もあり、基本的にそのような社員は経営側に自由に申請を出すことができます。これはたいてい初期段階に口頭で行われ、会社側が原則的に合意すれば、社員は正式な申請書に希望の理由を書いて提出するよう求められます。

MARCH 31ST (MONDAY)

This is my last entry of the year, and I have many things to report. I guess the biggest news is, Mr. Yonezawa will become the new president of the company from tomorrow! An internal memo announcing this was sent out last Thursday. It came as a complete surprise to everyone. The new head of the Global Logistics Department will be Ms. Uchiyama, and Ms. Hirai will take over her job as section manager.

The next item of news is that the president visited the department last Tuesday and presented me with my prize for winning the Kaizen competition. ¥100,000 in cash! Mr. Yonezawa introduced him, and he then gave a ten-minute speech on the importance of finding areas that require improvement. He then asked me to give a speech in front of everyone in the department, which embarrassed me greatly. I can't even remember what I said, but everybody gave me a round of applause at the end.

And, the most important news of all is that Mr. Yonezawa has deemed that my English has improved sufficiently over this year, so from tomorrow I will be an official member of the Global Logistics Department. **Mr. Yonezawa called me into his office (P.304)** last week and **presented me with a certificate (p.300)**. He also gave me a stack of **four books on business ethics (p.302)** as a gift (prize?) for completing the year successfully. Apparently, Misaki received the same books. This is an enormous relief. It would have been awful if I had been sent back to the General Affairs Department after working so hard this year. And, not only will I be able to stay in the Global Logistics Department, I have also been assigned to the Documentation Section!

But there is more! I have also been put in charge of reducing costs with the use of Computer Assisted Translation! In other words, I get the chance to try out my Kaizen proposal! Mr. Yonezawa rejected the nursery and freelance translator part of the proposal, but intends to use the money saved with CAT to establish an allowance for employees with pre-school children. And, on top of that, the person he has assigned to assist me is Aya Shibata! Whoopee!

What an amazing year it has been...

Nitobe

キーワード＆キーフレーズ→p.306

3月31日（月曜日）

　これは今年最後の日誌への記入になるのだけど、書くことがたくさんある。一番のビッグニュースは、米澤部長が明日から我が社の新社長になるということだ！　このことを発表する社内通知が先週の木曜日に配布された。これには皆が完全に驚かされた。新しい海外事業部長には内山課長がなり、平井さんが課長の座を引き継ぐことになる。

　もう1つのニュースは、火曜日に社長がうちの部署を訪れて、僕に改善コンペ優勝の賞金をくれたことだ。現金で10万円！　米澤部長が社長を紹介し、それから改善が必要な場所を見つけることの重要性について10分間のスピーチをした。その後、部長は僕にも部署の皆の前でスピーチをするように言ったので、ひどくまごついてしまった。自分が何を話したのかも覚えていないけど、最後には全員が大きな拍手をくれた。

　それから、中でも最も重要なニュースは、米澤部長が僕の英語力がこの1年間で十分上がったと判断したため、僕は明日から正式に海外事業部の一員になるということだ。先週、米澤部長は部長室に僕を呼んで、修了証を渡してくれた。この1年間でよい成果を上げたことを記念するプレゼント（賞品？）として4冊の企業倫理の本ももらった。どうやら、岬も同じ本をもらったらしい。これにはものすごくホッとした。この1年間あれだけ頑張ったのに総務部に戻されていたらひどくがっかりしただろう。そして、僕は海外事業部にい続けることができるだけではなく、何とドキュメンテーション課に配属されたのだ！

59

　でもそれで終わりではない！　僕はコンピュータ支援翻訳の利用によって経費を削減する仕事も任された！　つまり、自分の改善案を実際に試す機会をもらったのだ！　米澤部長は改善案の託児所とフリーランスの翻訳家の部分は却下したけど、CATで節約した金額を就学前の子どもがいる社員のための手当を設けることに使うつもりらしい。さらに、部長は僕を手伝ってくれる役として柴田彩さんを指名したのだ！　やったー！

　今年は本当に素晴らしい1年だったな…。

新渡戸

海外事業部
ドキュメンテーション課

presented me with a certificate ►

修了証明書を書いてみよう！

Certificate of Completion

This is to certify that **Shinnosuke Nitobe** has successfully completed one year of intensive English language training and will become a bona fide member of the Global Logistics Department as of April 1st.

Signed: *Osamu Yonezawa*

Tomizawa Integrated Solutions, Inc.

POINT

This is to certify that 〜が決まり文句。最後には発行人の名前を入れます。

修了証明書

　新渡戸慎之助　は1年間の集中英語研修を優秀な成績で修了し、4月1日付けで海外事業部の正社員となることをここに証明する。

署名: 米澤修

株式会社　富沢インテグレーテッド・ソリューションズ

クイックQ&A

Q〉 What is another word for "certify"? : announce, claim, or confirm
（「証明する」の別の言い方は「発表する」「主張する」「認証する」のどれですか）

59

POINT

本文2行目にあるbona fideはラテン語由来の語句で、「認可された」「本物の」または「心からの」という意味です。bona fidesという形で「誠意」「証明」という意味の名詞として使われることもあります。以下はその用例です。

・The committee made a bona fide effort to investigate the issue. （委員会はその問題の調査に誠意を持って取り組んだ）
・Only bona fide ink cartridges supplied by the manufacturer can be used in this printer. （このプリンターにはメーカーによって支給された真正のインクカートリッジしか使ってはいけない）
・The company checked his bona fides before employing him. （その会社は経歴を確認してから彼を雇用した）

A〉confirm（認証する）

推薦ビジネス書の紹介文を読んでみよう!

Recommended Books on Business Ethics

- *Natural Capitalism* (by Paul Hawken, L. Hunter Lovins, Amory B. Lovins)
  A book explaining how today's global businesses can be environmentally
  responsible while remaining profitable.

- *Ethics for the Real World: Creating a Personal Code to Guide Decisions in
  Work and Life* (by Ronald A. Howard, Clinton D. Korver, Bill Birchard)
  A book explaining the art of ethical decision-making by identifying and
  committing to ethical principles and generating creative alternatives for
  solving problems.

- *If Aristotle Ran General Motors: The New Soul of Business* (by Tom Morris)
  The practical application of ethics in everyday life. Concentrates on the
  philosophies of Aristotle, Confucius and other philosophers to demonstrate
  how ancient wisdom can be applied today.

- *The Sustainability Generation: The Politics of Change and Why Personal
  Accountability is Essential NOW!* (by Mark C. Coleman)
  A book providing clear directions for enlightening ourselves on the
  importance of social change targeting environmental responsibility.

企業倫理に関する推薦本

- **『自然資本の経済』**（ポール・ホーケン、L・ハンター・ロビンス、エイモリー・B・ロビンス著）
  今日のグローバル企業が、収益性を残しつついかに環境に配慮しうるかを解説している本。

- **『現実世界のための倫理学：仕事と生活で決断を導く個人コードをつくること』**（ロナルド・A・ハワード、クリントン・D・コーバー、ビル・バーチャード著）
  倫理原則を見分けて、それにコミットすること及び問題解決のための創造的な選択肢を生み出すことによる倫理的な意思決定の技法を解説している本。

- **『アリストテレスがGMを経営したら：新しいビジネス・マインドの探究』**（トム・モリス著）
  日常生活における倫理学の実用的な応用。アリストテレス、孔子、その他の哲学者の哲学に焦点を当て、古代の知恵が現代にいかに応用できるかを解説する。

- **『持続可能性の創出：変革の経営と個人の説明責任がなぜ「今」必須なのか』**（マーク・C・コールマン著）
  環境責任を目標とする社会変革の重要性について自身を啓蒙するための明確な方向性を与えてくれる本。

クイックQ＆A

Q Who wrote the book about changing society for environmental reasons?
（環境目的のために社会を変えることに関する本を書いたのは誰ですか）

59

POINT

ethicsという名詞は、その形容詞や副詞の形であるethicalやethicallyとともに、近頃ビジネスの場で頻繁に使われるようになっていて、これらの言葉の後ろにある基本概念は、決まりへの準拠やコンプライアンス、ガバナンス、社会的責任、世間が企業に要求するその他の社会倫理的な観念から切り離すことはできません。つまりethicsとは日常のあらゆる行動において善悪を区別できる能力とも言えます。以下はその用例です。
- Strong ethics are required by politicians when faced with the temptation of bribes. （賄賂という誘惑に遭ったとき、政治家には強い倫理観が要求される）
- He is well-known for being the most ethical journalists in the industry. （彼はこの業界で最も道徳的なジャーナリストとしてよく知られている）
- The president was forced to retire for unethically falsifying data. （その社長は非倫理的にデータを偽造したために辞めさせられた）

A Mark C. Coleman（マーク・C・コールマン）

Mr. Yonezawa called me into his office　▶　

実際の会話を聞いて話してみよう!

SETTING:

> Nitobe has been called into Mr. Yonezawa's office and is sitting opposite him.

Yonazawa: I just wanted to confirm what I mentioned the other day. You have successfully completed your English training, and will become a fully-fledged member of the Global Logistics Department from April 1st. Here is your certificate to prove it, as well as a few books that I think you may find useful.

Nitobe: Thank you, sir! A certificate! I'll hang it on my wall at home.

Yonazawa: You may find that people will make fun of you if you do that. Maybe you should just keep it in a drawer.

Nitobe: Ha, ha… Yes, sir. Thank you for the books, too.

Yonazawa: They all concern business ethics, which is an extremely important subject. Hopefully, they will give you a few ideas for the future as you move up the company ranks, as I'm sure you will.

Nitobe: Thank you. I'll study them carefully. May I ask what section I will be assigned to?

Yonazawa: The Documentation Section, as you hoped. But you will be working on something that you did not cover during your training. Your job will be to set up a system in which Computer-Assisted Translation software can be used for reducing operational costs.

Nitobe: You mean, like my Kaizen proposal?

Yonazawa: Yes. I studied your figures very closely, and decided that the CAT software would work. The freelance translation, however, would require too many people to operate successfully, so I have discarded that idea. That means that your proposal will not generate sufficient savings to operate a nursery, but I intend to use the sum saved through the use of CAT software to finance a child allowance for all employees with pre-school children.

Nitobe: That's wonderful news. Thank you, sir!

Yonazawa: You'll also need somebody to help you, so I will be assigning one of the current section members to work with you.

Nitobe: Thank you, sir! Who will that be?

Yonazawa: Aya Shibata.

Mr. Yonezawa called me into his office

場面：

> 新渡戸が米澤部長の部屋に呼ばれて、彼と向かい合って座っている。

Y：先日も触れたことを改めて言いたかったんだ。君は英語の訓練を無事終えたので、4月1日から海外事業部の一人前のメンバーになる。そのことを証明する修了証と、これから役に立つだろう本を何冊か贈る。

N：ありがとうございます、部長！　修了証ですね！　家で部屋の壁にかけます。

Y：そんなことをすると人にからかわれるぞ。引き出しにしまっておくだけにしたらどうかね。

N：はは…。そうしておきます、部長。この本も、ありがとうございます。

Y：それらはすべて企業倫理に関するもので、これは非常に重要なテーマだからね。きっと、君が社内で高い地位を得ていくうえで将来役立つことをいくつか教えてくれるだろう。私は君が出世していくだろうと信じているからね。

N：ありがとうございます。じっくり読み込んでおきます。僕がどの課に配属されるのかお尋ねしてもいいですか。

Y：君が希望していた通り、ドキュメンテーション課だよ。ただし、訓練中には触れなかったことに取り組むことになる。君の仕事はコンピュータ支援翻訳ソフトの使用によって経費を削減できる仕組みを立ち上げることだ。

N：つまり、僕の改善案のように、ということですか。

Y：そう。君の提示した数字をよく調べて、ＣＡＴソフトならうまくいくだろうと判断した。フリーランスの翻訳家という案は、問題なく機能するのに必要な人数が多すぎるから、却下したがね。そうすると君の案で託児所を運営するのに十分な金額は節約できないことになるが、ＣＡＴソフトの使用で節約できた金額を、就学前の子どもがいるすべての社員のための子ども手当に充てようと考えている。

N：それはとてもうれしく思います。ありがとうございます、部長！

Y：君を手伝ってくれる人間も必要だろうから、現在の課員の1人を君と一緒に仕事をするよう割り当てることにした。

N：ありがとうございます、部長！　それは誰になるんですか。

Y：柴田彩だ。

59

キーワードやフレーズをチェック！

come as a surprise　驚きである

It **came as a surprise** when he was promoted to senior sales manager.
彼が営業部長に昇進したのは驚きだった。

In light of the slowdown in the economy, this year's high profits **came as a surprise**.
景気低迷を考えると、今年大きな利益が出たのは意外な結果だった。

present *one* with ～　（人に）〜を贈る

The society **presented him with** an award for his report on environmental conservation.
学会は彼の環境保全に関する論文に対して賞を贈った。

The president **presented her with** a substantial golden handshake when she retired.
社長は彼女が退職する際、高額の退職金を与えた。

the importance of ～　〜の重要性

The importance of appropriate governance cannot be overstated.
適切なガバナンスの重要性はどんなに強調してもしすぎることはない。

The scandal taught the company **the importance of** double-checking figures.
そのスキャンダルは会社に数字の念入りな確認の重要性を教えた。

round of applause　拍手喝采

She received a **round of applause** after she finished her presentation.
彼女はプレゼンテーションを終えた後、大きな拍手をもらった。

The whole office gave him a **round of applause** when he was announced salesman of the month.
彼が月間最優秀セールスマンと発表されると、社内の皆が盛大な拍手を送った。

deem that ～　　～と判断する

It has been **deemed that** the company will never recover its real estate investment.
その会社が不動産投資の資金を回収することは不可能だろうと判断された。

The project was abandoned when it was **deemed that** it would certainly fail.
そのプロジェクトは確実に失敗するだろうと判断され中止された。

in other words　　つまり、言い換えれば

The company is liquidating its assets and is, **in other words**, nearby bankrupt.
その会社は資産を清算しており、言い方を変えると、じきに破産する。

I have to work late tonight. **In other words**, I won't be able to attend the party.
私は今夜遅くまで働かなければならない。つまり、パーティーには出席できない。

マナーのヒント

　英語の文章で引用符とイタリック体を使うときのルールは比較的簡単です。引用符はその名の通り、別にある元（人物、映画、テレビ番組、本、新聞記事など）ですでに言われた言葉を引用するときに主に使われます。一方、イタリック体は様々な状況で用いられ、その原則は以下の通りです。

1. 外国語の単語やフレーズを書くとき。
   例: The Japanese word [アンケート] originates from the French word *enquete*.（日本語の「アンケート」という言葉はフランス語のenqueteに由来する）

2. 本、映画、演劇、音楽アルバム、芸術作品などのタイトルを書くとき（例外的に、楽曲名には引用符が使われる）。
   例: Her favorite song is "My Heart Will Go On" from the movie *Titanic*.（彼女の好きな歌は映画『タイタニック』の「マイ・ハート・ウィル・ゴー・オン」だ）

3. 新聞、雑誌などのタイトルを書くとき。

4. 自動車、船、飛行機、ミサイルなどの名前を書くとき。

5. 文章中の特定の単語やフレーズを強調したいとき。
   例: I wrote to the company *six times*, but still haven't received a reply.（私はその会社に6回も手紙を書いたのに、まだ返事が来ない）

59

MARCH 31ST (MONDAY)

I'm sitting in my office in the Global Logistics Department for the last time, just soaking up the atmosphere. It's just after nine o'clock at night, and the office is mostly empty. Tomorrow, I will be sitting in the president's office on the 8th floor, and a name plate with my name on it will adorn the door. The final vote on the new president, which I won by a 3-1 majority, was taken on March 24th, and the **internal memo announcing my appointment (P.310)** was distributed last Thursday. The president held a **small party in his office (P.314)** this evening for all board members, and I think I drank a little too much champagne.

I still haven't completely come to terms with my new appointment, but I am determined to leave no stone unturned in order to make sure the company prospers while strictly maintaining its social responsibilities. I am looking forward to the new challenge.

My last task as director of the Global Logistics Department was to put my protégé Nitobe in charge of Computer-Assisted Translation in the Documentation Section. I checked through the figures he listed in his Kaizen proposal with a fine-tooth comb, and decided to run with his CAT idea. I instructed his boss, Hiroshi Takeda, to give him six months to make it work. If he fails, then the section will revert to its normal operations. I also decided to assign Aya Shibata to help him. I have been keeping my eye on them for some time, and I'm beginning to believe that maybe she is his bulbul after all. We'll see...

And, I have already decided on my first task as president. I will establish a monthly child allowance for all employees with children under elementary school age. Nitobe's idea of a nursery was too far-fetched and would cost an extraordinary amount of money, but I think his CAT proposal will cover the cost of a child allowance. I still need to check the figures, but I am thinking of ¥20,000 per child per month for everybody with pre-school children.

And so, another chapter of my life draws to a close, and a new chapter starts tomorrow. I may take a bottle of wine home to celebrate. I'll just **text my wife (P.312)** and see what she says.

Yonezawa

キーワード＆キーフレーズ→p.316

3月31日（月曜日）

　私はこれで最後となる海外事業部の部長室で座って、ただ雰囲気に浸っている。今は夜9時をちょうど過ぎたころで、社内に人はほとんどいない。明日には、私は8階の社長室に座っていて、そのドアには私の名前を書いた表札が取り付けられているはずだ。3月24日に行われた新社長を決める最終投票では3対1で私が選ばれ、先週の木曜日に私の任命を発表する社内通知が配られた。今日の夕方、社長が社長室で全役員に小さなパーティーを開いてくれ、そこで私はシャンパンを少々飲みすぎてしまったようだ。

　私はまだこの新たな任命を受け入れ切れていないが、我が社が社会的に責任を厳格に果たしつつ、しっかりと繁栄できるよう、あらゆる手を尽くすと決心している。この新しい挑戦は楽しみだ。

　私の海外事業部長としての最後の仕事は、教え子の新渡戸にドキュメンテーション課におけるコンピュータ支援翻訳の仕事を任せることだった。彼が改善案で挙げた数字を徹底的に調べた結果、彼のCATのアイデアを実行に移すことにしたのだ。彼の上司の武田宏さんに、彼がそれをうまく機能させるまで6か月の期間を与えるように言った。彼が失敗した場合、課は通常の運営方法に戻ることになる。それと、彼を手伝う役に柴田彩を指名することにした。あの2人のことをしばらく見守っていて、やはり彼のヒヨドリは彼女なのではと思い始めたのだ。まあいずれわかるだろう…。

　それから、私の社長としての最初の課題ももう決めてある。小学生以下の子どもがいる全従業員のための月々の子ども手当を設けるのだ。新渡戸の託児所のアイデアはかなり無理があってとんでもない金額が必要になってしまうが、CATの案なら子ども手当の分は確保できるだろう。まだ計算して確かめなければならないが、就学前の子どもがいる全員に毎月子ども1人につき2万円を考えている。

60

　こうして、私の人生の章がまた1つ終わりを迎え、明日から新しい章が始まる。祝いにワインをボトル1本買って帰るとするか。妻にメッセージを送って聞いてみよう。

　　　　　　　　　　　　　　米澤

新社長就任の社内通知を書いてみよう!

Tomizawa Integrated Solutions, Inc.

PO-000127

Attn :　All Staff Members
From:　The President's Office
Date :　March 27th

Important Announcement

It is with regret that we announce the retirement of Hideyuki Tomizawa, founder and president of Tomizawa Integrated Solutions, Inc., effective from March 31st. President Tomizawa has headed the company since it was first established in 1986, and he has now decided that it is time for him to move aside and pass the helm of the company over to someone else.

President Tomizawa will be succeeded by Osamu Yonezawa, who is currently director of the Global Logistics Department. Mr. Yonezawa will assume control of the company from April 1st. Kyoko Uchiyama, manager of the Legal Affairs Section, will take over Mr. Yonezawa's position as director of the Global Logistics Department, and Norika Hirai has been promoted to manager of the Legal Affairs Section.

President Tomizawa will remain in the company in an advisory capacity until May 31st, and he will also continue in his post as Chairman of the Board of Directors into the future.

Thank you

POINT

順序として最初に前社長の退任を、その業績や退任理由などとともに伝え、次に新社長の紹介、それに伴う新人事を発表します。

（株）富沢インテグレーテッド・ソリューションズ

PO-000127

宛先：　全社員
差出人：社長室
日付：　3月27日

重要なお知らせ

残念ながら、（株）富沢インテグレーテッド・ソリューションズの創業者であり、代表取締役社長の富沢秀幸が3月31日をもって退職することをお知らせいたします。富沢社長は1986年の創業以来会社を率いてこられましたが、このたび自身が引退し、他の人材に会社の指導を委ねることを決意されました。

富沢社長の職責は現在海外事業部長の米澤修氏に引き継がれます。米澤氏は4月1日から社長に就任いたします。法務課長の内山京子氏が米澤氏に代わって海外事業部長を引き継ぎ、法務課長には平井紀香氏が昇進します。

富沢社長は相談役として5月31日まで会社に残り、今後も役員会議長としての職務は続けます。

よろしくお願いいたします

クイックQ＆A

Q 〉 **How many positions will Tomizawa hold after retiring?**
（富沢は辞任した後、いくつの役職を持ちますか）

60

POINT

第1段落にあるheadは動詞として「～を管理する、制御する、指導する」という意味でよく用いられますが、リストの1位を占めるものや人々の先頭を切っている人を表すのにも使えます。以下はその用例です。
・Kyoto heads the list of most popular tourist destinations in Japan.（京都は日本で最も人気がある観光地のリストの1位を占めている）
・Mr. Grayson will head the inquiry into the company's shady affiliations.（グレイソン氏が先頭に立ってその会社のよそとの怪しい結びつきに関する取り調べをする）
・A car containing the athletes headed the procession through town.（選手たちを乗せた車が町中を通る行列の先頭を走った）

A 〉 Two (advisor and Chairman of the Board) (2つ（相談役と役員会議長）)

text my wife ▶

英語でLINEを読んでみよう!

Read 21:11
I'll be leaving the office in a few minutes. Shall I get some wine?

Good idea. Have you eaten?　21:14

Read 21:15
Yes. The president threw a party in his office. I had sushi, pizza and fried chicken. A snack would be nice with the wine, though. Cheese and crackers?

Okay. Congratulations, by the way. I've never served cheese to a president before... ☺　21:15

Read 21:16
I'm still a director, so don't worry. You can start serving the president from tomorrow. Naturally, I will expect better service.

Ha, ha, ha... You're asking for trouble. By the way, Aiko will be bringing Hikari over on Saturday to celebrate your promotion. She wants to take us out for dinner. Any preferences?　21:17

Read 21:18
How about that new Italian restaurant by the station? It's not too expensive, and we can walk (no driving = I can drink).

Sounds good. So, Mr. President. What time will you be home?　21:18

Read 21:19
In about 45 minutes. I'll take a taxi and drop by the liquor store to get the wine.

Okay. See you then...!　21:19

既読 21:11 あと数分で会社を出るよ。ワインを買っていこうか？

いいわね。ご飯は食べた？ 21:14

既読 21:15 うん。社長が会社でパーティーをしてくれたんだ。すしとピザとフライドチキンを食べた。ワインには軽いものがいいと思うけど。チーズとクラッカーかな？

了解。ところで、おめでとう。社長にチーズを出したことは今までにないわ…☺ 21:15

既読 21:16 まだ部長だから心配ご無用。社長には明日から出せばいい。当然、もっといいサービスを期待してるよ。

ははは・・・。面倒なことになるわね。ところで、愛子があなたの昇進を祝って土曜日に光を連れて来るそうよ。私たちをディナーに連れて行ってくれるって。どこか行きたいところある？ 21:17

既読 21:18 駅のそばの新しいイタリアンレストランはどうかな？ 高すぎないし歩いて行ける(運転しない＝飲める)。

いいわね。では社長様。ご帰宅は何時でしょうか。 21:18

既読 21:19 あと45分後くらい。タクシーを拾ってワインを買うのに酒屋に寄って行くよ。

了解。じゃあ後でね！ 21:19

クイックQ&A

Q ⟩ When will Yonezawa require better service?
（米澤はいつからより良いサービスを要求すると言っていますか）

60

POINT

動詞throwはボールなどを投げる動作を表すのに加え、3番目のメッセージにあるthrow a partyなど様々な行為に使えます。例えば、throw open a door「ドアを勢いよく開ける」、throw a scarf around one's neck「首にサッとスカーフを巻く」、throw a criminal into jail「犯罪者を刑務所にぶち込む」、throw an angry glare「怒りの視線を投げかける」、throw into a panic「パニックに陥らせる」、throw on the lights「パッと明かりで照らす」、throw a game「試合を放棄する」などです。以下はそのいくつかの用例です。
・He threw open the door and stormed inside. (彼はドアを乱暴に開けて勢いよく中に入った)
・He was accused of car theft and thrown into jail. (彼は自動車盗の罪に問われ、刑務所にぶち込まれた)
・He was thrown into a panic when he noticed that his passport was missing. (彼はパスポートが見当たらないことに気づいてパニックに陥った)

実際の会話を聞いて話してみよう！

SETTING:

> Yonezawa is eating sushi and sipping from a glass of champagne at a small party held in the president's office for all board directors and other executives when the president approaches him.

Tomizawa: Congratulations again, Osamu. I know you will do an exceptional job. I can leave the company with peace of mind knowing that you are in charge.

Yonezawa: Thank you. I wish I shared your confidence. I can assure you that I will do my best to live up to your expectations, but whether I can or not is another matter.

Tomizawa: Still shell-shocked, huh?

Yonezawa: Oh, yes! I feel as if I stepped on a rake and the handle bounced up and hit me in the face. I guess it'll take a few months for me to get used to the idea.

Tomizawa: Well, I'll be here for another couple of months, so let me know if there is anything I can do.

Yonezawa: That's comforting to know. Thank you.

Tomizawa: No hard feelings about me setting up that job offer with Toru Sano at SJF Engineering?

Yonezawa: No, not at all. I was shocked at first, but the more I thought about it, the more it reminded me of a lesson I learned while in the London office.

Tomizawa: Tell me more.

Yonezawa: Well, to cut a long story short, a girl who should have been selected for a study trip to Japan was overlooked in favor of another less-experienced girl who was thinking of quitting the company. It was a political decision to keep both girls on the payroll, and the girl who was overlooked accepted the situation when the reason was carefully explained to her. Thinking back on the meeting with Sano, I realized that you had made a political decision, but then, although you could have kept it a secret, you had the decency to admit to it. In the same way as the girl in London, I was honored by the fact that you thought me worthy of the test.

Tomizawa: You know what, Osamu? You're going to make an excellent president!

small party in his office

場面:

> 全役員とその他の重役たちのために社長室で開かれた小さなパーティーで、米澤がすしを食べてシャンパンをグラスでちびちび飲んでいると、社長が話しかけてくる。

T：改めておめでとう、修。君は良い仕事をしてくれると信じているぞ。俺は君に任せて安心して会社を去ることができるよ。

Y：ありがとうございます。その自信がうらやましいですよ。社長の期待に応えられるようベストを尽くすことはお約束しますが、実際にできるかどうかはまた別です。

T：まだショックから立ち直れてないようだな。

Y：ええ、その通りですよ！　鍬を踏んづけたら柄が跳ね上がってきて顔面を直撃されたような気分です。慣れるまでには何か月かかかると思います。

T：まあ、俺もあと2か月ほどはここにいるから、できることがあれば何でも言ってくれ。

Y：それは心強いです。ありがとうございます。

T：SJFエンジニアリングの佐野徹からのスカウトの件で君をだましたことは恨んでないのかい？

Y：いえ、全く。初めは驚きましたが、そのことについて考えれば考えるほど、私がロンドン支社で得た教訓のことを思い出すんですよ。

T：詳しく話してくれ。

Y：そうですね、かいつまんで話すと、日本への研修旅行に選ばれるはずだった女性社員が、会社を辞めることを考えていたもっと経験の浅い女性社員を行かせるためにそれを見送らされたんです。これは両方の女性社員を会社にとどめるための政治的な判断だったのですが、理由を丁寧に説明されて、研修が見送りになった女性社員はその状況を受け入れたんです。佐野氏との会話について思い返して、社長が政治的な判断をしたのだと気づいたのですが、それでも、社長は秘密にしておくことができたにもかかわらず、それを打ち明けて誠意を示してくださいました。私もロンドンの女性社員と同様に、社長が私を試すに値すると評価してくださったことを光栄に思いました。

T：なあ、修。君はきっと素晴らしい社長になるぞ！

60

キーワードやフレーズをチェック!

☐ **soak up the atmosphere** 雰囲気に浸る

I love overseas business trips as they allow me to **soak up the atmosphere** of other cultures.

私は外の文化の雰囲気を満喫できるので海外出張が大好きだ。

She loves being the center of attention, and **soaked up the atmosphere** as she gave her presentation.

彼女は注目の的になるのが大好きで、プレゼンテーションを行っている間その場の空気を楽しんでいた。

☐ **come to terms with ～** ～を受け入れる

He still hasn't **come to terms with** the fact that he was demoted to a lower position.

彼は低い地位に降格されたことをまだ受け入れられていない。

The company must **come to terms with** the fact that environmental conservation is important.

その会社は環境保全が重要だという事実を認めなければならない。

☐ **leave no stone unturned** あらゆる手を尽くす

The investigative committee **left no stone unturned** during their investigation.

調査委員会はその調査で草の根を分けて調べ尽くした。

The department will **leave no stone unturned** to guarantee that the campaign is a success.

部署はそのキャンペーンを確実に成功させるためにあらゆる手を尽くすつもりだ。

☐ **put *one* in charge** （～に）管理を任せる

The manager **put** him **in charge** of organizing a farewell party.

部長は彼に送別会の準備を任せた。

She was **put in charge** of telephone sales from April.

彼女は4月から電話営業の管理を任された。

with a fine-tooth comb　細密に

She searched through the report **with a fine-tooth comb** to obtain more evidence.

彼女はもっと証拠を集めるためその報告書を徹底的に調べた。

He checked through the contract **with a fine-tooth comb** before he signed it.

彼はその契約書を入念に確認してからサインした。

far-fetched　形 無理な

The idea of the company launching an IPO is not as **far-fetched** as I thought.

その会社がIPOを行うというのは私が思ったほど無理な話ではない。

The original sales target was a little **far-fetched**, so it was revised later in the year.

元々の売上目標は少し非現実的だったため、その年の後になって修正された。

マナーのヒント

　昇進した人に祝いの言葉を述べるには、相手が互いによく交流している同僚なら、以下のように言えば気持ちが十分に伝わるでしょう。通常、そんなに頻繁に関わらない（あるいは知らない）人や自分より社内の階級が上の人に祝いの言葉を述べる必要はありません。

- Congratulations on your promotion. I'm sure you'll be very successful in your new job. （昇進おめでとう。新しい仕事でも成功すると信じているよ）
- Good luck in your new job. I'm sure you'll be very successful. （新しい仕事頑張ってね。成功すると信じているよ）
- Congratulations on your promotion. I look forward to working with you. （昇進おめでとう。一緒に働くのが楽しみだよ）

60

『ビジネス英語奮闘記』を
読んでくださった皆さま、
ありがとうございます。
新渡戸新之助と米澤修の奮闘記は
楽しんでいただけましたか。

この２人の主人公と同じように、
突然仕事で英語が必要になった
方々が辛さや退屈さを
感じるのではなく、

楽しく前向きに英語と付き合って
いけることを切に願います。

そしてその身につけた英語が
皆さんのビジネスの現場で
大いなる助けとなり、
世界で活躍できるビジネスパーソン
が1人でも多く生まれますように…。

またいつかお会いしましょう！

CD と同内容の音声をダウンロードできます

❶ PC・スマートフォンで音声ダウンロード用のサイトにアクセスします。
QR コード読み取りアプリを起動し左の QR コードを読み取ってください。
QR コードが読み取れない方はブラウザから
「http://audiobook.jp/exchange/sanshusha」にアクセスしてください。

❷ 表示されたページから、audiobook.jp への会員登録ページに進みます（既にアカウントをお持ちの方はログインしてください）。　※ audiobook.jp への会員登録（無料）が必要です。

❸ 会員登録後❶のページに再度アクセスし、シリアルコードの入力欄に「05968」を入力して「送信」をクリックします。

❹ 「ライブラリに追加」のボタンをクリックします。

❺ スマートフォンの場合はアプリ「audiobook.jp」をインストールしてご利用ください。
PC の場合は、「ライブラリ」から音声ファイルをダウンロードしてご利用ください。

編集協力	仲慶次
装丁・本文デザイン	上坊菜々子
本文・カバーイラスト	田渕正敏
翻訳協力	土志田あいり
DTP	小林菜穂美
企画協力	ドナチアン・アルフォンス・K、田中聡子

CD2枚+DL付
ストーリーを楽しむ(たの)だけでいい！
ビジネス英語奮闘記(えいごふんとうき) 31日目(にちめ)〜60日目(にちめ)

2020 年 1 月 30 日　第 1 刷発行

著　者	晴山陽一，クリストファー・ベルトン
発行者	前田俊秀
発行所	株式会社 三修社
	〒 150-0001　東京都渋谷区神宮前 2-2-22
	TEL03-3405-4511　FAX03-3405-4522
	http://www.sanshusha.co.jp
編集担当	本多真佑子
印刷・製本	壮光舎印刷株式会社

©2020 Yoichi Hareyama, Christopher Belton　Printed in Japan
ISBN 978-4-384-05968-7 C2082